MORALITY, JUSTICE,
AND THE
LAW

MORALITY, JUSTICE, AND THE LAW

The Continuing Debate

edited by
M. Katherine B. Darmer and Robert M. Baird

Prometheus Books

59 John Glenn Drive
Amherst, New York 14228-2119

Published 2007 by Prometheus Books

Inquiries should be addressed to

Prometheus Books
59 John Glenn Drive
Amherst, New York 14228–2119
VOICE: 716–691–0133, ext. 210
FAX: 716–691–0137
WWW.PROMETHEUSBOOKS.COM

11 10 09 08 07   5 4 3 2 1

Library of Congress Cataloging-in-Publication Data

Morality, justice, and the law : the continuing debate / edited by M. Katherine Baird Darmer and Robert M. Baird.
        p. cm.
Includes bibliographical references.
ISBN 978–1–59102–524–5 (alk. paper)
1. Law and ethics. I. Darmer, M. Katherine B. II. Baird, Robert M., 1937–.

K247.6.M676 2007
340'.112—dc22   2007001596

Printed in the United States of America on acid-free paper

CONTENTS

ACKNOWLEDGMENT

The editors wish to thank Amelia J. Uelmen for helpful suggestions as to the content of this book.

INTRODUCTION

M. Katherine B. Darmer
and Robert M. Baird

P hilosophers and legal scholars have long debated whether and to what degree law and morality are or should be connected. Several related questions are suggested by that debate. What is the primary function of "the law"? When is it legitimate to break the law? Do lawyers, judges, and lawmakers have a duty to "morality" that transcends their duty to law? What role should religion play in lawyering and the law?

The opening book in this series on contemporary issues, *Morality and the Law*, published in 1988, focused on the famous Hart-Devlin debate on laws dealing with homosexuality and civil disobedience. This new volume, initially conceived as an "update" of that earlier volume, instead grew into an entirely different book. Indeed, one of the goals of this volume is to illustrate that questions about morality, justice, and the law transcend sexual morality and similar issues that are traditionally linked with the term "morality." Questions about morality and justice permeate all aspects of the law.

This book starts with a theoretical discussion of law and morality. The initial essay in section one is a landmark piece by

Oliver Wendell Holmes. Published in the *Harvard Law Review* in the waning years of the nineteenth century, it is the starting point of twentieth-century legal philosophy—so says Robert George, author of the second piece in this section. Holmes's "The Path of the Law" emphasizes the difficulties that result from confusing morality and the law. Acknowledging that the two are related in a variety of ways, Holmes's argument that the two are distinct employs his "bad man" imagery. A bad man may not care at all about the morality of his act, but he cares considerably about its legality, which is a separate issue. The bad man cares, Holmes maintains, because the law is simply a prediction of what the bad man will suffer should he behave in certain ways.

Disagreements over the relationship between law and morality gave birth to a variety of positions in the twentieth century. George's essay "What is Law? A Century of Arguments" begins with a discussion of Holmes's essay and then addresses other views that emerged in jurisprudence such as legal realism and its emphasis on the indeterminacy of the law (its subjectivity), the varied expressions of the natural law position, and the legal positivism of John Austin and H. L. A. Hart. George is most interesting in his discussion of ambiguities in the views of Holmes and the consequent ambiguous connection between the views of Holmes and the twentieth-century legal realists with whom he is often identified. Concerning the "separation thesis" of law and morality, George acknowledges the truth in it, but he also recognizes the insight of the natural law position with regard to the derivation of just positive law from the natural law.

Ira Peak's essay on Hart and Ronald Dworkin interprets these two giants in the philosophy of law as positioning themselves between the natural law position of Thomas Aquinas and the legal positivism of John Austin—with Dworkin having more affinity with natural law and Hart with legal positivism. Peak's primary concern is to show that difficulties faced by both Dworkin and Hart can be rectified by applying some of Michael Polanyi's insights regarding the nature of science and the scientific community to an understanding of law and the legal community. In the process, Peak helpfully explicates the positions of both Dworkin and Hart.

Dworkin is also the focus of the next essay, Cass Sunstein's review of Dworkin's recently published *Justice in Robes*. Contrasting Dworkin with the judicial philosophies of Justices Antonin Scalia and Clarence Thomas, Sunstein discusses such distinctions as semantic originalism (Dworkin) and expectation originalism (Scalia and Thomas). Sunstein also provides a helpful discussion of Dworkin's critique of the legal pragmatism of Richard Posner. While Sunstein accepts Dworkin's claim that moral principles inevitably play a role in legal interpretation, he rejects on grounds of the fallibility of judges the suggestion that judges, in a grand way, should "deploy their own moral and political judgments" in judicial interpretations.

The book then turns to more concrete questions of morality and lawyering, an area rich for ethical debate. The first piece in this section is John J. Worley's foreword to a law review symposium exploring the lawyer's duty to promote the "public good." Worley uses a lawyer's dilemma in the novel *The Just and the Unjust* as a point of reference: the lawyer has been asked to represent a college, the beneficiary of a will, to the detriment of four sympathetic and deserving sisters whom the testator sought to disinherit out of spite. Worley contrasts two competing visions of the lawyer's role: the "neutralist conception," which endorses the view that the lawyer zealously pursue his client's objectives, and the "perfectionist theory," which advocates that the lawyer promote values beyond those of his clients. Worley then critiques the contributions of theorists from both camps; in the excerpt here, we include Worley's analyses of the contributions of John M. Finnis and Robert J. Araujo.

Finnis uses natural law principles to defend a neutralist position. In his view, lawyers have no duty to ensure that clients "conform to communal norms," but at the same time, lawyers are constrained by natural law principles, such as an absolute injunction against lying. Thus, a lawyer may zealously defend a client who is guilty of heinous crimes, but he may not resort to perjury to get him off. Araujo writes from the perfectionist view, arguing that lawyers should be judged by the virtues of justice, prudence, courage, and wisdom. While finding much to admire in Finnis's and Araujo's work, Worley criticizes Finnis's absolutist position against lying, which would forbid lying even in a situation where a lie might save a life. However, Worley acknowledges that an "absolutist objection" to lying in court proceedings is justified because of the extraordinary negative consequences for the justice system if lying became pervasive. Regarding Araujo, Worley questions whether his virtue-centered theory provides enough practical guidance for lawyers, but he acknowledges the importance of Araujo's reminder that we should not simply ask, "What is the right thing for the good lawyer to do?" but also "What kind of person is the good lawyer to be?"

Linda Meyer's article, "Between Reason and Power: Experiencing Legal Truth," follows. Meyer begins her piece by quoting a question frequently asked of lawyers: "How can you defend the guilty?" Meyer goes on to discuss the role of rhetoric in lawyering, offering a persuasive defense of rhetoric as being much more than just sweet talk or a means of manipulation. She makes the important point that in court the ultimate questions are not questions of fact (which are often disputed) but questions of *action*. Juries must decide, for example, whether to convict or acquit a defendant. Given that decision makers are forced to make decisions based on incomplete and sometimes conflicting information, rhetoric plays an important role in seeking common ground with the listener and in seeking to share the speaker's version of truth.

Meyer suggests that "the truth" can transcend narrow facts such as whether the defendant pulled the trigger. This theme is also present in the following article, Charles Ogletree's "Beyond Justifications: Seeking Motivations to Sustain Public Defenders." When asked how he could defend guilty clients, Ogletree says that he used to respond, "with pleasure." He acknowledges, however, that the work of criminal defense advocacy often leads to disillusion and burnout. Therefore, he sets out in his article to provide motivations, as opposed to justifications, for pursuing such work. He starts by analyzing conventional justifications for criminal defense work—including the Sixth Amendment right to counsel provided by the Constitution and professional standards calling for zealous representation. He then tells the compelling story of his own personal experience as a defense lawyer deeply shaken by the news that his beloved sister had been brutally murdered. Shortly after the murder—which remained unsolved—he was asked to defend a man who himself was accused of rape and murder. Despite newfound empathy for victims of crime, Ogletree accepted the representation and indeed threw himself into it. He believed that the client (referred to as Craig Strong) had been treated wrongly by the police, and when he first met Strong, he found a frightened man who needed help. Ogletree was devastated by his client's ultimate conviction.

In the concluding section of his article, Ogletree describes both empathy and a vision of heroism as sustaining motivations for defending his clients. By empathizing with a client, Ogletree was able to look beyond what the client may have done: "I viewed Strong as a person and as a friend, and thus I was able to disassociate him from the person who had murdered my sister. I did not blame him, nor did I resent him because I had been victimized by crime. Instead, I viewed Strong as a victim as well." Moreover, by seeing the work of defending indigent criminal defendants as heroic, it provided an ability to argue persuasively: "[B]y extending the definition of heroism to encompass the listener, the lawyer may be able to convince the jury to adopt that course of action that will produce the noblest and most just result."

Taken together, Meyer's and Ogletree's articles provide a compelling response to those who view defense lawyers as unethical manipulators who simply seek to "trick" juries into finding their clients not guilty. Such lawyers are not "lying," they are simply arguing for a broader version of the truth as they see it—a truth that takes into account injustices suffered by clients with whom the lawyers strongly identify.

The next selection in this lawyering section is an excerpt from Russell Pearce and Amelia Uelmen's article, "Religious Lawyering in a Liberal Democracy: A Challenge and an Invitation." In the section excerpted here, Uelmen explains why a "neutralist" approach to lawyering, where the lawyer is simply a "hired gun" for her client, is ultimately unsatisfying. She explains that this particular conception of lawyering (which is also discussed in Worley's opening piece) is not consistent with the view of lawyers at the time of the Federalist Papers, when lawyers were considered part of the elite group of "learned professionals" charged with pursuing the public good. The shift to a hired-gun conception troubles many, especially because unequal access to legal service then results in unequal justice. The religious lawyering movement, she argues, provides a "robust framework" for helping lawyers to integrate their personal morality and to consider the public good in their work for clients. Religious lawyering, for example, can provide a compelling reason for a person of religious background to provide services to the poor. Uelmen goes on to defend religious lawyering against objections that it is unfair to clients and dangerous for a liberal democracy.

In "Reflections on the Practice of Law as a Religious Calling, From a Perspective of Jewish Law and Ethics," Samuel Levine notes that lawyers face unique challenges both substantively and procedurally. He suggests that lawyers even on opposing sides may "serve justice" consistent with Jewish law. For example, prosecutors can work for justice while defense lawyers can embrace the role of representing society's most vulnerable. Procedurally, lawyers may be challenged by, for example, being called upon to cross-examine witnesses in hostile and embarrassing ways. Such challenges do not lend themselves to easy resolution, but Levine suggests that individual circumstances and conditions must be considered and that it may be "particularly appropriate" for a lawyer's religious and personal values to provide guidance.

The final piece in this section is Martha Minow's essay "On Being a Religious Professional: The Religious Turn in Professional Ethics," which was originally published in the *University of Pennsylvania Law Review*. Minow acknowledges the growing trend in discussions of religion in professional contexts and posits that the last two centuries saw a period of secularization followed by a period of increased religiosity. Moreover, she points out that "left-leaning parents" have found common ground with religious groups in social justice and cultural issues.

Minow describes her reaction to the increased role of religion in the professions as "ambivalent," an ambivalence that she says is embodied in the First Amendment of the Constitution, which simultaneously protects free exercise but also prohibits the establishment of religion. Minow acknowledges that religious teachings have informed movements she admires, such as the civil rights and antiwar movements and the War on Poverty. She also believes that the "boundaries of reasonable liberal conceptions of justice" evolve over time, shaped by life experiences and "multiple sources of values and beliefs," including religious beliefs.

At the same time, Minow believes that political discourse must be accessible to those who do not share the speaker's religious views. She warns that "triumphalism," which she acknowledges infects secular as well as religious "true believers," may insulate some from rational response. She also worries that if lawyers working within a religious framework eschew an adversarial posture in favor of conciliation, our current system, which is predicated upon "competitive fact-finding and argument," will not work. She also expresses concern about bias and exclusion of those who do not share the religious professional's beliefs. Ultimately, she concludes that resisting the view that one's religion provides all the answers for either the religious professional or her clients is possibly "the most critical challenge" for those in the religious lawyering movement.

The book's third section then turns to civil disobedience. Ronald Dworkin's thoughtful article, "On Not Prosecuting Civil Disobedience," was written during the height of the Vietnam War but remains relevant today. Dworkin starts with the proposition that not all instances of lawbreaking are punished; prosecutors have discretion to forbear prosecution for a variety of reasons. He then asks what the thoughtful citizen should do in the face of a law whose legitimacy is unclear. He examines three possibilities: (1) that the citizen should obey doubtful laws, even if he thinks they are wrong; (2) that the citizen may follow his own judgment and disobey doubtful laws until an institutional authority such as a court has ruled the other way; and (3) that he may continue to follow his own judgment with regard to doubtful laws, even in the face of a contrary court ruling (even from the Supreme Court), while taking that court ruling into account. Ultimately, he supports position three, making clear that even the Supreme Court sometimes reverses itself (as on the question of whether a person should be compelled to salute the flag), and thus that a reasonable citizen may follow his judgment if he has a reasoned belief that a law is unconstitutional.

The other selection in this short section is William H. Pryor's "Christian Duty and the Rule of Law." Pryor, writing as the attorney general of Alabama, defends his decision to obey the law by not resisting a court order calling for the removal of a monument depicting the Ten Commandments, which had been placed in a state judicial building. While Pryor believes that the display of the Ten Commandments is constitutional, he argues that in this case it was both his legal duty and his duty as a Christian to comply with the court order. Citing several biblical texts, Pryor argues that the Bible supports respect for government authority. Pryor acknowledges that the Bible also justifies disobeying the government at times in the interest of Christian duty or obligation. He quotes with approval Martin Luther King Jr.'s reliance on St. Augustine and St. Thomas Aquinas in support of the proposition that "[a]n unjust law is a human law that is not rooted in eternal or natural law." Pryor also underlines King's injunction that "[o]ne who breaks an unjust law must do so openly, lovingly and with a willingness to accept the penalty." In short, Pryor agrees that civil disobedience is justified in some contexts. However, he is concerned to distinguish between King's resistance to segregation and the activity of those who compared themselves to King in preparing to defy the court order banning the Ten Commandments monument from the judicial building. Segregation "distort[ed] the soul and damage[d] the personality," but the existence or nonexistence of a monument in a government building does not have such consequences. And perhaps more importantly, argues Pryor, segregation denied individuals the right to vote and, therefore, denied them political means of redress. Such a fundamental infringement of human rights could justify civil disobedience. In the injunction calling for the removal of the Ten Commandments monument from a public building, however, no one's fundamental rights had been abridged. In such cases, if one thinks that the court has made a mistake, the proper recourse is the political arena where one can urge the overruling of erroneous precedents or even amend the Constitution.

The fact that the Constitution is subject to different interpretations that are frequently shaped by moral views is very much at issue in the next section, which turns to an examination of capital punishment. We first excerpt two Supreme Court cases where justices had widely divergent views about the "right result." In capital cases, which turn on the Eighth Amendment's proscription of cruel and unusual punishment, the Supreme Court has conventionally looked at "evolving standards of decency," which surely implies consideration of conventional standards of morality and justice. Whether capital punishment is constitutional at all is an issue that the Court has struggled with, with further debate emerging about particular aspects. Recently, the risk of executing the innocent has come to the fore in the capital punishment debate, and that risk is discussed in all three of the selections in this section.

In *Herrera v. Collins*, the condemned prisoner claimed to be "actually innocent" of his crime of conviction and sought to present newly discovered evidence that he said would exonerate him. The relevant state statute, however, forbade consideration of the new evidence because of a strict time limit on the presentation of new evidence. As a moral matter, the execution of an actually innocent man would be barbaric. It was not as clear, however, that the Constitution—"the law"—would forbid it. As the Court explains, freestanding claims of innocence based on newly discovered evidence, absent an "independent constitutional violation" have not traditionally been a ground for relief on a federal habeas corpus claim, although the case upon which the majority chiefly relied, *Townsend v. Sain*, did not involve a defendant facing execution. Ultimately, however, the majority "assume[d], for the sake of argument in deciding this case, that in a capital case a truly persuasive demonstration of 'actual innocence' made after trial would render the execution of a defendant unconstitutional." Because of the "disruptive" effect of entertaining innocence claims after the fact, however, the Court notes further that the "threshold showing for such an assumed right would necessarily be extraordinarily high." Because the petitioner in *Herrera v. Collins* did not satisfy the Court's majority that he had met that high burden, his claim was rejected.

In a controversial concurring opinion, Justice Scalia takes a much harder line, making clear that the Constitution itself would not forbid the execution of an innocent. According to Scalia, the Constitution simply does not demand that the courts consider "newly discovered evidence of innocence" after conviction. In other words, so long as the underlying trial was consistent with due process, even compelling evidence of innocence need not be considered—though Scalia notes it would likely lead to an executive pardon. He ultimately joined the opinion of the majority, even though the majority was unwilling to say that the execution of an innocent would be constitutional. In that regard, Scalia notes: "I can understand, or at least am accustomed to, the reluctance of the present Court to admit publicly that Our Perfect Constitution lets stand any injustice, much less the execution of an innocent man who has received, though to no avail, all the process that our society has traditionally deemed adequate" (footnote omitted).

In a dissenting opinion very different in tone, three justices led by Justice Blackmun take the position that "[n]othing could be more contrary to contemporary standards of decency, or more shocking to the conscience, than to execute a person who is actually innocent." According to the dissenters, the Eighth Amendment to the Constitution, which forbids "cruel and unusual punishment," itself provides a mechanism for a person to challenge capital punishment on the basis of innocence, as does the Due Process Clause. The dissenters further found that the affidavits presented by the petitioner warranted consideration by the lower courts in the first instance. Acknowledging prior doubts about the constitutionality of capital punishment under current law, Blackmun concludes as follows: "Of one thing, however, I am certain. Just as an execution without adequate safeguards is unacceptable, so too is an execution when the condemned can prove that he is innocent. The execution of a person who can show that he is innocent comes perilously close to simple murder."

The *Herrera* case, which has been the subject of debate for some time, is followed in this volume by a more recent Supreme Court opinion on capital punishment, *Kansas v. Marsh*, which was decided on June 26, 2006. In that case, the Court considered the constitutionality of Kansas's sentencing scheme, which provides that the death penalty "shall be imposed" if the jury finds aggravating and mitigating circumstances to be in equipoise.

Respondent Marsh was convicted of brutal murders of a woman and her toddler. The jury found the existence of three aggravating circumstances and did not find those circumstances to be outweighed by mitigating circumstances. In accordance with the sentencing statute, the jury then sentenced Marsh to death. Marsh appealed, arguing that the Kansas statute created an unconstitutional "presumption in favor of death" by providing for the death penalty where mitigating and aggravating circumstances are equally balanced. The Kansas Supreme Court agreed with Marsh, but a majority of the United States Supreme Court disagreed.

In the majority opinion written by Justice Thomas, Thomas explains that a jury's process of weighing aggravating and mitigating circumstances is simply a means to decision. Because the jury knows that the consequence of a decision finding the circumstances to be in equipoise will mean that a death sentence will be imposed, its conclusion that the factors are in fact equally balanced "is a *decision for death* and is indicative of the type of measured, normative process in which a jury is constitutionally tasked to engage" when determining whether a death sentence is appropriate.

Responding to the dissent's concerns about the error rate in capital sentencing, Thomas writes that the logical consequence of that argument is that the death penalty itself can only be just in an error-free system. "Because the criminal justice system does not operate perfectly," he goes on, "abolition is the only answer to the moral dilemma the dissent poses. This Court, however, does not sit as a moral authority." Finding that the Court's precedents permit states to authorize capital punishment even in an imperfect system, he ultimately found no constitutional violation.

As he had in *Herrera*, Scalia wrote a separate concurring opinion in *Marsh*, in which he responded specifically to the claims of the dissent about the risks inherent in capital punishment. In his *Marsh* opinion, he notes that he found it inappropriate for judges to "heap either praise or censure" upon legislation it confronts, "lest it be thought" that the judges' interpretation was driven by their own personal policy choices. Plainly believing that the dissent was driven by such a policy choice, he laments that the dissent's claims about the condemnation of innocents would be "trumpeted abroad" as vindication of "sanctimonious criticism" that America's death penalty is "somehow unworthy of a civilized society." His opinion goes on to document, in some detail, questions and limitations regarding the studies and other authority relied upon by the dissent to support its views about the risks of capital punishment.

While acknowledging the imperfection of the system, he concludes that the possibility of mistake in imposing the death sentence under the current American system "has been reduced to an insignificant minimum." Given the support of a majority of Americans for capital punishment, it is not the Court's "proper business" to impose "judicially invented obstacles to its execution."

Four justices, led by Souter, dissented, making numerous references to moral considerations in capital sentencing. While states have leeway in devising a capital-sentencing scheme, a sentence of death must be a "reasoned moral response" to the defendant's circumstances: the death penalty must be reserved for the "worst of the worst." The dissent deems it "morally absurd" that the Kansas law would require execution even if aggravating factors did not outweigh mitigating ones.

Moving beyond the Court's prior precedent calling for "reasoned moral judgment" in sentencing, the dissenters next argue that new factual considerations must be considered in assessing the Eighth Amendment prohibition of cruel and unusual punishment—namely, the repeated exonerations of inmates sentenced to death in recent years. Going into some details regarding studies of wrongful convictions, the dissent concludes as follows:

> In the face of evidence of the hazards of capital prosecution, maintaining a sentencing system mandating death when the sentencer finds the evidence pro and con to be in equipoise is obtuse by any moral or social measure. And unless application of the Eighth Amendment no longer calls for reasoned moral judgment in substance as well as form, the Kansas law is unconstitutional.

In the various opinions of the justices excerpted from the *Herrera* and *Marsh* cases, it is clear that the justices take very different positions about the morality of an imperfect capital-sentencing system. Scalia, for example, who believes that the chances of a wrongful execution have been reduced to an "insignificant minimum" also believes that the system, even given its inevitable errors, remains constitutional and that the Court is not empowered to "invent obstacles" to a system supported by a majority of voters. Taking a similar view, Thomas explicitly states that the Court does not sit as a "moral authority" to resolve the moral dilemma posed by the risk of wrongful executions. Other justices, however, plainly take the view that the risk of error is relevant in determining whether the constitutional prohibition on "cruel and unusual punishment" is violated by aspects of capital sentencing and, particularly in *Marsh*, the dissenters explicitly use the language of morality to support their view.

The final piece in this section is Mark Osler's provocative new article, "Christ, Christians, and Capital Punishment." Starting with the point that both Bill Clinton and George Bush support capital punishment and that both presidents also made their Christian faith a part of their "public and political personae," Osler argues that Christ's execution should inform the modern debate about capital punishment. Initially, he argues that Christ's trial provides a "moral basis for eliminating capital punishment" because it involves the execution of an innocent, a risk that Osler describes as a compelling objection to the capital-punishment system today. Moreover, Osler likens aspects of Christ's trial—including a rush to judgment, the role of the mob, and inadequate representation— to modern capital procedures. Using Texas's procedures as an illustration, Osler argues that the sentencing process is too rushed, that there is inadequate political insulation for Texas judges who must respond to an electorate, and that representation is not fully effective and sometimes conflicted. (It is interesting to recall that Texas's sentencing system, with strict time limits on the consideration of new evidence, is at issue in the *Herrera* case.) Ultimately, Osler concludes powerfully that "[i]n holding the sacred story of Christ's trial up to the profane capital processes used in the United States . . . one sees that present procedure, and perhaps the existence of the death penalty at all . . . do not match up with the lessons to be gleaned from the trial of Christ himself."

Finally, this volume examines the current raging debate on immigration. Indeed, as this book goes to press the US Senate has just defeated a highly controversial new immigration bill. Issues of morality and the law are plainly intertwined in this context. On a fundamental level, when a person makes the choice to cross a border without sanction, he is choosing to break a law. Many people are virulently opposed to "amnesty" for such persons because it appears to condone the flouting of our laws. On the other hand, some believe that there is a *moral imperative* to help the less fortunate. One bill proposed in Congress would actually criminalize the providing of such assistance. Is such a law moral?

The awareness of several social realities and several value commitments are at the heart of the essay by Mary Ann Glendon. Among the social realities are the inevitability of migration and this country's need for immigrants who can contribute to our declining work force. Among the values she emphasizes are the rights of individuals in adverse circumstances to migrate from one country to another in the pursuit of work and the importance of the United States as a society for whom operating under the rule of law is fundamental—a matter relevant to the illegal immigrant problem. Glendon expresses concern that tensions over immigration are exacerbated both by immigration alarmists who inflame nativist sentiments and immigration advocates who fail to appreciate the significance of the strains involved in integrating immigrants into social structures and institutions. Glendon calls for a "fuller and better-informed" public discussion of the immigration issue with the hope that a solution can be reached that mediates between amnesty without qualification and punitiveness.

George Friedman argues in "Borderlands and Immigrants" that the current immigration debate is a question that needs to be separated into two inquiries. He distinguishes among immigrants to the United States from other parts of the world such as Asia or the Middle East, immigrants from Mexico who move to areas of the United States far removed from the border between Mexico and the States, and Mexican immigrants who move into "borderlands that were created by US conquests." Friedman emphasizes that historical experience has repeatedly shown that those who recognize the economic advantage of absorbing immigrants have been correct in their dispute with those who fear immigrants. But, he argues, the issues arising as a result of migration to borderlands that once were under the control of the country from which the immigrants are coming need to be considered in their particularity.

In his essay "Immigration Quotas vs. Individual Rights," Harry Binswanger explicitly defends "phasing-in open immigration into the United States." Individuals should be legally permitted to move to the United States, seek employment, and purchase property at will. His normative legal claim is grounded in a moral claim about individual rights—rights one has, he emphasizes, by virtue of being a human being not because one is an American. Binswanger is not advocating automatic citizenship, and he does recognize the need for protection against criminals, terrorists, and those who have infectious diseases. But he is convinced of and argues for the economic and spiritual advantage of unlimited immigration.

Victor Hanson maintains that illegal immigration is a moral issue, and he poses a series of questions as a way of emphasizing his point. Is it ethical for the Mexican government to assist her citizens in migrating illegally to the United States by providing them with survival guidelines? Is this encouragement not an immoral way for Mexico to avoid needed social reform in its own country? Is it moral to hire illegal aliens? Is it fair to unemployed US citizens to have to compete for jobs with illegal immigrants? Is it moral to require that some obey the law but permit illegal aliens an exemption? These questions, Hanson argues, are legitimate, and to raise them does not entail that one is a racist or nativist.

The brief piece by Cardinal Theodore E. McCarrick, archbishop of Washington, DC, agrees with Hanson that the immigration issue is a moral one, but McCarrick's moral focus is quite different. He is fundamentally concerned that faith communities respond to immigrants as newcomers, many of whom are downtrodden and oppressed. He specifically opposes the Border Protection, Anti-Terrorism, and Illegal Immigration Act of 2005 passed by the House of Representatives on the grounds that it is punitive and unfair in its scope; he supports the Secure America and Orderly Immigration Act introduced in the Senate by John McCain (R-AZ) and Edward Kennedy (D-MA). While Cardinal McCarrick does not explicitly support civil disobedience in this context, it is interesting to note that others have argued that any law that forbids helping immigrants should be disobeyed on moral, including religious, grounds. Especially in light of Congress's recent failure to agree on legislation, issues related to immigration reform remain a source of ongoing disagreement in the political arena and elsewhere.

The concluding opinion piece by Kathleen Parker is in response to recent immigrants taking to US streets to protest and demand rights "in Spanish while waving Mexican flags." Despite her "over-the-top pro-Latino and pro-immigrant" proclivities, she surmises that such actions on the part of illegal aliens will be counterproductive. Acknowledging the complexity of the immigration issue, she notes that the right of political protest is a citizen's right and that the responsibility of legislators is to pass laws serving the interests of US *citizens*.

The issues represented in this volume are complex and multifaceted, and we acknowledge that there are further dimensions to all of them that are not explored in this volume. Moreover, space permitted inclusion of only a handful of the topics covered by the subject "morality, justice, and the law." By providing materials that address underlying philosophical issues as well as concrete modern moral dilemmas, we hope that this volume contributes to ongoing discussions of the extent to which morality and the law are and should be connected.

EDITORS' NOTE

Many of the selections included herein have been edited in the interest of space. Among other alterations, many footnotes were eliminated without indication, particularly in law review articles and in opinions of the United States Supreme Court. Otherwise, editors' omissions are generally reflected with ellipses and alterations with brackets. The publishers have made minor additional alternations to some selections. Where footnotes are included, the publishers have endeavored to conform the footnotes to the Chicago Manual of Style. In some instances, however, not all information normally required by the Chicago Manual was available. Information provided in footnotes in those instances is consistent with information required by the Blue Book for Legal Citations, though footnotes still appear in the style of the Chicago Manual rather than the Blue Book. For those readers wishing to read the selections herein in unedited form, information as to the original source of each selection is provided.

PART ONE

THE RELATIONSHIP BETWEEN MORALITY AND THE LAW

THE PATH OF THE LAW

Oliver Wendell Holmes

When we study law we are not studying a mystery but a well-known profession. We are studying what we shall want in order to appear before judges, or to advise people in such a way as to keep them out of court. The reason why it is a profession, why people will pay lawyers to argue for them or to advise them, is that in societies like ours the command of the public force is entrusted to the judges in certain cases, and the whole power of the state will be put forth, if necessary, to carry out their judgments and decrees. People want to know under what circumstances and how far they will run the risk of coming against what is so much stronger than themselves, and hence it becomes a business to find out when this danger is to be feared. The object of our study, then, is prediction, the prediction of the incidence of the public force through the instrumentality of the courts.

The means of the study are a body of reports, of treatises, and

10 *Harvard Law Review* 457 (1897)

of statutes, in this country and in England, extending back for six hundred years, and now increasing annually by hundreds. In these sibylline leaves are gathered the scattered prophecies of the past upon the cases in which the axe will fall. These are what properly have been called the oracles of the law. Far the most important and pretty nearly the whole meaning of every new effort of legal thought is to make these prophecies more precise, and to generalize them into a thoroughly connected system. The process is one, from a lawyer's statement of a case, eliminating as it does all the dramatic elements with which his client's story has clothed it, and retaining only the facts of legal import, up to the final analyses and abstract universals of theoretic jurisprudence. The reason why a lawyer does not mention that his client wore a white hat when he made a contract, while Mrs. Quickly would be sure to dwell upon it along with the parcel gilt goblet and the sea-coal fire, is that he foresees that the public force will act in the same way whatever his client had upon his head. It is to make the prophecies easier to be remembered and to be understood that the teachings of the decisions of the past are put into general propositions and gathered into textbooks, or that statutes are passed in a general form. The primary rights and duties with which jurisprudence busies itself again are nothing but prophecies. One of the many evil effects of the confusion between legal and moral ideas, about which I shall have something to say in a moment, is that theory is apt to get the cart before the horse, and consider the right or the duty as something existing apart from and independent of the consequences of its breach, to which certain sanctions are added afterward. But, as I shall try to show, a legal duty so called is nothing but a prediction that if a man does or omits certain things he will be made to suffer in this or that way by judgment of the court; and so of a legal right.

The number of our predictions when generalized and reduced to a system is not unmanageably large. They present themselves as a finite body of dogma which may be mastered within a reasonable time. It is a great mistake to be frightened by the ever-increasing number of reports. The reports of a given jurisdiction in the course of a generation take up pretty much the whole body of the law, and restate it from the present point of view. We could reconstruct the corpus from them if all that went before were burned. The use of the earlier reports is mainly historical, a use about which I shall have something to say before I have finished.

I wish, if I can, to lay down some first principles for the study of this body of dogma or systematized prediction which we call the law, for men who want to use it as the instrument of their business to enable them to prophesy in their turn, and, as bearing upon the study, I wish to point out an ideal which as yet our law has not attained.

The first thing for a businesslike understanding of the matter is to understand its limits, and therefore I think it desirable at once to point out and dispel a confusion between morality and law, which sometimes rises to the height of conscious theory, and more often and indeed constantly is making trouble in detail without reaching the point of consciousness. You can see very plainly that a bad man has as much reason as a good one for wishing to avoid an encounter with the public force, and therefore you can see the practical importance of the distinction between morality and law. A man who cares nothing for an ethical rule which is believed and practiced by his neighbors is likely nevertheless to care a good deal to avoid being made to pay money, and will want to keep out of jail if he can.

I take it for granted that no hearer of mine will misinterpret what I have to say as the language of cynicism. The law is the witness and external deposit of our moral life. Its history is the history of the moral development of the race. The practice of it, in spite of popular jests, tends to make good citizens and good men. When I emphasize the difference between law and morals I do so with reference to a single end, that of learning and understanding the law. For that purpose you must definitely master its specific marks, and it is for that that I ask you for the moment to imagine yourselves indifferent to other and greater things.

I do not say that there is not a wider point of view from which the distinction between law and morals becomes of secondary or no importance, as all mathematical distinctions vanish in presence of the infinite. But I do say that that distinction is of the first importance for the object which we are here to consider—a right study and mastery of the law as a business with well understood limits, a body of dogma enclosed within definite lines. I have just shown the practical reason for saying so. If you want to know the law and nothing else, you must look at it as a bad man, who cares only for the material consequences which such knowledge enables him to predict, not as a good one, who finds his reasons for conduct, whether inside the law or outside of it, in the vaguer sanctions of conscience. The theoretical importance of the distinction is no less, if you would reason on your subject aright. The law is full of phraseology drawn from morals, and by the mere force of language continually invites us to pass from one domain to the other without perceiving it, as we are sure to do unless we have the boundary constantly before our minds. The law talks about rights, and duties, and malice, and intent, and negligence, and so forth, and nothing is easier, or, I may say, more common in legal reasoning, than to take these words in their moral sense, at some state of the argument, and so to drop into fallacy. For instance, when we speak of the rights of man in a moral sense, we mean to mark the limits of interference with individual freedom which we think are prescribed by conscience, or by our ideal, however reached. Yet it is certain that many laws have been enforced in the past, and it is likely that some are enforced now, which are condemned by the most enlightened opinion of the time, or which at all events pass the limit of interference, as many consciences would draw it. Manifestly, therefore, nothing but confusion of thought can result from assuming that the rights of man in a moral sense are equally rights in the sense of the Constitution and the law. No doubt simple and extreme cases can be put of imaginable laws which the statute-making power would not dare to enact, even in the absence of written constitutional prohibitions, because the community would rise in rebellion and fight; and this gives some plausibility to the proposition that the law, if not a part of morality, is limited by it. But this limit of power is not coextensive with any system of morals. For the most part it falls far within the lines of any such system, and in some cases may extend beyond them, for reasons drawn from the habits of a particular people at a particular time. I once heard . . . [it said] that a German population would rise if you added two cents to the price of a glass of beer. A statute in such a case would be empty words, not because it was wrong, but because it could not be enforced. No one will deny that wrong statutes can be and are enforced, and we would not all agree as to which were the wrong ones.

The confusion with which I am dealing besets confessedly legal conceptions. Take the fundamental question, [w]hat constitutes the law? You will find some text writers telling you that it is something different from what is decided by the courts of Massachusetts or England, that it is a system of reason, that it is a deduction from principles of ethics or admitted axioms or what not, which may or may not coincide with the decisions. But if we take the view of our friend the bad man we shall find that he does not care two straws for the axioms or deductions, but that he does want to know what the Massachusetts or English courts are likely to do in fact. I am much of this mind. The prophecies of what the courts will do in fact, and nothing more pretentious, are what I mean by the law.

Take again a notion which as popularly understood is the widest conception which the law contains—the notion of legal duty, to which already I have referred. We fill the word with all the content which we draw from morals. But what does it mean to a bad man? Mainly, and in the first place, a prophecy that if he does certain things he will be subjected to disagreeable consequences by way of imprisonment or compulsory payment of money. But from his point of view, what is the difference between being fined and taxed a certain sum for doing a certain thing? That his point of view is the test of legal principles is proven by the many discussions which have arisen in the courts on the very question whether a given statutory liability is a penalty or a tax. On the answer to this question depends the decision whether conduct is legally wrong or right, and also whether a man is under compulsion or free. Leaving the criminal law on one side, what is the difference between the liability under the mill acts or statutes authorizing a taking by eminent domain and the liability for what we call a wrongful conversion of property where restoration is out of the question? In both cases the party taking another man's property has to pay its fair value as assessed by a jury, and no more. What significance is there in calling one taking right and another wrong from the point of view of the law? It does not matter, so far as the given consequence, the compulsory payment, is concerned, whether the act to which it is attached is described in terms of

praise or in terms of blame, or whether the law purports to prohibit it or to allow it. If it matters at all, still speaking from the bad
man's point of view, it must be because in one case and not in the
other some further disadvantages, or at least some further consequences, are attached to the act by law. The only other disadvantages thus attached to it which I ever have been able to think of are
to be found in two somewhat insignificant legal doctrines, both of
which might be abolished without much disturbance. One is, that
a contract to do a prohibited act is unlawful, and the other, that, if
one of two or more joint wrongdoers has to pay all the damages,
he cannot recover contribution from his fellows. And that I believe
is all. You see how the vague circumference of the notion of duty
shrinks and at the same time grows more precise when we wash it
with cynical acid and expel everything except the object of our
study, the operations of the law.

Nowhere is the confusion between legal and moral ideas more
manifest than in the law of contract. Among other things, here
again the so-called primary rights and duties are invested with a
mystic significance beyond what can be assigned and explained.
The duty to keep a contract at common law means a prediction
that you must pay damages if you do not keep it—and nothing
else. If you commit a tort, you are liable to pay a compensatory
sum. If you commit a contract, you are liable to pay a compensatory sum unless the promised event comes to pass, and that is all
the difference. But such a mode of looking at the matter stinks in
the nostrils of those who think it advantageous to get as much
ethics into the law as they can. . . .

I have spoken only of the common law, because there are some
cases in which a logical justification can be found for speaking of
civil liabilities as imposing duties in an intelligible sense. These are
the relatively few in which equity will grant an injunction, and will
enforce it by putting the defendant in prison or otherwise punishing him unless he complies with the order of the court. But I
hardly think it advisable to shape general theory from the exception, and I think it would be better to cease troubling ourselves
about primary rights and sanctions altogether, than to describe our
prophecies concerning the liabilities commonly imposed by the
law in those inappropriate terms.

I mentioned, as other examples of the use by the law of words drawn from morals, malice, intent, and negligence. It is enough to take malice as it is used in the law of civil liability for wrongs what we lawyers call the law of torts—to show that it means something different in law from what it means in morals, and also to show how the difference has been obscured by giving to principles which have little or nothing to do with each other the same name. Three hundred years ago a parson preached a sermon and told a story out of Fox's *Book of Martyrs* of a man who had assisted at the torture of one of the saints, and afterward died, suffering compensatory inward torment. It happened that Fox was wrong. The man was alive and chanced to hear the sermon, and thereupon he sued the parson. Chief Justice Wray instructed the jury that the defendant was not liable, because the story was told innocently, without malice. He took malice in the moral sense, as importing a malevolent motive. But nowadays no one doubts that a man may be liable, without any malevolent motive at all, for false statements manifestly calculated to inflict temporal damage. In stating the case in pleading, we still should call the defendant's conduct malicious; but, in my opinion at least, the word means nothing about motives, or even about the defendant's attitude toward the future, but only signifies that the tendency of his conduct under known circumstances was very plainly to cause the plaintiff temporal harm.

In the law of contract the use of moral phraseology led to equal confusion, as I have shown in part already, but only in part. Morals deal with the actual internal state of the individual's mind, what he actually intends. From the time of the Romans down to now, this mode of dealing has affected the language of the law as to contract, and the language used has reacted upon the thought. We talk about a contract as a meeting of the minds of the parties, and thence it is inferred in various cases that there is no contract because their minds have not met; that is, because they have intended different things or because one party has not known of the assent of the other. Yet nothing is more certain than that parties may be bound by a contract to things which neither of them intended, and when one does not know of the other's assent. Suppose a contract is executed in due form and in writing to deliver a lecture, mentioning no time. One of the parties thinks that the promise will be construed to mean at once, within a week. The other thinks that it means when he is ready. The court says that it means within a reasonable time. The parties are bound by the contract as it is interpreted by the court, yet neither of them meant what the court declares that they have said. In my opinion no one will understand the true theory of contract or be able even to discuss some fundamental questions intelligently until he has understood that all contracts are formal, that the making of a contract depends not on the agreement of two minds in one intention, but on the agreement of two sets of external signs—not on the parties' having meant the same thing but on their having said the same thing. Furthermore, as the signs may be addressed to one sense or another—to sight or to hearing—on the nature of the sign will depend the moment when the contract is made. If the sign is tangible, for instance, a letter, the contract is made when the letter of acceptance is delivered. If it is necessary that the minds of the parties meet, there will be no contract until the acceptance can be read; none, for example, if the acceptance be snatched from the hand of the offerer by a third person.

This is not the time to work out a theory in detail, or to answer many obvious doubts and questions which are suggested by these general views. I know of none which are not easy to answer, but what I am trying to do now is only by a series of hints to throw some light on the narrow path of legal doctrine. . . . I hope that my illustrations have shown the danger, both to speculation and to practice, of confounding morality with law, and the trap which legal language lays for us on that side of our way. For my own part, I often doubt whether it would not be a gain if every word of moral significance could be banished from the law altogether, and other words adopted which should convey legal ideas uncolored by anything outside the law. We should lose the fossil records of a good deal of history and the majesty got from ethical associations, but by ridding ourselves of an unnecessary confusion we should gain very much in the clearness of our thought.

WHAT IS LAW?

A CENTURY OF ARGUMENTS

Robert P. George

There is a sense in which twentieth-century legal philosophy began on January 8, 1897. On that day, Oliver Wendell Holmes, then a justice of the Supreme Judicial Court of Massachusetts, spoke at a ceremony dedicating the new hall of the Boston University School of Law. In his remarks, which were published that spring in the *Harvard Law Review* under the title "The Path of the Law," Holmes sought to debunk the jurisprudence of the past and to propose a new course for modern jurists and legal scholars. Holmes' themes—the question of law's objectivity and the relationship between law and morality—have preoccupied legal philosophy in the century that was then dawning and has now drawn to a close.

The opening sentence of Holmes' lecture invited his audience —lawyers, law professors, and law students—to consider what it is we study when we study law. We are not, he said, studying a "mys-

Copyright © 2001 *First Things* 112 (April 2001): 23–29.

tery," but, rather, "a well–known profession." People are willing to pay lawyers to advise and represent them because "in societies like ours the command of the public force is entrusted to the judges in certain cases, and the whole power of the state will be put forth, if necessary, to carry out their judgments and decrees." Now, this is a fearsome power. So people "will want to know under what circumstances and how far they will run the risk of coming against what is so much stronger than themselves, and hence it becomes a business to find out when this danger is to be feared." The object of the study of law, therefore, "is prediction, the prediction of the incidence of the public force through the instrumentality of the courts."

This was the thesis of "The Path of the Law." It was intended, I believe, as a provocation. And so Holmes formulated it in provocative ways:

> A legal duty so called is nothing but a prediction that if a man does or omits certain things he will be made to suffer in this or that way by judgment of the court. . . . The prophecies of what the courts will do in fact, and nothing more pretentious, are what I mean by the law. . . . The duty to keep a contract at common law means a prediction that you must pay damages if you do not keep it—and nothing else.

The power of provocation is usually enhanced to the extent one obscures one's intention to provoke. And so Holmes claimed merely to be proposing a "businesslike understanding of the matter." Such an understanding, he insisted, requires us strictly to avoid confusing moral and legal notions. This is difficult, Holmes suggested, because the very language of law—a language of "rights," "duties," "obligations," "malice," "intent," etc.—lays a "trap" for the unwary. "For my own part," he declared in another famously provocative sentence, "I often doubt whether it would not be a gain if every word of moral significance could be banished from the law altogether, and other words adopted which should convey legal ideas uncolored by anything outside the law."

Holmes' implicit denial of law's objectivity is not unconnected to his insistence on the strict separation of moral and legal notions. "One of the many evil effects of the confusion between legal and moral ideas," he stated, "is that theory is apt to get the cart before the horse, and to consider the right or the duty as something existing apart from and independent of the consequences of its breach, to which certain sanctions are added afterward." A corrective, according to Holmes, was to adopt the viewpoint of a "bad man" when trying to understand the law as such:

> If you want to know the law and nothing else, you must look at it as a bad man, who cares only for the material consequences which [legal] knowledge enables him to predict, not as a good one, who finds his reasons for conduct, whether inside the law or outside of it, in the vaguer sanctions of conscience.

And what exactly is being corrected by adopting the bad man's point of view?

> You will find some text writers telling you that [the law] is something different from what is decided by the courts of Massachusetts or England, that it is a system of reason, that it is a deduction from principles of ethics or admitted axioms or whatnot, which may or may not coincide with the decisions. But if we take the view of our friend the bad man we shall find that he does not care two straws for the axioms or deductions, but that he does want to know what the Massachusetts or English courts are likely to do in fact.

"I am," Holmes declared, "much of his mind."

Still for all his skepticism—legal and moral—Holmes denied that his was "the language of cynicism":

> The law is the witness and external deposit of our moral life. Its history is the history of the moral development of the race. The practice of it, in spite of our popular jests, tends to make good citizens and good men. When I emphasize the difference between law and morals I do so with reference to a single end, that of learning and understanding the law.

Going still further, Holmes claimed to "venerate the law, and especially our system of law, as one of the vastest products of the human mind." It was not, he assured his readers, disrespect for the law that prompted him to "criticize it so freely," but rather a devotion to it that expresses itself in a desire for its improvement.

Holmes' aim was merely, he said, to expose some common fallacies about what constitutes the law. For example, some people—Holmes doesn't tell us who they are—hold that "the only force at work in the development of the law is logic." This erroneous way of thinking is, Holmes advised his audience, "entirely natural" for lawyers, given their training in logic with its "processes" of analogy, discrimination, and deduction, but it is erroneous nevertheless. Moreover, "the logical method and form flatter that longing for certainty and for repose which is in every human mind. But," Holmes went on to say,

> certainty generally is an illusion, and repose is not the destiny of man. Behind the logical form lies a judgment as to the relative worth and importance of competing legislative grounds, often an articulate and unconscious judgment, it is true, and yet the very root and nerve of the whole proceeding.

Now, this is getting interesting. The man who would later utter, in another connection, the famous aphorism that "the life of the law has not been logic, it has been experience," has already told his audience in this lecture that law is a matter of prediction, of prophecies of what courts will do in fact. He has also expressed great skepticism about the role of logic in guiding the decision-making of judges whose rulings, one way or the other, will constitute the law. So, how are those decisions to be rationally guided? What is "the law" from the perspective, not of the "bad man," but of the "good judge" who, facing a disputed question of law, will not be comforted by the assurance that "the law" is a prediction of how he will in fact resolve the case?

In fact, what he wishes to do is to resolve the case according to the law. That, he supposes, is his job. He wants to rule on the matter favorably to the litigant whose cause is supported by the superior *legal* argument. But what constitutes *legal* argument? What are the sources of law upon which legal reasoning operates?

Of course, one candidate for inclusion in the list of legal

sources is history. And according to Holmes, "The rational study of law is still to a large extent the study of history." Is this good or bad? "History must," Holmes says, "be a part of the study, because without it we cannot know the precise scope of rules which it is our business to know." But then comes the punch line: "It is a part of the rational study, because it is the first step toward an enlightened skepticism, that is, toward a deliberate reconsideration of the worth of those rules."

So, history is not a source in the sense that the legal rules uncovered (and whose meaning is clarified) by historical inquiry are authorities that guide the reasoning of the conscientious judge. On the contrary, such study has its value in exposing such rules to "an enlightened skepticism" regarding their value. But then, by appeal to what standards are such judgments of value to be made? And—most critically—are these standards internal to the law or external? Does the judge discover the proper standards *in* the legal materials—the statutes, the cases, the learned treatises—or bring them *to* those materials? If the latter, then what is the discipline from which he derives them?

These are questions that will be central to the theoretical reflections of jurists and legal scholars throughout the twentieth century. They will be answered one way by Jerome Frank and his fellow "legal realists" in the first half of the twentieth century, and precisely the opposite way by Ronald Dworkin and his followers in the second half. H. L. A. Hart—the greatest of the English-speaking legal philosophers of the century—will refer to the realists' answer as the "nightmare" that law does not exist, and to Dworkin's answer as the "noble dream" that law as such provides a "right answer"—a single uniquely correct resolution—to every dispute that makes its way into the courtroom.

Holmes' own answer was tantalizingly ambiguous. In "The Path of the Law" he said at one point, "I think . . . the judges themselves have failed adequately to recognize their duty of weighing considerations of social advantage." At another point he made this remarkable statement:

> I look forward to a time when the part played by history in the explanation of [legal] dogma shall be very small, and instead of

ingenious research we shall spend our energy on a study of the ends sought to be attained and the reasons for desiring them. As a step toward that ideal it seems to me that every lawyer ought to seek an understanding of economics.

Three-quarters of a century later, Richard Posner, Frank Easter-brook, Richard Epstein, Guido Calebresi, and other theorists and practitioners of the "economic analysis of law" would take this last piece of advice quite literally. Their books, law review articles, and—in the cases of Posner, Easterbrook, and, most recently, Cale-bresi—judicial opinions would subject legal rules and social policies to cost-benefit tests and other forms of economic analysis to assess their instrumental rationality and thus, in some cases, their legal validity. What these scholars and jurists do fits pretty well with Holmes' desire for lawyers and judges to "consider the ends which the several rules seek to accomplish, the reasons why those ends are desired, what is given up to gain them, and whether they are worth the price." But, one must ask, would Holmes really approve their doing it?

Although Holmes was, in his politics, "a moderate, liberal reformer," he was resolutely determined, as a judge, not to "legislate from the bench." Indeed, during a period of unprecedented "judicial activism," he became the symbol of opposition to the judicial usurpation of legislative authority under the guise of interpreting the Constitution. As a Justice of the Supreme Court of the United States, he drew as sharp a line as any jurist of his time between "law" and "politics"—even when the politics in question concerned political economy. In what is perhaps his most celebrated dissent, Holmes castigated the majority in the 1905 case of *Lochner v. New York* for invalidating a state law setting maximum working hours for employees in bakeries on the ground that such a regulation violated the "freedom of contract" that was held to be implicit in the Due Process Clause of the Fourteenth Amendment. Holmes argued that this so-called "substantive due process" doctrine was an invention designed to authorize what was, in fact, the illegitimate judicial imposition of a theory of economic efficiency and a morality of economic relations on the people of the states and the nation. His claim was not that there was anything defective in that theory; on the contrary, its "Social Darwinist" dimensions held considerable appeal to him. Rather, it was that judges had no business substituting their judgments of efficiency and value for those of the people's elected representatives in Congress and the state legislatures. They, he famously said, should be able to go to hell in their own way.

It is not that any of this is flatly inconsistent with what Holmes asserted in "The Path of the Law." Indeed, at one point in that lecture he seems to suggest that training in economics and a due weighing of considerations of social advantage will have the salutary effect of encouraging judicial restraint. "I cannot but believe," he declared, "that if the training of lawyers led them habitually to consider more definitely and explicitly the social advantage on which the rule they lay down must be justified, they sometimes would hesitate where now they are confident, and see that really they were taking sides upon debatable and often burning questions."

But plainly Holmes, as a judge—and, above all, as a dissenting judge—is supposing that the law is something more than merely a prophecy of what the courts will in fact decide. As a dissenter, he holds that the courts have decided the case incorrectly. Of course, he does not deny that their rulings—even where incorrect—have the binding force of law, at least until they are reversed by higher courts of appeal; but he does suppose that the judges in the majority "got the law wrong." So, apparently, judges in resolving disputes should be guided, in some significant sense, by law. And this presupposes the reality of law, and indeed, the *preexistence* of law, as something more than a "prophec[y] of what courts will do in fact."

So we must press the question: To what standards of legal correctness should the judge look in reasoning to the resolution of a case? Are the standards internal to the legal materials and discoverable, by some method, in them? Or are they external? Do judges "find" the law? Or do they, necessarily, "create" it? Can lawyers predict or "prophesy" what a good and conscientious judge will do by figuring out what he should do in light of the legal materials that should control his reasoning? If that is all Holmes means by "prediction" and "prophecy," then his debunking exercise is, for all its provocative language, far less skeptical than it appeared.

Drawing their inspiration from Holmes, however, there soon

emerged a group of legal scholars who were prepared, for a while at least, to expose the idea of law to truly radical skepticism. The legal realist movement, which reached the peak of its influence in the 1930s and '40s, advanced the debunking project well beyond the point at which Holmes had left things in "The Path of the Law." Felix Cohen, Karl Llewellyn, Jerome Frank, and others pressed to an extreme the idea of jurisprudence as an essentially "predictive" enterprise. "Law," according to Llewellyn, was what *officials do about disputes.*" In accounting for their decisions, he insisted, it could only rarely be true to say that they are guided by rules. The trouble is not—or not just—that judges and other officials are willful, and thus willing to lay aside the clear command of legal rules in order to do as they please. It is that legal rules are necessarily vague and susceptible of competing reasonable interpretations and applications. Even the problem of selecting which rule to apply to a given set of facts can only rarely be solved by looking to a clear rule of selection. The result is a measure of indeterminacy that makes nonsense of the idea of legal objectivity. The key to understanding the phenomenon of law—accounting for what judges and other officials do or predicting what they will do about disputes—is not the analysis of legal rules. It must be something else. True, judges and other officials cite the rules in justifying their decisions. But if we are to be realistic about what is going on, according to Llewellyn, we must recognize that this is the mere legal rationalization of decisions reached on other grounds.

Frank's realism was, if anything, still more extreme in its denial of legal objectivity. Going beyond Llewellyn's "rule-skepticism," Frank declared himself to be a "fact-skeptic" as well. Thus he denied law's objectivity even in the rare cases in which a clear rule was clearly applicable. Since rules must be applied to facts in order to generate a legal outcome, everything depends on findings of fact in trial courts and other fact-finding tribunals. And facts are, in most cases, virtually as indeterminate as legal rules. In statements that seem eerily, well, realistic in the aftermath of the O. J. Simpson trial, Frank argued that our perceptions of facts are deeply influenced by conscious and subconscious beliefs, attitudes, and prejudices that vary among groups and individuals. So the key to understanding law—understood in legal realist terms—is understanding people's beliefs, attitudes, and prejudices, and why they hold them. Since law is a sort of epiphenomenon of human psychology, legal scholarship should be directed to scientific (e.g., psychological) and social scientific studies of human motivation. To be realistic, it should abandon the idea that law preexists and is available to guide legal decisions.

The legal realists' insistence on the indeterminacy of law would, in our own time, be reasserted by advocates of "critical legal studies," though this time in the service of a "new left" political agenda and with nothing like the realists' faith in the objectivity and explanatory power of the natural and social sciences. The realists themselves were, like Holmes, political progressives—moderate liberals—eager to bring instrumental rationality to bear to solve social problems. Many were New Dealers. A few became judges, and those who did were, like Holmes, far less radical in practice than their theoretical views would have led one to predict. Although appeals to the alleged findings of social science became an increasingly common feature of judicial opinions as the twentieth century wore on, realists who became judges rarely cited their own subjective views or prejudices or psychological predilections as grounds for their decisions. Rather, they cited legal rules as the ultimate reasons for their decisions and claimed, at least, to lay aside their own preferences in fidelity to the law. (Interestingly, in the aftermath of the revelation of Nazi atrocities in Europe, Frank declared himself, in the Preface to the Sixth Edition of his *Law and the Modern Mind*, to be a follower of the natural law teaching of St. Thomas Aquinas on the basic questions of law and morality. Nothing in his earlier writings, he insisted, was ever meant to suggest otherwise.)

Of course, realism had its appeal precisely because it was, from a certain vantage point, realistic. Trial lawyers take issues of venue and voir dire very seriously because they know—and knew long before the O. J. Simpson case—that who is on the jury can be critical to whether facts are found favorably to their clients. And one of the first questions lawyers at any level of litigation want to know the answer to is who the judge or judges are who will be making determinations of law at the trial or on appeal. Often enough, different jurors or a different judge or judges means different results. Clearly, then, the phenomenon of law includes strong elements of "subjectivity."

But the realists overstated their case. Their argument falters under the same question we put to Holmes a little while ago. From the point of view of conscientious judges, the law is not—for it cannot be—a prediction of their own behavior. Often they, like Holmes, will be faced with what they themselves perceive to be a duty to follow rules whose application generates outcomes that run contrary to their personal preferences. True, a willful judge can simply give effect to his prejudices under the guise of applying the law, at least until reversed by a higher court of appeal (if there is one). But this is no modern discovery. And it is no more a threat to the possibility of law's objectivity than is the fact that people sometimes behave immorally a threat to the objectivity of morals. Just as a conscientious man strives to conform his behavior to what he judges to be the standards of moral rectitude, the conscientious judge strives to rule in conformity with the controlling rules of law. And no account of the phenomenon of law which ignores the self-understanding of such a judge—no account which, that is to say, leaves his point of view out of account—can do justice to the facts.

This, I think, was clear to H. L. A. Hart. He above all other English-speaking juridical thinkers in the wake of legal realism recognized that the shortcomings of legal skepticism had mainly to do, not with the dangers of its capacity to undermine the public's faith in the rule of law, but rather with realism's inability realistically to account for the phenomenon of law as it functions in human societies. Realist theories failed to fit the facts. And they failed to fit the facts because they approached the phenomenon of law from a purely external viewpoint. The problem, according to Hart, was not that legal realists were bad lawyers; it was that they were bad psychologists and social scientists, even as they looked to psychology and social science to explain the phenomenon of law.

Social phenomena—phenomena created or constituted, at least in part, by human judgment, choice, cooperation, etc.—can never adequately be understood, Hart argued, without adopting what he called the "internal point of view." This is the point of view of those who do not "merely record and predict behavior conforming to rules" or understand legal requirements as mere "signs of possible punishment," but rather *"use* the rules as standards for the appraisal of their own and others' behavior."

On this score, Hart faulted not only the legal realists, but also the leading figures in his own intellectual tradition, the tradition of analytical jurisprudence inspired by Thomas Hobbes and developed by Jeremy Bentham and his disciple John Austin. The problem with their jurisprudential theories, Hart observed, is that they too fail to fit the facts. And they fail to fit the facts because they do not take into account the practical reasoning of people whose choices and actions create and constitute the phenomenon of law—people for whom legal rules function as reasons for decisions and actions.

Hart in no way denied the wide variability of legal rules. Beyond some basic requirements of any legal system—what Hart called the "minimum content of natural law"—there is a great deal of variation from legal system to legal system. But in all societies that have achieved a legal order—that is, moved from a prelegal order to a regime of law—law exhibits a certain objectivity and autonomy from other phenomena, including other normative systems. And the law of any system is not truly understood by the theorist until he understands the practical point of the law from the perspective of actors within the system who understand themselves to be making laws for reasons and acting on reasons provided by the laws.

In his masterwork, *The Concept of Law*, Hart invited his readers to treat his analysis as "an essay in descriptive sociology." But his was a sociology designed to make possible the understanding of legal systems "from the inside." So what he proposed, and what the tradition of analytical jurisprudence has now more or less fully accepted as Hart's most enduring contribution, is that even "the descriptive theorist (whose purposes are not practical) must proceed . . . by adopting a practical point of view. . . . [He must] assess importance or significance in similarities and differences within his subject matter by asking what would be considered important or significant in that field by those whose concerns, decisions, and activities create or constitute the subject matter."

If Hart rejected the externalism of Bentham and Austin—with its understanding of law (in Hobbesian fashion) as constituted by commands of a sovereign ("orders backed by threats") who is habitually obeyed by a populace but who in turn obeys no one—he retained their commitment to "legal positivism." He described this much-misunderstood commitment as the acknowledgment of a "conceptual separation" of law and morals. Although he was yet another moderate liberal in his politics, Hart did not mean by "positivism" the idea that law ought not to embody or enforce moral judgments. True, in his famous debate with Patrick Devlin over the legal enforcement of morals, Hart defended a modified version of J. S. Mill's "harm principle" as the appropriate norm for distinguishing legitimate from illegitimate state enforcement of morality; but he fully recognized that this principle itself was proposed as a norm of political morality to be embodied in, and respected by, the law.[1] Moreover, he understood perfectly well that the content of legal rules reflected nothing so much as the moral judgments prevailing in any society regarding the subject matters regulated by law. So Hart cheerfully acknowledged the many respects in which law and morality were connected, both normatively and descriptively. In what respect, then, did he insist on their "conceptual separation"?

As I read *The Concept of Law*, as well as Hart's later writings, the "conceptual separation" thesis seems rather modest. It has to do above all, I think, with the legitimate aspiration of the descriptive sociologist to keep his descriptions, to the extent possible, free of coloration by his own normative moral views. One can recognize a law, or even a whole legal system, *as* a law or legal system, irrespective of whether one believes that that law or legal system is just; indeed, even a gravely unjust legal system can be, from a meaningful descriptive viewpoint, a legal system. And what is true of the descriptive sociologist or legal theorist can also be true of the judge who may conclude in a given case that the law—identified by authoritative criteria or standards of legality—provides a rule of decision in the case at hand which is, from the moral point of view, defective. In repudiating what he took—wrongly, in my view—to be the defining proposition of the natural law theorist, Hart denied in an unnecessarily wholesale fashion the proposition *lex iniusta non est lex* (an unjust law is not law).

Although his views in fundamental moral theory are frustratingly elusive, nothing in Hart's positivism commits him in any way to the moral skepticism, subjectivism, or relativism characteristic of the positivism of, say, Hans Kelsen or that one detects in the extrajudicial writings of Oliver Wendell Holmes. In fact, the student of Hart's who has remained closest to his views in legal theory, Joseph Raz, combines Hartian legal positivism with a robust moral realism. Hart and Raz have both insisted—rightly, in my view—on the necessity of some conceptual separation of law and morality for the sake of preserving the possibility of moral criticism of law. As John Finnis has recently observed, the necessary separation "is effortlessly established [by Aquinas] in the *Summa* [by] taking human positive law as a subject for consideration in its own right (and its own name), a topic readily identifiable and identified *prior* to any question about its relation to morality."

Nevertheless, Hart's positivism generated one of the century's most fruitful jurisprudential debates when it was challenged by Lon L. Fuller in the late 1950s. Fuller—whose careful explication and working out of the diverse elements of the Aristotelian ideal of the Rule of Law constitutes a genuine achievement of twentieth-century legal philosophy—proposed an argument to show that law and morality are, as a matter of brute fact, more tightly connected than Hart's positivism would allow. He sought to show that law necessarily embodies an "internal morality" that defies Hart's "conceptual separation" thesis. He offered to argue the point, not as a normative matter about moral standards that positive law *ought* to meet, but rather on Hart's own terms, as a descriptive proposition about moral standards that law has to embody before even the purely descriptive theorist can recognize it as law.

In *The Morality of Law*, Fuller offered an apparently "value free" definition of law that any legal positivist ought to be able to accept: "Law is the enterprise of subjecting human behavior to the governance of norms." Nothing in this definition demands that those who make and enforce the laws be wise, virtuous, benign, or concerned in any way for the common good. Still, some things follow from it. For example, people cannot conform their behavior to rules that have not been promulgated, or that lack at least some measure of clarity, or that apply retrospectively. So promulgation, clarity, and prospectivity are aspects of the Rule of Law. Where they are absent, no legal system exists or, at most, only a highly defective legal system exists. And there are other requirements, including some significant measure of reliable conformity of official action with stated rules. Taken together, Fuller argued, the Rule of Law constitutes a *moral* achievement.

While adherence to the Rule of Law does not guarantee that a legal system will be perfectly just—in fact, all legal systems contain elements of injustice—it does mean that a certain minimum set of moral standards must be met before a legal system actually exists. And, sure enough, or so Fuller supposed, grave injustice is rarely found in systems in which the rulers—whatever their personal vices and bad motives—govern by law. It is in societies in which the Rule of Law is absent that the most serious injustices occur. Of course, Hart wasn't buying this for a moment. While he admired and for the most part accepted Fuller's brilliant explication of the Rule of Law, he saw no reason to refer to its content as an internal *morality*. He contended, moreover, that there is no warrant for supposing that a system of law could not be gravely unjust, or that the Rule of Law provided any very substantial bulwark against grave injustice. Indeed, Raz later argued against Fuller that the Rule of Law was analogous to a sharp knife—valuable for good purposes, to be sure, but equally useful to rulers in the pursuit of evil objectives.

The Hart/Fuller debate (like the Hart/Devlin debate) was an illuminating one. I count on it every year for one or two lively meetings of my seminar in Philosophy of Law at Princeton. My own judgment is that Fuller scored a powerful point in establishing a certain moral value of the Rule of Law, but that Hart rightly resisted Fuller's somewhat exaggerated moral claims on its behalf. In any event, I do not think that Fuller undermined the central appeal of the "conceptual separation" thesis: the methodological aspiration to avoid confusing "law as it is" with "law as it ought to be."

For Hart, the question of how much law-creating (or "legislative") authority a judge has, if any, or where that authority obtains, is not to be resolved at the level of general jurisprudence. Legal systems differ—indeed, reasonably differ—on the question of how such law-making authority is to be allocated among judges and other actors in the overall political system. To be sure, Hart observes that legal rules are inevitably "open textured" and, thus, in need of authoritative interpretation in their concrete application; and this entails a certain measure of judicial discretion and law-making authority as a matter of fact, even in those systems which exclude it in theory. This means that the wall between legal validity and the moral judgment of judges is porous, even in systems (such as the British one) of avowed legislative supremacy. Hart's legal positivism is, in fact, completely compatible with the recognition that judges in some legal systems are invited or even bound under the positive law of the Constitution to bring moral judgment to bear in deciding cases at law. Hart's is not a theory designed to show judges how they can resolve cases without making moral judgments, though neither is it a theory offering to justify their doing so. The theory simply isn't addressed to such questions.

What I think Hart *is* to be faulted for is a failure to see and develop fully the implications of his own refutation of Benthamite and Austinian positivism and of his adoption of the internal point of view. (Some of these implications are acknowledged by Raz in his recent work.) The central or focal case of a legal system, to borrow a principle of Aristotle's method in social study, is one in which legal rules and principles function as practical reasons for citizens, as well as judges and other officials, because the citizens appreciate their moral value.

Yet Hart himself, in *The Concept of Law* and elsewhere, declined to distinguish central from peripheral cases of the internal point of view itself. Thus, he treated cases of obedience to law by virtue of "unreflecting inherited attitudes" and even the "mere wish to do as others do" no differently from morally motivated obedience of fidelity to law. These "considerations and attitudes," like those which boil down to mere self-interest or the avoidance of punishment, are, as Finnis says, "diluted or watered-down instances of the practical viewpoint that brings law into being as a significantly differentiated type of social order and maintains it as such. Indeed, they are parasitic upon that viewpoint."

This is in no way to deny any valid sense to the positivist insistence on the "conceptual separation" of law and morality. It is merely to highlight the ambiguity of the assertion of such a separation and the need to distinguish, even more clearly than Hart did, between the respects in which such a separation obtains and those in which it does not. Still less is it to suggest that belief in natural law or other forms of moral realism entails the proposition that law and morality are connected in such a way as to confer upon judges as such a measure of plenary authority to enforce the requirements of natural law or to legally invalidate provisions of positive law they judge to be in conflict with these requirements. Important work by Finnis and others has clearly identified the misguidedness of such a suggestion. The truth of the proposition *lex iniusta non est lex* is a moral truth, namely, that the moral obligation created by authoritative legal enactment—that is to say, by positive law—is conditional rather than absolute; our prima facie obligation to obey the law admits of exceptions.

What about law's objectivity? Does law "exist" prior to legal decision? Can judicial reasoning be guided by standards internal to the legal materials? At the dawn of the twenty-first century we can, I think, affirm a position more subtle than the one Holmes asserted at the end of the nineteenth. Yes, the standards to guide judicial reasoning can be internal to the law of a system that seeks to make them so, though never perfectly. Positive law is a human creation—a cultural artifact—though it is largely created for moral purposes, for the sake of justice and the common good. That is to say, law exists in what Aristotelians would call the order of technique, but it is created in that order precisely for the sake of purposes that obtain in the moral order. So, for moral reasons, we human beings create normative systems of enforceable social rules that enjoy, to a significant extent, a kind of autonomy from morality as such. We deliberately render these rules susceptible to technical application and analysis for purposes of, for example, fairly and finally establishing limits on freedom of conduct, as well as resolving disputes among citizens, or between citizens and governments, or between governments at different levels. And to facilitate this application and analysis we bring into being a legal profession, from which we draw our judges, that is composed of people trained in programs of study that teach not, or not just, moral philosophy, but the specific tools and techniques of research, interpretation, reasoning, and argument relevant to *legal* analysis.

To stress law's objectivity and relative autonomy from morality is by no means to deny the Thomistic proposition that just positive law is derived from the natural law. For Thomas himself did not suppose that positive law was anything other than a cultural artifact, a human creation, albeit a creation of great moral worth brought into being largely for moral purposes. Nor did he suppose that a single form or regime of law was uniquely correct for all times and places. His stress on *determinationes* by which human lawmakers give effect to the requirements of natural law in the shape of positive law for the common good of his community— enjoying, to a considerable extent, the creative freedom Aquinas analogized to that of the architect—reveals his awareness of the legitimate variability of human laws. Whomever Holmes may have had in mind in criticizing those "text writers" who saw law as a set of deductions from a few axioms of reason, the charge does not apply to Aquinas. In this, as in so many other respects, the Angelic Doctor was a man of the twentieth century and—if I may engage in a bit of prediction and prophecy myself—of the twenty-first and beyond.

NOTES

1. Editors' note: The Hart-Devlin debate was the focus of part one of an earlier volume in the Prometheus Books Contemporary Issues in Philosophy Series. See Robert M. Baird and Stuart E. Rosenbaum, ed., *Morality and the Law* (Amherst, NY: Prometheus Books, 1988), pp. 15–53.

DWORKIN AND HART ON "THE LAW"

A POLANYIAN RECONSIDERATION

Ira H. Peak Jr.

INTRODUCTION

I t is the purpose of this paper to propose and defend a potential resolution of a long-standing conundrum in the philosophy of law. The conundrum is posed by the conceptual impasse emerging from the debate between H. L. A. Hart and Ronald Dworkin over the nature of "the law." The paper is developed in three sections. The first contextualizes the debate between these giants in the field of jurisprudence. The second section develops in some detail the positions of each thinker on this central issue in legal philosophy, the "rules" approach of Hart and the "principles" approach of Dworkin. This section also sharpens these differences in terms of the broader issues which their debate poses for the larger field of philosophy of law. A third section proposes a Polanyian model for reconsidering this apparent impasse. The model develops an

Tradition & Discovery: The Polanyi Society Periodical 18, no. 2 (1991–1992): 22–32.

approach to decision-making in terms of "universal intent." The paper's conclusion seeks to establish that this model can be applied to the philosophy of law and effectively forge a compromise between the competing views of Hart and Dworkin.

I.

Perhaps the simplest way to contextualize the Hart-Dworkin debate is to sketch (all too) briefly the poles between which each sought to position himself, i.e. natural law theory (exemplified preeminently by St. Thomas) and "legal positivism" (articulated classically by the 19th century British jurist John Austin).

In *Summa Theologica*, St. Thomas organizes his discussions of "the nature of law" around his notion of "natural law." Law, in this view, is universal because it springs from reason possessed by all people. It is this natural law that shapes the positive law of which we ordinarily speak in referring to "the law." Positive law stands in contrast both to natural law and to divine law, and the relations among the three in the ordering of human life are explained by St. Thomas. In this connection the question of special importance is whether (and in what way) human law is derived from natural law.

Positive law, for St. Thomas, is determined by the natural law for the common good. It is binding upon the conscience, because it is just. The "angelic doctor's" concept of law, then, is of an ideal to be found in laws. It is absent when unjust exercise of power produces laws in name only. For the most part these need not be obeyed. St. Thomas's views on law and morality actually anticipate more modern views regarding conscientious objection to unjust laws. For, on his understanding, only moral wrongs that are socially significant, such as harm to others, properly concern the law.

John Austin's work in jurisprudence has long been regarded in the Anglo-American tradition as the leading work in opposition to natural law theory. Austin seeks to define positive law, and this he does by distinguishing "laws properly so called" from other law-like utterances and other things called laws.

Laws properly so called turn out to be "commands" requiring conduct; and some, called positive laws, issue from a sovereign to

members of an independent political society over which sovereignty is exercised. Commands entail a purpose and a power to
impose sanctions on those who disobey; a sovereign is a determi-
nate human superior (that is, one who can successfully compel
others to obey) who is not in a habit of obedience to such a superior and who also receives habitual obedience. An independent
political society, then, is one in which the bulk of society habitually
obeys a sovereign.

Accordingly, Austin's "legal positivism" sees the issue of "the
law" reducing to the issue of who sets the rule (i.e., "command")
and how the command is enforced (i.e., by force or threat of force).
Oversimplified, and crudely so, Austin sees the operative principle
in determination of "the law" as something like, (successfully and
effectively exercised) *"might makes* (properly 'legal') *right."*

Hence, whereas for St. Thomas positive law could be said to be
grounded, in some sense, axiologically, for Austin law's only
"grounding" is the effective exercise of power to enforce commands. Stated alternatively, while St. Thomas defines the law in
terms *de jure*, Austin does so in terms *de facto*.

II.

As one might suppose, much of the literature in this domain of the
philosophy of law has been given over to attempts to define mediating positions between these "extremes." Two such mediating
views are articulated by Hart and Dworkin.

The work now generally regarded as the most important twentieth-century statement of the positivist position in the Anglo-
American tradition is H. L. A. Hart's book, *The Concept of Law*.[1] In
it, Hart does not seek to defend a narrow, partisan tradition, but
rather departs from Austin's version of positivism by undertaking
a broad reexamination of the fundamental questions of jurisprudence, clarifying them and securing their importance.

Hart's analysis of the concept of law is based on several inter-
related ideas.[2] He maintains that a legal system—in contrast to a
set of unrelated laws—consists of a union of primary rules of obligation and secondary rules. The most important secondary rule,

which Hart calls "the rule of recognition," specifies the criteria for identifying a law within the system (e.g., the United States Constitution). Other secondary rules specify how primary rules are changed or modified and when primary rules have been violated.

Furthermore, in distinguishing primary rules of obligation from secondary rules, Hart takes the position that there is at least one type of law that imposes an obligation.[3] This type tells citizens that they must not do this or must do that. Raising the crucial question of what an obligation with respect to legal rules means, Hart rejects the idea that to say that law imposes an obligation is merely to assert a prediction (about likely behavior of citizens). Nor does he accept the view that laws imposing an obligation are simply coercive orders.

Hart attempts to provide a general analysis of obligation in terms of social pressure.[4] He sees this analysis as clearly distinguishing his view from those of Austin and other positivists.

Finally, in order to understand secondary and primary rules and the obligation the law imposes, Hart insists that the point of view of people who follow and apply the law must be considered.[5] In particular, he emphasizes the importance of an internal point of view of the law, that is, the point of view of those who operate within the law rather than of external observers of the law. So, according to Hart, a legal theorist who wishes to understand a legal system must view the legal system from the point of view of an actor *in* the system.[6] In Wittgenstein's categories, perhaps, we might say that Hart views the legal system as a "form of life," rather than merely as a formal system.

How then, one might inquire, do Hart's notions of "law" and "legal system" impact the crucial issue of judicial interpretation? Clearly, he has moved away from a strict legal formalism, the view that legal interpretation is always simply the straightforward application of a legal rule to a case. Hart does believe that there are instances where this formalist approach is appropriate, but he denies that it always is. Sometimes the judge must exercise discretion, and a mechanical application of rule to case is impossible.

Note the difficulty which this issue poses for a legal positivist who is equally displeased with a natural law form of "legal foundations" and the extreme position of rule skepticism (the notion that judges always have wide discretion and that the application of rules to cases plays no significant role in judicial decision). I will return to this issue a bit later. For the present, I will merely note that across the years Hart's position on this issue has undergone change. To be fair, therefore, I will attempt to characterize his position on judicial interpretation in terms of his mature thought on this problem, some of which has evolved in his ongoing debate with Ronald M. Dworkin.

Dworkin, the most famous critic of Hart's theory of judicial interpretation, was Hart's successor to the Chair of Jurisprudence at Oxford University. Against Hart, Dworkin maintains that even in unclear cases there is always one correct decision, although what this decision might be is unknown. In addition, Dworkin argues that a judge's decision in unclear cases is characteristically determined, and should be, entirely by principles specifying rights and entitlements. But I am here getting ahead of myself. I must first summarize in more specific terms exactly how Dworkin's position differs from Hart's.

Professor Ronald Dworkin has presented a fascinating critical tool in philosophy of law for critiquing legal positivism, i.e., his notion of "legal principles."[7] He describes principles as "a standard that is to be observed, not because it will advance or secure an economic, political, or social situation deemed desirable, but because it is a requirement of justice or fairness or some other dimension of morality."[8] He argues that the difference between "principles" and "rules" is (1) "logical"; (2) related to the fact that principles (not rules) differ in their "weightiness"; but (3) not always recognizable from their form.[9]

Although "principles" are sometimes well established (for example, by judicial precedent), at times they do not become established until there is adjudication of "hard cases."[10] Yet these *principles* become (indeed are used for) the justification of decisions in cases, which (in turn) become *rules* of law.[11]

Although Dworkin defends his concept of "legal principles" with explicit intent and systematic vigor in "The Model of Rules," the nature and subtlety of his position emerges more clearly from his more popular article "On Not Prosecuting Civil Disobedience."[12] For our purposes here, however, the foregoing summary of Dworkin's position will suffice.

It would appear that the net effect of Dworkin's firm opposition to legal positivism is a kind of conundrum for philosophy of law. On the one hand, Dworkin is able to demonstrate that the "rules" (or "pedigree") approach of H. L. A. Hart to "certifying" valid positive law does not account for the presence of (and appeal to) "principles" (not reducible to "rules") within jurisprudence. Indeed, it does appear that "principles" in fact play a role in some judges arriving at decisions, interpreting their reasoning, and justifying their claims.

On the other hand, Dworkin is unable to identify all such principles (since some remain unnoticed/undiscovered until a judge is forced to rule on a "hard case"). Moreover, he cannot specify their status, although he believes quite clearly that they are "legally binding" upon judges in making rulings or handing down decisions.

Hence, the conundrum. It would appear that there is a functioning critical apparatus at work within our legal system (and, perhaps, beyond), the legal status of which cannot be established.

In "On Not Prosecuting Civil Disobedience," Dworkin does at least begin to lay bare why this anomaly exists. He argues that there is what he calls "doubtful law," law the validity of which is in dispute (or is otherwise suspect).[13] "In the US, at least, almost any law which a significant number of people would be tempted to disobey on moral grounds would be doubtful, if not clearly invalid, on constitutional grounds as well. The constitution makes our conventional political morality relevant to the question of validity: any statute that appears to compromise that morality raises constitutional questions, and if the compromise is serious, the constitutional doubts are serious also."[14] Moreover, Dworkin believes that in draft resistance cases of the late 1960s, the connection between moral and legal issues were made especially (even starkly) clear.

Draft dissenters, in Dworkin's view, were not asserting a privilege to disobey valid laws. They believed firmly that the laws being broken were unconstitutional. Under these conditions, it is not always clear how such dissenters in a complex society are to "play the game."[15] This metaphor is ironic. It is the legal positivists who have relied heavily on images and metaphors like "playing a game" to emphasize the law's rule-like character and process. Yet,

Dworkin has presented a challenge, asking now what (or whose?) move is next.[16] How then does Hart's position respond to Dworkin's challenge? We must recall that Hart sees law as an institution within a larger social system. It is a form of rule-making, rule-applying, and rule-enforcing behavior. These rules do indeed have connection to morality, both in origin (on occasion) and in interpretation, as well as in application and enforcement. This overlapping of differing kinds of rules, in this case moral ones and legal ones, does not imply the dependence of one upon the other in any "ultimate" sense, any more than other social rules (e.g., "rules of etiquette") might be.[17] What alternative, then, does Hart offer for explaining the "foundations" of law? Hart introduced the notion of "rules of recognition."[18] The "rule of recognition" is a secondary rule used to identify primary rules of obligation.[19] This rule of recognition is more complex in modern legal systems where there are a variety of "sources" of law.[20] The relationship of one set of rules to the other is one of "relative subordination," not derivation. In his more mature thought, Hart has broadened his concept of "rules" applied by judges in their decisions to embrace "legal standards."[21] Although Hart now believes that these legal standards constrain a judge's decision in unclear cases, he maintains that there may be alternative decisions in such cases that are equally justified in terms of these standards. In Dworkin's view, Hart's position remains truncated and unsatisfying.

Hence, the conundrum cited above remains. It can be summarized as follows. If Hart's positivist account of the nature of "the law," a system of primary and secondary rules, validated by a (secondary) "rule of recognition" and supplemented by emerging "legal standards" in the process of judicial interpretation, is accepted, his approach seems unable to account for the role played by principles in many judicial decisions, especially "hard cases." If, by contrast, Dworkin's claims that some principles appealed to in judicial decisions and opinions are in fact "legal principles" and "obligatory" for judges to follow are accepted, then it would seem that he should be able to identify these principles or to state how they are themselves justified or validated. But, alas, he cannot. How then is "the law" to be related to "principles"?

It would appear that the impasse reached by Hart and Dworkin remains. Yet, there may be another alternative. The key to identifying that alternative may be lurking in Dworkin's characterization of judicial decisions in "hard cases." Dworkin admits that judges sometimes face cases where the "right" principle of law (to which appeal should be made in determining the case) is not known. Not only is it not known by the particular judge presiding; but it is not known by anyone else as well! In fact, says Dworkin, it is only when such hard cases are adjudicated that a judge's attention can be directed to that principle (which is the right principle). In other words, it is only in the judicial process itself that some such principles emerge. They are actual, but previously unrecognized, principles of law. The principle for deciding the case rightly, it would seem, given this characterization, is present only *tacitly*, not *explicitly*.

Yet, this hypothesizing takes us outside the parameters of either Hart's position or Dworkin's. To develop a model, then, for moving beyond their conundrum, I propose that we consider a model for decision-making developed from the thought of Michael Polanyi.

III.

The model to be developed here out of Polanyi's thought was anticipated in, and suggested to me by, a paragraph from Richard Gelwick.[22] Following Carl Friedrich's analysis, Gelwick suggests a new possibility for discussing natural law.[23] "Even though Polanyi does not discuss natural law, his grounding of cultural values in a society of universal intent suggests a 'natural law theory in human nature.'"[24] "His [Polanyi's] thought, therefore, bears *a fortiori* upon the enterprise and its interpretation of attempting to embody justice in law. . . ."[25]

In the analysis which follows, I will develop a model of decision-making which parallels, in some respects the position articulated by Friedrich; but it is not dependent upon his notion of "natural law." Hence, while being appreciative of Friedrich's illuminating insights, I have developed a model which is independent of his and more closely tied to the phenomenology of moral experience than to the venerable history of natural law theory. (I have

developed the connections between a Polanyian model for decision making and the phenomenological analysis of moral experience more explicitly in an unpublished paper, "Can a Moral Judgment Be Both Contextual and Objective?")

Taking the conundrum bequeathed to the philosophy of law by
Hart and Dworkin as our point of departure, I ask that you recall
the plight of the judge hypothesized above, who must decide a
"hard case" in which the strict application of rules will not suffice.
Moreover, he or she may not have access even to a specific principle of law, because the "right" principle has not yet been articulated (or otherwise discovered) in the history of judicial interpretation. Yet, in order to become the basis for the adjudication of the
case at hand, the judge must appeal to a *legal* principle, one
derived from, and inherent in, the body of existing law (both leg-
islated and interpreted).

Since what is called for then is a kind of "discovery" on the part
of our hypothetical judge, I would . . . [note] Polanyi's discussion of
that issue in *Science, Faith and Society* . . . [where] "discovery" is
described by Polanyi . . . as a process . . . which he summarizes in
the four words "Preparation, Incubation, Illumination, and Verification," a process not unlike consistent efforts at "guessing and exper-
imenting," in creating a work of art, ". . . solving riddles, inventing
practical devices, . . . diagnosing of an illness," and perhaps, prayer-
fully "searching for God."[26] Rather than attempting merely to
"achieve results," the scientist is attempting to make contact with
reality. Therefore, the guiding and constraining force by which
he/she seeks and sorts evidence must be his/her own conscience—
since there are not set rules for procedure to which he/she can
appeal for validation of his/her choices and conclusions.

Polanyi devotes the balance of this work (*SFS*) to showing how
the community of scientific discovery and inquiry protects its tradition against mere subjectivism and blatant error and to describing the necessary freedom under which science must operate to
prohibit the encroachment of either skepticism or totalitarianism.
He is concerned to show that the loyalty of scientists to the discovery of truth for its own sake must not be abdicated to the tran-
sient interests of any lesser authority.

Polanyi notes that the seemingly subjective judgments of scientists are guided by the premises of science which are twofold. These are (1) "naturalistic assumptions concerning the nature of every day life"; and (2) "more particular assumptions underlying the process of scientific discovery and verification."[27] These premises are learned and passed on to succeeding generations of scientists in the manner of artistic tradition and practice. Hence, there is not a set of cold facts which can be captured in language and memorized by the novice in science. He or she must be guided beyond techniques and principles to a grasping of reality, whereby his/her own judgment can become operative in both assessment of data and recognition of problems.

In a similar vein, Polanyi demonstrates the way in which mutual discipline in the scientific community protects against the admission of error into premises and tradition. He does so by indicating the kind of self-government in science which exercises the authority of scientific opinion. He summarizes thus, "It is clear enough then that the self-governing institutions of science are effective in safe-guarding the organized practice of science which embodies and transmits its premises."[28] He argues that the functions of these institutions are mainly protective and regulative and based themselves on a "general harmony of views among scientists." This general harmony is seen as growing out of a common tradition in science, as being maintained by the acceptance of mutual bonds of loyalty to scientific ideals, and as depending ultimately on the common exercise of scientific conscience. There can be no appeal for validity in scientific inquiry, other than to scientific opinion itself, without jeopardizing the entire scientific enterprise. The kind of authority operative in the scientific community demands not obedience, but freedom.

The exercise of decision by which new theories are to be screened and competing theories evaluated must not be usurped.

> There are divisions among scientists, sometimes sharp and passionate, but both contestants remain agreed that scientific opinion will ultimately decide right; and they are satisfied to appeal to it as their ultimate arbiter . . . A common belief in the reality of scientific ideals and a sufficient confidence in their fellow scientists' sincerity resolves among scientists the apparent

internal contradiction in the conception of freedom. It establishes government by scientific opinion, as a General Authority, inherently restricted to the guardianship of the premises of freedom.[29]

Hence, Polanyi can affirm that the goal of scientific inquiry must never be exclusively utilitarian. Rather, its goal must be the discovery of the truth to which it is committed. This can be done only within the context of a society which guarantees the freedom and encourages the dedication of its members to the pursuit of transcendent obligations, "particularly to truth, justice and charity."[30]

Nevertheless, Polanyi's belief that knowledge is grounded in personal and tacit commitments does not mean that he thinks that "knowledge" is simply subjective. It is true that there is no such thing as perfect objectivity in knowledge. No perfect detachment, nothing perfectly explicit is possible, even in the ideal case of knowledge.

The knower, however, is not thereby condemned to whimsical subjectivity, by the fact that his/her *intent* in knowledge is universal.[31] The intent is inescapably universal, Polanyi thinks, because the quest for knowledge is a quest for an impersonal reality.[32] To suppose that one has found it is to suppose that others "similarly equipped," would also be able to find it.[33] The knower, therefore, does make use of the rules and standards that he/she supposes to be universal, in the sense of being the "proper" ones for anyone to use.[34] On Polanyi's view the scientific community functions as a kind of moral association of persons by exercising mutual authority. It welds tradition and freedom together in a pursuit of the truth. It upholds the personal, tacit component but also the universal intent of knowing. This touches the central nerve of Polanyi's epistemology. He is purposing nothing less than the attempt to overcome the split between the subjective and the objective, an attempt which is based on the distinction between

... the personal in us, which actively enters into our commitments, and our subjective states, in which we merely endure our feelings. This distinction establishes the conception of the *personal*, which is neither subjective nor objective. In so far as the personal submits to requirements acknowledged by itself as independent of itself, it is not subjective; but insofar as it is an action guided by individual passions it is not objective either. It transcends the disjunction between subjective and objective.[35]

The mutual correlation between the personal and the universal within the framework of commitment, then, is the "solution" to the paradox of standards which are determined by personal commitment and belief. The answer to the objection to Polanyi's view that it implies that "you can believe whatever you like" is, quite simply, that you cannot, if you wish to be responsible within a community of universal intent.

> While compulsion by force or by neurotic obsession excludes responsibility, compulsion by universal intent establishes responsibility. . . . While the choices in question are open to egocentric decisions, a craving for the universal sustains a constructive effort and narrows down this discretion to the point where the agent making the decision finds that he cannot do otherwise. *The freedom of the subjective person to do as he pleases is overruled by the freedom of the responsible person to act as he must.*[36]

It is in this limited sense, then, of what Polanyi has called "personal knowledge" that any scientific judgment can lay claim to being "objective."

How, then, does this account of "discovery" and exercise of judgment underwrite a model of decision-making which could be employed by a judge deciding a "hard case"?

Both Polanyi's scientist and the judge presuppose that the respective principles with which each is concerned are ultimately rooted in beliefs and commitments (ones foundational to scientific inquiry and the practice of jurisprudence, respectively). Yet, in the nature of the case (for each enterprise) these beliefs and commitments are nondemonstrable.

Moreover, each of these projects, in its own way, asserts that its judgments represent attempts to make contact with reality, based on informed perceptions of patterns or "shapes" in the real which manifest themselves to inquiry—whether the inquiry be into the observable behavior of phenomena or into "the facts of the case." Each kind of judgment is informed by norms or principles embraced by a community of people who share mutual commitments (to the premises of science/to the rule of law) and universal intent (in the pursuit of truth/in the pursuit of justice). Each one's judgments claim to be public and authoritative, even if they are original or novel; because they are made with universal intent and with the expectation of being ultimately vindicated within the community.

Lest one be inclined to decry this attempt to develop a model for decision-making out of Polanyi's philosophy of science and epistemology, one which can apply to a judge's interpretation of "the law," ... [note] Polanyi's discussion of "systems of spontaneous order" and "systems of intellectual order" in the tenth chapter of *The Logic of Liberty*.[37]

The section of this chapter entitled "Systems of Intellectual Order" takes as its first example "... the Law, and in particular Common Law."[38]

> Consider a judge sitting in court and deciding a difficult case. While pondering his decision, he refers consciously to dozens of precedents and unconsciously to many more. Before him numberless other judges have sat and decided according to statute, precedent, equity and convenience, as he himself has to do now; his mind, while he analyses [sic] the various aspects of the case, is in constant contact with theirs. And beyond the purely legal references, he senses the entire contemporary trend of opinions, the social medium as a whole. Not until he has established all these bearings of his case and reasoned to them in the light of his own professional conscience, will his decision acquire force of conviction and will he be ready to declare it.[39]

The operation of Common Law constitutes a "sequence of adjustments," both between succeeding judges and (as well) between the judges and the general public. "The result is the ordered growth of the Common Law, steadily reapplying and reinterpreting the same fundamental rules and expanding them thus to a system of increasing scope and consistency."[40]

In this process of discovery of legal principles "embedded" in the matrix of legal precedent, relevant law, facts brought to light by testimony in court, etc., Friedrich rightly affirms that in law, as in science, "... tacit knowing plays a decisive role. Polanyi's insistence that 'there are vast domains of knowledge that exemplify in various ways that we are generally unable to tell what particulars we are aware of when attending to a coherent entity which they constitute,' while written with scientific experiment in the foreground of attention, applied equally well to the law."[41]

IV.

The forgoing analysis, utilizing the categories of Polanyi's thought, indicates that there is, indeed ". . . a functioning critical apparatus at work within our legal system," the legal status of which we can now establish. (In so doing, we will demonstrate that the Hart-Dworkin conundrum is subject to resolution.)

The values of a society have a "fiduciary grounding" in the personal backing given to them ". . . by men who, moved as they are by moral and intellectual passions, perceive and uphold these values with universal intent within a convivial order."[42] Quite clearly, however, the embodiment of justice in laws and in judicial decisions is both necessarily incomplete and yet also achieved in part by more or less skillful judicial assessment.

> These skillful feats, supported by moral and intellectual passions with universal intent, are accredited by and subject to the superintendency of the convivial order within which they are achieved and whose very basis is in turn precisely these same passions.[43]

Hence, both Hart and Dworkin are right, but incomplete, in their interpretations of "the law." Hart is correct that law is legitimated by appeal to secondary rules and a "rule of recognition." Yet, as Dworkin rightly argued, some decisions regarding the nature of "the law" can only be settled by appeal to principles (not reducible to rules) within jurisprudence. It certainly appears that "principles" in fact play a role in some judges arriving at decisions, interpreting their reasoning and justifying their claims.

At the same time, we now can account for why Dworkin was unable to identify all such principles, as well as why some legal principles remain unnoticed or undiscovered until a judge is forced to rule on a "hard case."

Important legal principles implicit within the legal framework of legislation, judicial interpretation, etc., are present only tacitly. The principles are present and operative within the jurisprudential community, a community of universal intent. In certain "hard cases," one or more members of the community are forced (by the incompleteness of explicit case law) to render a decision which requires the application of the tacitly held principle. Under these conditions, that which is "tacit" becomes the object of focal awareness. Accordingly, the "right legal principle," thus discovered, was present all along.

NOTES

1. H. L. A. Hart, *The Concept of Law* (Oxford: Clarendon, 1961).

2. See especially ibid., "Law As the Union of Primary and Secondary Rules," p. 77ff.

3. Ibid., p. 80ff.

4. Ibid., p. 84ff.

5. Ibid., pp. 86–87.

6. Ibid., p. 88ff.

7. Ronald M. Dworkin, "The Model of Rules," in *Philosophy of Law*, ed. Joel Feinberg, Hyman Gross, Jules Coleman, 3rd ed. (Belmont, CA: Wadsworth, 1986), p. 153ff.

8. Ibid., p. 153.

9. Ibid., pp. 154, 156.

10. Ibid., p. 157.

11. Ibid.

12. Ronald M. Dworkin, "On Not Prosecuting Civil Disobedience," *New York Review of Books* 10 (June 6, 1968), pp. 14–21.

13. Ibid., p. 15ff.

14. Ibid., p. 16.

15. Ibid., p. 17.

16. For a detailed examination of these issues in a format comparing Hart and Dworkin, see Philip E. Soper, "Legal Theory and the Obligation of the Judge: The Hart/Dworkin Dispute," in *Ronald Dworkin and Contemporary Jurisprudence*, ed. Marshall Cohen (Totowa, NJ: Rowman and Allenheld, 1984), pp. 3–27.

17. H. L. A. Hart, "Positivism and the Separation of Law and Morals," in *Philosophy of Law*, ed. Joel Feinberg, Hyman Gross, Jules Coleman, 3rd ed. (Belmont, CA: Wadsworth, 1986), p. 82.

18. Hart, *The Concept of Law*, p. 94.

19. Ibid., p. 94ff.

20. Ibid., p. 97ff.

21. Soper, "Legal Theory," pp. 7–9.

22. Richard Gelwick, *The Way of Discovery: An Introduction to the Thought of Michael Polanyi* (New York: Oxford University Press, 1977), pp. 127–28.

23. Thomas A. Langford and William H. Poteat, *Intellect and Hope* (Durham, NC: Duke University Press, 1968), pp. 91–110.

24. Gelwick, *The Way of Discovery*, p. 127.

25. Carl Freidrich, quoted in Langford and Poteat, *Intellect and Hope*, p. 92.

26. Michael Polanyi, *Science, Faith, and Society* (Chicago: University of Chicago Press, 1964), p. 34.

27. Ibid., p. 42.

28. Ibid., p. 50.

29. Ibid., p. 63.

30. Ibid., p. 85.

31. Michael Polanyi, *The Tacit Dimension* (Garden City, NY: Doubleday, 1967), pp. 77–78.

32. Michael Polanyi, *Personal Knowledge: Towards a Post-Critical Philosophy* (New York: Harper and Row, 1964), p. 300ff.

33. Ibid., p. 324.

34. Ibid., p. 343.

35. Ibid., p. 300.

36. Ibid., p. 309.

37. Michael Polanyi, *The Logic of Liberty: Reflections and Rejoinders* (Chicago: University of Chicago Press, 1951), p. 154ff.

38. Ibid., p. 162.

39. Ibid.

40. Ibid.

41. Langford and Poteat, *Intellect and Hope*, pp. 103–104.

42. Ibid., p. 91.

43. Ibid., p. 92.

SOURCES CONSULTED

Dworkin, Ronald M. "The Model of Rules." In *Philosophy of Law*, 3rd ed., edited by Joel Feinberg, Hyman Gross, and Jules Coleman, 149–66. Belmont, CA: Wadsworth, 1986.

————. "Is There Really No Right Answer In Hard Cases?" In *Philosophy of Law*, 3rd ed., edited by Joel Feinberg, Hyman Gross, and Jules Coleman, 174–91. Belmont, CA: Wadsworth, 1986.

————. *The Philosophy of Law*. London and Oxford: Oxford University Press, 1977.

————. "On Not Prosecuting Civil Disobedience." *New York Review of Books* 10 (June 6, 1968): 14–21.

————. "Lord Devlin and the Enforcement of Morals." *Yale Law Review* 75 (1966): 986–1005.

Gelwick, Richard. *The Way of Discovery: An Introduction to the Thought of Michael Polanyi*. New York: Oxford University Press, 1977.

Gill, Jerry H. "Reasons of the Hearts: A Polanyian Reflection." *Religious Studies* 14 (1978): 143–57.

————. "Tacit Knowing and Religious Belief." *International Journal for the Philosophy of Religion* 6 (1975): 73–88.

————. "The Case for Tacit Knowledge." *Southern Journal of Philosophy* 9 (1971): 49–60.

Grant, Patrick. "Michael Polanyi: The Augustinian Component." *New Scholasticism* 48 (1974): 438–63.

Grene, Marjorie. "Polanyi et la Philosophie Francaise." *Archives de Philosophie* 35 (1972): 3–5.

Hart, H. L. A. "Positivism and the Separation of Law and Morals." In *Philosophy of Law*, 3rd ed., edited by Joel Feinberg, Hyman Gross, and Jules Coleman, 69–87. Belmont, CA: Wadsworth, 1986.

————. *Essays in Jurisprudence and Philosophy*. Oxford: Clarendon Press, 1983.

————. "Social Solidarity and the Enforcement of Morality." *University of Chicago Law Review* 35 (1967): 1–13.

————. *The Concept of Law*. Oxford: Clarendon Press, 1961.

Jensen, A. D. "Polanyi's Personal Language." *Southwestern Journal of Philosophy* 6 (1975): 95–107.

Kroger, Joseph. "Polanyi and Lonergan on Scientific Method." *Philosophy Today* 21 (1977): 2–20.

Langford, Thomas A., William H. Poteat. *Intellect and Hope*. Durham, NC: Duke University Press, 1968.

Mackie, John. "The Third Theory of Law." In *Ronald Dworkin and Contemporary Jurisprudence*, edited by Marshal Cohen, 161–70. Totowa, NJ: Rowman and Allenheld, 1984.

Martin, Michael. *The Legal Philosophy of H. L. A. Hart*. Philadelphia: Temple University Press, 1987.

Polanyi, Michael. *Meaning*. Chicago: University of Chicago Press, 1975.

————. "On the Introduction of Science into Moral Subjects." In *Scientific Thought and Social Reality*, edited by Fred Schwartz. New York: International Universities Press, 1974.

————. *Knowing and Being*, edited by Marjorie Grene. London: Routledge G. K. Paul, 1969.

————. *The Tacit Dimension*. Garden City, NY: Doubleday, 1967.

————. *Personal Knowledge: Towards a Post-Critical Philosophy*. New York: Harper and Row, 1964.

————. *Science, Faith, and Society*. Chicago: University of Chicago Press, 1964.

————. *Beyond Nihilism*, 32. Cambridge: Cambridge University Press, 1960.

————. *The Study of Man*. Chicago: University of Chicago Press, 1959.

————. *The Logic of Liberty: Reflections and Rejoinders*. Chicago: University of Chicago Press, 1951.

Soper, E. Philip. "Legal Theory and the Obligation of a Judge: The Hart/Dworkin Dispute." In *Ronald Dworkin and Contemporary Jurisprudence*, edited by Marshal Cohen, 3–27. Totowa, NJ: Rowman and Allenheld, 1984.

VIRTUES AND VERDICTS

A REVIEW OF RONALD DWORKIN'S
JUSTICE IN ROBES

Cass R. Sunstein

During their recent confirmation hearings, John Roberts and Samuel Alito insisted on the importance of "following the law," and of distinguishing between a judge's personal moral commitments and his views about the Constitution. In drawing this distinction, both nominees recapitulated a discussion in the presidential debates of 2004, when the candidates were asked what kind of person they would appoint to the Supreme Court. President Bush replied, "I would pick somebody who would not allow their personal opinion to get in the way of the law. I would pick somebody who would strictly interpret the Constitution of the United States." Senator Kerry agreed. He said, "I don't believe we need a good conservative judge, and I don't believe we need a good liberal judge. . . . I want to make sure we have judges who interpret the Constitution of the United States according to the law."

For over three decades, Ronald Dworkin has been the most

The New Republic 234, no. 4766 (May 22, 2006).

influential and illuminating analyst of the view that judges can or should merely "follow the law." In this collection of recent essays, Dworkin explores the relationship between law and morality, elaborating his previous arguments and replying to a number of prominent objections. Dworkin agrees that judges generally must be faithful to existing legal materials, but he insists that they are not merely "following" something. The law is often unclear. Dworkin contends that when resolving real disputes, judges must select the principle that puts previous decisions in their most attractive light. For this reason, the task of interpretation requires judges to think seriously about what morality requires, and they might well end up moving the law in dramatic and novel directions. On these grounds, Dworkin argues that some of the most controversial decisions of the Supreme Court, commonly challenged as forms of "liberal activism," are perfectly defensible. *Roe v. Wade*, protecting the right to choose abortion, is just one example; and Dworkin leaves little doubt that he would welcome judicial decisions broadening the right of privacy.

To see how Dworkin's approach works, suppose that the Supreme Court is asked to decide whether the Constitution guarantees terminally ill patients a right to physician-assisted suicide. The text of the Constitution bans states from depriving people of "life, liberty, or property, without due process of law." Over a span of decades, the Court has issued many decisions interpreting the due process clause. In some of those decisions, the Court has said that the government may not intrude on certain intensely private choices (such as the right to live with members of one's family). Faced with a legal ban on physician-assisted suicide, Dworkin thinks that the Court has to make a moral judgment. It has to ask, what principle makes best sense of the previous decisions? Dworkin's approach imposes a requirement of what he calls "integrity." Judges must not only fit previous rulings but also "justify" them, by identifying the principle that puts them in the best light.

Many people do not like Dworkin's method. These critics seek to eliminate moral judgments from judicial rulings. Justices Antonin Scalia and Clarence Thomas believe that the Constitution should be read to mean what it meant at the time of ratification. At one point in his confirmation hearings, Alito too spoke in frankly originalist terms, saying, "I think we should look to the text of the Constitution, and we should look to the meaning that someone would have taken from the text of the Constitution at the time of its adoption." Originalists believe that their view captures what it means to be faithful to the founding document. They accuse their opponents, those committed to a "Living Constitution," of infidelity to the document as it stands.

In one of his most vigorous discussions, Dworkin explains why he rejects Scalia's approach in favor of one that authorizes judges to make ambitious moral claims. He accepts "semantic originalism," or the view that it is important to begin "by asking what—on the best evidence available—the authors of the text in question intended to say." But he rejects "expectation originalism," which understands the Constitution to conform to the founders' original expectations about how their words would be interpreted.

To appreciate the difference between the two forms of originalism, consider the constitutional provision that prevents states from denying people "the equal protection of the laws." It is clear that the authors of this provision did not mean to ban discrimination on the basis of sex or sexual orientation. For expectation originalists, such discrimination is acceptable. But for semantic originalists, this conclusion is far less clear. The answer turns on whether discrimination on the basis of sex or sexual orientation actually does deprive people of "equal protection of the laws." That question, in Dworkin's view, calls for a moral judgment, not a historical one.

Dworkin says that when we are asking about the meaning of constitutional terms such as "cruel and unusual punishment" or "equal protection of the laws," we must choose between "an abstract, principled, moral reading" and "a concrete, dated reading." The abstract, principled, moral reading would insist "that the authors meant to prohibit punishments that are in fact cruel as well as unusual." The concrete, dated reading would ban punishments that were thought to be cruel and unusual at the time they wrote. Dworkin argues in favor of the abstract reading, on the ground that it best fits what the Constitution actually says. "The framers were careful statesmen who knew how to use the language they spoke," and they "presumably . . . used abstract language because they intended to state abstract principles." Scalia and Thomas are expectation originalists, and Dworkin accuses them of a kind of infidelity to the Constitution itself.

Dworkin does not think that the abstract reading allows judges to do whatever they want. Their obligation to "fit" the document, and previous judicial decisions, imposes real constraints. Dworkin himself believes, for example, that in principle the idea of equal citizenship requires "at least a decent minimum standard of housing, nutrition, and medical care." But courts cannot insist on such a standard, because doing so would "graft into our constitutional system something that (in my view) doesn't fit at all." Yet if judges are allowed to produce a principle to make best sense of past decisions, they might well move the law in novel and surprising directions. Thus Dworkin thinks that the Court was wrong to refuse to recognize a right, on the part of dying patients, to physician-assisted suicide. He emphasizes that according to his approach, those who interpret the Constitution must "make fresh moral judgments about issues that deeply divide citizens, such as abortion, assisted suicide, and racial justice." But they make those decisions in the interest of fidelity to the Constitution, not in opposition to it.

Dworkin is aware that many people object to the judicial role that he espouses on the ground that it is fatally undemocratic. Why should judges, rather than citizens, make the relevant moral judgments? He responds by distinguishing between two conceptions of democracy. In the first, political majorities are entitled to answer all questions of politics and morality. In the second, the democratic ideal "means self-government by all of the people acting as members of a cooperative joint venture with equal standing." This conception of democracy, which he calls one of partnership, requires that citizens have "not only an equal franchise but an equal voice both in formal public deliberations and in informal moral exchanges." Partnership democracy also requires that people have "an equal stake in the government" and "a private sphere within which they are free to make the most religious and ethical decisions for themselves." Dworkin agrees that the judicial role that he supports is inconsistent with majoritarian democracy, but he rejects that conception of democracy as unattractive. By contrast, constitutional courts, seeking integrity, actually promote partnership democracy, because they help to secure its preconditions.

Dworkin also knows that some people do not want judges to "construct large-scale interpretations of grand moral principles." (I am one of Dworkin's principal targets here.) According to those who favor judicial "minimalism," judges should allow the law to "grow slowly, incrementally, by analogy rather than grand principle, testing its steps one by one, attempting bit by bit to make the law work better." The problem is that we cannot know whether any particular step "works" without reference to general principle. Minimalists want judges to avoid ambitious theoretical claims, but they cannot always do that, because their answers will sometimes presuppose an ambitious theoretical position. This is the problem with analogical reasoning: "analogies without principles are blind. Which analogy should the Supreme Court have adopted when asked whether women have a right to an early abortion? An abortion is in some ways like infanticide, in others like an appendectomy, and in others like the destruction of a work of art." Analogical reasoning might well require a kind of theoretical ascent in which judges end up taking controversial stands even if they try to avoid them.

Dworkin's rejection of minimalist judging is tied to his general rejection of pragmatism as an account of legal reasoning. Thus he devotes a good deal of space to the work of Richard Posner, who has long described himself as a pragmatist, and who is an especially sharp critic of the use of moral theory in law. Posner contends that judges do not and should not decide cases on the basis of controversial moral arguments; they should think instead about the consequences of one or another course of action. Dworkin mounts a blistering attack on Posner, arguing that he does not really avoid moral theory, and that he has no plausible argument for his claim that judges can and should do so. How can judges possibly rule on segregation, or privacy, or same-sex marriage, without resorting to moral claims of one or another sort? Posner's version of pragmatism "is empty, because though he insists that judges should decide cases so as to produce the best consequences he does not specify how judges should decide what the best consequences are."

For more than thirty years, Dworkin has been engaged in a complex and elaborate debate with the legal positivists, H. L. A. Hart and his various followers. Legal positivists typically insist on a sharp separation between law and morality; they believe that a statement about what the law is need not involve any moral judgment at all. Hart attempted to produce a purely descriptive, and morally neutral, account of the concept of law. One of his most influential claims was that the law qualifies as such by virtue of a "rule of recognition," which is a social convention, not a matter of morality. It is a convention, for example, that establishes that the US Constitution is law in the United States, as the Universal Declaration of Human Rights is not.

Dworkin objects that Hart's theory "is not a neutral description of legal practice" and indeed that no such description is possible. To defend that objection, Dworkin re-asserts his claim that on complicated issues, judges asked "to decide what the law is . . . must interpret past law to see what principles best justify it, and then decide what those principles require in the fresh case." Moral principles, not recognized by any convention, can be central to judicial rulings about whether a contract is valid, whether an injured person may receive compensation for an alleged wrong, whether a school may fire someone on the basis of sexual orientation. Responding to Dworkin, some positivists say that when the legal sources leave gaps, judges simply have discretion to make up the law. Other positivists contend that moral arguments are admissible if and only if the relevant rule of recognition makes them admissible. Hart himself acknowledged that "the rule of recognition may incorporate as criteria of legal validity conformity with moral principles or substantive values," as the Constitution appears to do.

Dworkin believes that these responses are quite inadequate. The reason is that a society may lack any "convention" to establish the rule of recognition. Hence people's disagreements about the governing law cannot be resolved by reference to any such rule; it can be resolved only by answering the relevant moral questions. Judges who decide in favor of a privacy right, or same-sex marriage, are unable to rely on a convention. They must think about what morality requires. When the Supreme Court ultimately pro-

vides answers to the most controversial questions, its task is interpretive in Dworkin's particular sense. The Court must attempt
both to fit and to justify the pre-existing legal materials.

In a discussion that does not involve law but that turns out to
be closely related to his critique of Hart, Dworkin challenges the
claim, associated with Isaiah Berlin, that our deepest moral commitments are plural and conflicting. Many people believe that they
are committed to both liberty and equality, but they know that the
two ideals might conflict. A sharply progressive income tax, for
example, might promote the goal of equality, but it might also
compromise liberty. Berlin contends that conflicts between deeply
held values can create a kind of tragedy, or at least some important
damage, as we are forced to sacrifice one in favor of another.
Dworkin is skeptical of this claim. Whether there is any conflict
"depends on how we conceive these abstract values." If we conceive of them properly, we may face no conflict. If we offer "an
account that shows us what is good about liberty or equality or
democracy, so that we can see why any compromise of these
values is not merely inconvenient but bad," the apparent conflict
may well disappear. It may be that a sharply progressive income
tax does not compromise liberty at all.

Dworkin contends that it is possible that "the most attractive
conceptions of the leading liberal values do hang together in the
right way." Against Berlin, Dworkin makes the same claim that he
makes against Hart—that "definitions or analyses of the concepts
of equality, liberty, law, and the rest are as substantive, normative,
and engaged as any of the contending opinions in the political battles that rage about those ideals." The reason is that such definitions and analyses are interpretive rather than merely descriptive.

Though Dworkin's arguments in this book range over
numerous topics, his main focus is on constitutional law, and
much of the book reads as a series of extended replies to the many
people (including Scalia and Posner) who have rejected his claim
that controversial moral judgments are important in determining
the Constitution's meaning. Dworkin's timing is extraordinarily
good, for we are living in a period in which that claim is under
immense pressure. Moreover, Dworkin is convincing on two large
points. First, he is right to emphasize the importance of both "fit"

and "justification." Any argument about the meaning of the Constitution is generally obliged to account for previous decisions, and to do so in a way that tries to make the best possible sense of them. This claim greatly helps to illuminate what legal argument is all about. And second, Dworkin is right to say that any theory of constitutional interpretation must be defended in moral, or at least political, terms. Those who select one theory of interpretation and reject others cannot claim that they are simply following the document or those who made it; they must be prepared to make moral or political arguments of their own.

The problem is that, from these two important points, Dworkin's more particular claims do not follow. Judges need not treat the Constitution as embodying abstract ideals, or as licensing them to strike down democratic enactments that offend their own best judgments about how those ideals are properly understood. Suppose that those judgments are highly unreliable—and that judges are entirely aware of their own limitations in the domain of moral theory. For that very reason, judges might adopt an approach to interpretation that limits their ability to make moral judgments in particular cases, or to wield those judgments as weapons against the democratic process. Indeed, judges might adopt that approach on the ground that it best fits and justifies our own practices. This, I think, is the real blind spot in Dworkin's account of constitutional law, and it requires a re-thinking of his approach to law in general.

To see the problem, let us begin with originalism. Dworkin favors "semantic originalism," which requires judges to follow what the Constitution's Framers meant to say. He does not favor "expectation originalism," which means that judges must follow what the Framers hoped, or expected, that their words would be taken to mean. But Dworkin misunderstands his adversaries. Sophisticated originalists such as Scalia are not much interested in the Framers. They care about the ratifiers—We the People—who were authorized to make the Constitution law. Nor do the best originalists focus on the "intentions," or hopes, or expectations, of the Framers. Instead they focus on the original public meaning of the document. Originalists believe that the Constitution must be construed to fit with its original public meaning to those who ratified it. Originalists insist that words have public meanings, and that the task of constitutional interpretation is to uncover those meanings at the time of ratification.

Dworkin could easily use this point to his advantage. He could contend that the original public meaning consists of abstract moral commitments, not concrete judgments. But if he is playing the originalists' game here, as he seems to be doing, his contention stands or falls on the answer to a historical question: did the original public meaning consist of abstract commitments or concrete ones? Dworkin seems unaccountably confident that, as a matter of history, the Constitution was understood to contain abstract ideals. As it happens, there is a considerable historical literature on this, to which Dworkin does not refer; and it is not at all clear that Dworkin's conclusion is right on historical grounds.

But perhaps Dworkin does not really believe that history should have the final word. He might believe that the question is how we should take the Constitution's words, and perhaps that question is interpretive, not a simple matter of history. Dworkin might well think that if we would make best sense out of the Constitution by treating it as embodying abstract commitments, then that is exactly what we should do. But why, exactly, is that what we should do? Suppose that originalists can claim that their approach fits, well or wonderfully, with many important areas of law—that for the most part the Court's most important decisions, in those areas, correspond fairly well to the original understanding. Suppose, too, that originalists can argue that their approach would lead to far better results than one that asks judges to ask, and answer, large-scale moral questions. Originalists might well emphasize that judges are not experts on moral and political questions, and their judgments about what is required by justice (not to mention "partnership democracy") may be unreliable, confused, biased, or even perverse. If so, perhaps we make the best sense out of the Constitution if we read it to fit with the ratifiers' understandings.

Dworkin does not give a clear argument against this position. He does not show that Scalia's brand of originalism fails to fit and to justify existing constitutional law. Still, he is right to say that the Constitution should not be interpreted to fit with the concrete expectations of people long dead. In many areas, existing constitutional law goes well beyond the original understandings of the Framers and ratifiers, and thank goodness for that. The Constitution is now understood to forbid race and sex discrimination by the national government, even though none of its provisions was originally understood to forbid such discrimination. The Constitution is now taken to include broad protection of freedom of speech, going far beyond the original understandings. In many domains, originalism fails to fit our practices. And in most of those areas, originalism would make our constitutional system worse, not better.

But even if we reject originalism, it does not follow that judges should adopt and impose large-scale moral principles of their own (and call what they are doing "fidelity"!). Suppose that we insist that when judges strike down legislation because of their own moral judgments, they might well err. In American history, it is easy to find examples. As candidates, we might emphasize not *Brown v. Board of Education*, but instead, say, *Lochner v. New York* (invalidating maximum-hour legislation), *Adkins v. Children's Hospital* (invalidating minimum-wage legislation), *Buckley v. Valeo* (invalidating campaign finance reform), *First National Bank of Boston v. Bellotti* (invalidating restrictions on corporate speech), *Lucas v. South Carolina Coastal Council* (invalidating the Beachfront Management Act), *City of Boerne v. Flores* (invalidating the Religious Freedom Restoration Act), *United States v. Morrison* (invalidating part of the Violence Against Women Act), *Adarand Constructors v. Pena* (invalidating an affirmative action program). I am confident that Dworkin would reject most of these decisions on moral grounds.

Puzzlingly, Dworkin does not come to terms with the risk of judicial error in the moral domain. To their great credit, Scalia and other originalists are greatly concerned with that risk; but there are more appealing ways of ensuring that the Court operates in a way that is attuned to its own fallibility. Posner wants to offer one. Against Posner, Dworkin is correct to say that moral disagreement can break out over the question of whether consequences are good. But Posner hopes that if we are able to have an accurate sense of consequences, diverse people might well be brought into agreement with one another, whatever they think on the largest moral issues. Suppose that a significant increase in the minimum wage would reduce employment, because it would become so much more expensive to hire people. If this is so, people of diverse views might reject significant increases in the minimum wage. Or suppose that certain voucher programs greatly improve education, and do so without causing religious strife or favoring any particular religious creed. If so, the Supreme Court might be led to uphold such programs (as in fact it did), notwithstanding fundamental disagreements about theology and the meaning of the Constitution's religion guarantees. Dworkin rightly chastises legal pragmatists for neglecting the difficulty of evaluating consequences without taking a moral stand; but sometimes an understanding of consequences can lead diverse people, with quite different moral views, to the same conclusion.

It is for similar reasons that the Court might try, whenever it can, to base its decisions on the least contentious principles—those that can be accepted by citizens having competing views about morality and politics. In many contexts, social life and law are both made possible by what I have called incompletely theorized agreements—agreements on practices or judgments amid uncertainty or disagreement about the abstract moral or political theory that justifies them. People who disagree on the meaning of "equal protection of the laws" are now able to agree that the government cannot discriminate against women. People with different views about the foundations of the free speech principle are now able to agree that the government cannot censor political dissent without showing a clear and present danger. Judges' efforts to avoid the most controversial questions, and their reluctance to invalidate laws on the basis of the most abstract principles, need not be based on a crudely majoritarian conception of democracy. Such efforts can be based instead on humility about judges' own capacity for abstract moral reasoning. Dworkin is quite right to say that analogy is blind without principle, but some principles are more controversial than others. Often it is possible for the Court to rule in a way that avoids the largest controversies.

It is important, for this reason, to distinguish between two different claims. The first is that any approach to legal interpretation requires some kind of moral or political defense. On this point, Dworkin's central arguments are right. Legal reasoning typically works by attempting both to "fit" past decisions and to "justify" them, by making them into sense rather than nonsense. Too much of the time, politicians and judges ignore the fact that judicial judgments, about principle and policy, play an inevitable role in determining what the law is. In controversial cases, the voting patterns of Republican appointees are systematically different from the voting patterns of Democratic appointees, and it is ludicrous to say that this is because one or another group "follows the law." Contrary to a popular myth (sometimes repeated in the pages of this magazine), judges generally adhere to the views of the president who nominated them. Dworkin's emphasis on the role of moral judgments in law helps to explain why.

Dworkin's second claim is that the Supreme Court should adopt an approach that calls on the justices to make large-scale judgments about the meaning of our highest ideals. I think that the Court should, most of the time, refuse to assume such a role. It should refuse to do so because fallible judges ought to avoid engaging, in particular cases, with the most fundamental problems in morality and politics. No theory of interpretation can avoid moral and political controversy, but it is possible to adopt, on moral and political grounds, a theory of interpretation that asks judges to decline to deploy their own moral and political judgments as weapons against the democratic process.

PART TWO

MORALITY AND LAWYERING

NEUTRALISM, PERFECTIONISM, AND THE LAWYER'S DUTY TO PROMOTE THE COMMON GOOD

John J. Worley

TWO RIVAL CONCEPTIONS OF THE LAWYER'S MORAL OBLIGATIONS

In his novel *The Just and the Unjust,* James Gould Cozzens poses a moral predicament for lawyer Abner Coates.[1] Senator Enoch Little, a friend of Abner's father's and a man of great influence, asks Abner to represent Peck College, of which Senator Little is an alumnus and Chairman of the Board of Trustees. Herbert Blessington has died, and he has named Peck College in his will. During life, Blessington had been a prosperous businessman, but he "had often been described as an eccentric; a short way of saying that he was a stubborn, vindictive, selfish, and unreasonable old bastard." His only heirs were four sisters, each of whom had at one time

Foreword to "Symposium on the Lawyer's Duty to Promote the Common Good," *South Texas Law Review* (Spring, 1999) copyright © 1999 South Texas Law Review, Inc.; John J. Worley.

lived with him and served as his housekeeper, but he had had violent arguments with all the sisters and at his death was estranged from three of them. The fourth sister, Elvira, had been living with and caring for Blessington when he died. Blessington's will left his estate in trust for Elvira, provided that she never live with or make any gifts to the other three sisters. The will went on to provide that, should the condition of the bequest to Elvira be held invalid, Blessington's estate would go to Peck College, with which Blessington's only other connection was that a friend of his had attended it. Senator Little and the Peck College Trustees asked Abner to contest the conditional devise to Elvira so that the college could take under the alternative bequest.

Abner has certain misgivings about representing the college's cause. Seeking to prevent Elvira's taking under the will "might not offend right and justice; but it did do a certain violence to one's sense of fairness or human decency." Blessington's motivation in cutting his sisters out of the will certainly was impure; there could be no doubting that he had adopted the condition out of spite, malice, and vindictiveness toward the sisters with whom he had bitterly quarreled during his life. Moreover, he had no reason to select the college as the object of his beneficence: he had no association with Peck College and created the contingent bequest to the college only because his lawyer had advised him that if the condition were held invalid the estate would go unconditionally to Elvira, who inevitably would have provided for her three sisters. In addition, the college had no expectation of receiving anything from Blessington; the trustees learned about the college being mentioned in the will only after Blessington died. By contrast, the sisters were deserving. All four women had kept house for the querulous and vengeful Blessington at one time or another and had undoubtedly suffered his abuses while doing so. All were old and in distressed financial circumstances. Two of them had never married, in part because Blessington had made them work for him. One was widowed, and another had an invalid husband.

Despite his reservations about doing so, Abner agrees to represent the college. Taking the case allows him to do a favor for the powerful Senator. The issue raised by the will had not definitively been settled, so that the case would, in all likelihood, give him a

chance to argue before the Supreme Court, an opportunity beneficial to his developing legal career. Although not poor, Abner is
contemplating marriage and could use the money his fee would
bring. But, troubled by his decision, he consults with his father,
himself a respected lawyer and judge. Judge Coates explains to
Abner why he has acted rightly in taking the college's case:

> It's provided by law, primarily by statute, that one of a man's
> rights which the courts shall protect him in, is the disposal of his
> property after his death according to his intentions expressed in an
> attested will. It is a very important right. It is part and parcel of
> human freedom and dignity. . . . [W]e have to hold that a man
> must be free, if he has the legal capacity to make a will, to make an
> unequal, unjust and unreasonable will. . . . The intention to realize
> is not the intention of the Court, nor the intention of Abner Coates,
> Counselor at Law. In ethics and morals their intentions may be
> demonstrably better and wiser and fairer than the testator's inten-
> tion. You've been saying, in effect, that you'd like to devise a better
> and juster disposal of Blessington's goods. You have no right to do
> it. The Court has no more right. The point for you is not whether
> you personally think the will just and good, but whether you can
> dispassionately and disinterestedly submit to the Court reasons in
> law and equity that bear out what you feel to be the testator's
> intention to leave the money to the clients you represent.

Though first published in 1942, Cozzens' novel depicts one of
the central disputes in contemporary theorizing about the
lawyer's role. Abner's uncertainty about representing Peck College's challenge to Elvira's taking under the Blessington will and
Judge Coates' explanation for why Abner should not give into his
moral scruples about doing so reflect two rival conceptions of the
lawyer's ethical responsibilities found in the recent legal and
philosophical literature. The traditional view defended by Judge
Coates endorses what William Simon has called the "ideology of
advocacy."[2] This ideology has two principal tenets: (1) the lawyer
is neutral or detached from the client's purposes, and (2) the
lawyer is an aggressive partisan for the client who works only to
advance the client's objectives. Under the neutrality principle, the
lawyer uses a moral filter to screen out all values, commitments,

and considerations other than those identified by the client. Just as a physician should not judge the moral worth of his patient but work only to preserve or to protect his health and physical well-being, so too should the lawyer not judge the value of his client's pursuits but work only to accomplish the client's aims. No more than does the engineer take into account the purpose to which the client will put his design should the lawyer consider what end his services will achieve for the client. As Judge Coates tells Abner, the lawyer has no right to substitute his own moral judgment for the client's. So long as the client's goal is permitted by law, the lawyer need not, indeed, should not, pass judgment on it. Monroe Freedman, one of the most influential proponents of the traditional model of the lawyer's role, puts it like this: "Once the lawyer has chosen to accept responsibility to represent a client . . . the zealousness of that representation cannot be tempered by the lawyer's moral judgments of the client or of the client's cause."[3]

This neutralist model of the lawyer's role, which Susan Wolf calls the lawyer as "the Arm of the Client," conceives the lawyer's moral and professional duty primarily as a faithful and competent commitment to advancing the client's self-identified interests, goals, and projects.[4] The lawyer is simply a legal expert acting at the direction of the client. The client employs the lawyer to advance or protect some interest; the lawyer provides legal services to accomplish the client's objective. The lawyer not only acts for or on behalf of the client, but also acts under the client's direction. As the pejorative vernacular expression would have it, the lawyer is the client's "mouthpiece" or "hired gun." In representing the client, the lawyer does not thereby necessarily endorse or ascribe to the client's goals. He or she is nothing more than an agent or an employee hired to perform some discrete task. If the client's aims are unreasonable, unjust, or immoral, the lawyer bears no responsibility for the unreasonable, unjust, or immoral outcome. The blame lies with the client, whose decision it was to pursue the project, or perhaps with the legal system itself, which countenances the client's objective. As Charles Fried explains, the lawyer "acts in your interests, not his own; or rather he adopts your interests as his own."[5] Some critics find the neutralist conception of the lawyer's role morally debased. Richard Wasserstrom, for example, criticizes the traditional conception as one in which "the lawyer's world is a simplified moral world; often it is an amoral one; and more than occasionally perhaps, an overtly immoral one."[6] Wasserstrom locates the problem in what he calls "role-differentiated morality." The lawyer, acting in his professional capacity, is guided by norms of behavior that may differ significantly from the norms of ordinary morality. Wasserstrom points out that "it is the nature of role-differentiated behavior that it often makes it both appropriate and desirable for the person in a particular role to put to one side considerations of various sorts—and especially various moral considerations—that would otherwise be relevant if not decisive."[7] Wasserstrom illustrates how the traditional view of the lawyer's role inappropriately brackets moral considerations relevant to his representation with a hypothetical example strikingly reminiscent of Cozzens' fictional one: he asks us to imagine a client who seeks assistance in preparing a will disinheriting her children because they opposed the Vietnam War. Although Wasserstrom is not unequivocal in his critique of the neutralist lawyer's disregarding considerations that ordinary morality would deem relevant, he suggests that the lawyer should refuse to draft the will for the client if the lawyer believes that opposition to the war in Vietnam is a "bad reason" to disinherit one's children.[8]

In Cozzens' fictional account, Bill Fuller, the lawyer who drafted the will for Blessington, struggled with his own crisis of conscience in advising Blessington on how to ensure that the three estranged sisters would see none of his estate. He tells Abner how he almost permitted Blessington to prepare his will containing the conditional bequest to Elvira without any alternative bequest, knowing that the condition would very likely be held invalid, thereby allowing Elvira to inherit the estate unconditionally and defeating Blessington's vengeful intentions.

[W]hen Herb told me what he was planning to do, I had a good mind to let him. Then I said to myself, "Now, Bill, my friend," I said, "evil communications are kind of corrupting you! This rat in pants here's come for legal advice; and to the best of your knowledge you've got to give it to him straight." . . . Well, I did my duty, Ab; though it damn near killed me.[9]

Presumably, Wasserstrom would say that Fuller's duty lay, not in giving Blessington the advice necessary to accomplish his morally corrupt plan, but in refusing to draft the will for him. If the lawyer believed that Blessington's intention to disinherit his sisters was morally unjustified, then he should decline the representation.

This alternative view, which Susan Wolf calls the lawyer as an "Arm of Society,"[10] rejects the principle of lawyer neutrality and advocates a broadly perfectionist view of the lawyer's professional obligations. Perfectionist theories generally claim that certain ways of living embody "excellence" or "perfection," and that such ways of life should be promoted while less worthy ways of life should be discouraged. Perfectionist theories of the lawyer's moral obligations claim that the lawyer should not limit his role merely to promoting the client's subjectively determined and self-defined interests. They advocate, instead, a view of the lawyer's responsibilities that recognizes the claims of the wider range of persons affected by the lawyer's representation and a wider range of values implicated by his conduct.

Perfectionist critics of the traditional neutralist conception thus locate the lawyer's moral and professional responsibility in promoting some value beyond simply realizing the client's aims—in achieving truth or justice or some other broad social goal. Wasserstrom, for example, suggests that the lawyer's duty ought to be rooted in principles of ordinary morality. He says, "I am inclined to think that we might all be better served if lawyers were to see themselves less as subject to role-differentiated behavior and more as subject to the demands of the moral point of view."[11] Judge Frankel evinces a similar concern for raising a lawyer's sight beyond the narrow preoccupation with amorally promoting the client's interests, and argues that the legal system pays too little attention to the pursuit of truth. David Luban advocates lawyers adopting the principle of "moral activism": "lawyers have the opportunity to make the law better by law reform activity, and to make their clients better by using their advisory role to awaken the clients to the public dimension of their activities, to steer them in the direction of the public good."[12]

Doubtless, characterizing neutralist and perfectionist conceptions of the lawyer's moral obligations in such categorical and unqualified terms so oversimplifies matters as to risk caricature. Neither view is as stark and inflexible as the foregoing exposition suggests—neutralists recognizing that social and institutional demands and the rights of third parties constrain the lawyer's zealous pursuit of the client's objectives, and perfectionists acknowledging the client's special claims on the lawyer's fidelity. This simplistic categorization of views fails to do justice to the sometimes complex and subtly nuanced views represented in the literature. But this way of looking at the lawyer's obligations does provide a useful framework for better understanding the different approaches contributors have taken to the subject of this Symposium, "The Lawyer's Duty to Promote the Common Good." For it would be a grave mistake to assume that neutralists are indifferent to the common good, while perfectionists are committed to it. Instead, neutralist and perfectionist theorists both affirm the idea of the common good, and both recognize a place for the lawyer in promoting it. Nevertheless, they assume rather different conceptions of what constitutes the common good.

For partisans of the neutrality principle, the common good is the product of that process by which individuals pursue their own goals, achieve their own interests, and realize their own values. The common good is achieved in this process of combining individual preferences. The traditional conception of the lawyer's role is roughly analogous to the liberal conception of the state's role: they both reflect a belief that discriminating against or discouraging the projects or plans that people believe are most valuable to them is an inappropriate or undesirable way to promote people's interest in leading a good life. The neutralist lawyer believes that enabling individuals to act on and realize their own preferences and their own conceptions of the good life best conduces to the common good.

Perfectionist theorists, by contrast, hold that the common good consists in some particular substantive conception of the good life. The best act, institution, or political or social arrangement is that which promotes the perfection or excellence of people. The common good is not merely a function of individuals realizing their subjectively determined preferences, but is instead the achievement or approximation of what is, in fact, good for people.

The perfectionist starts with some account of what constitutes the objectively good life—certain traits or characteristics or properties—and then holds that the common good consists in promoting or developing these traits, characteristics, or properties in some significant way. The common good consists in the shared ends of a community, and the perfectionist lawyer claims that one can and should encourage people, including clients, to adopt and act on a true conception of the good life while discouraging flawed or erroneous conceptions of the good life.

Understanding these differences between neutralist and perfectionist conceptions of the lawyer's moral obligations illuminates the differences among . . . contributors to [South Texas Law Review's 1999] Ethics Symposium. . . . John M. Finnis[, for example]—defend[s] a neutralist conception. Yet [he] introduces qualifications of or limitations to the general view that makes his view distinctive . . . Finnis deploy[s] perfectionist principles in defense of the traditional neutralist position that the lawyer is not morally accountable for the client's end. The remaining . . . contributors[, including] . . . Robert J. Araujo . . . advance perfectionist considerations for moral evaluation of attorney conduct. . . . Araujo . . . advocate[s] reforms to . . . legal education . . .

Neutralist View: John M. Finnis

John Finnis is one of the most important and influential moral and legal philosophers working today, and together with Germain Grisez and others he has defended a modern version of natural law theory. In his contribution to this Symposium, Finnis employs natural law principles in defense of what is largely the standard conception of the lawyer's role. He argues that lawyers have a duty to promote the common good, but that the principal way they discharge this obligation is by engaging in a partisan representation of the client; exercising sound professional judgment in performing that representation; and facilitating the client's vindication of his legal rights, so long as this representation is performed in accordance with the law and the rules governing lawyers' professional conduct. Notwithstanding his natural law commitments, Finnis rejects any universalist, perfectionist obligation for the lawyer: "There is no general duty of the lawyer to ensure that clients conform to communal norms, or even to common law or statute, but there is a stringent duty not to assist in crime or fraud or in any kind of misconduct in legal proceedings with which the lawyer is professionally concerned."[13] For Finnis, a lawyer promotes the common good in a manner reminiscent of the injunction expressed in Canon 7 of the Model Code of Professional Responsibility: "A Lawyer Should Represent a Client Zealously Within the Bounds of the Law."

But Finnis reaches this conclusion by a distinctively natural law route. He postulates that there are basic human goods which provide persons with reasons for action. Although some reasons for acting are purely instrumental, merely means to ends, others are intrinsic. These intrinsic human goods are a part of the common good in two senses. First, each is good for any and for all individual persons, for the pursuit of these goods constitutes the means to human fulfillment for individual persons; and second, "each can be an aspect of the flourishing of a group, a community, big or small, formal or informal, and can be a reason for that community or group to act in the way that groups do. . . ."

The common good, therefore, operates as a part of any rationally deliberative activity. When one acts fully reasonably, his intrinsic reasons for action direct him toward these basic human goods. But, since these goods are goods for all persons and for all communities, rational actions promote the flourishing of all people and all communities. This line of reasoning leads Finnis to formulate the philosophical version of the "master principle of morality" as follows: "In voluntarily acting for human goods and avoiding what is opposed to them, one ought to choose and otherwise will those and only those possibilities whose willing is compatible with a will toward integral human fulfillment." This general principle generates (a) negative moral norms and rules which absolutely prohibit actions that subvert or do injury to any basic human good in any person, as well as (b) positive moral norms and rules which identify a person's obligations to promote the common good in communities as wide and varied as families, friendships, businesses, professions, and political groups.

This respect for the common good has several components.

First, it requires respect for one's self, i.e. for one's true interests. Second, it demands respect for others and for the rights of others. Third, it entails respect for the requirements of successful social coordination and cooperation.

Finnis explains why lying is always wrong in view of these three aspects of the common good. The liar asserts a proposition to be true while believing it to be false. In so doing, he projects a false picture of himself and conceals from his audience his true self behind a veil of a feigned revelation. Finnis argues that every act of lying is "profoundly disrespectful to oneself" because it "denies the basis on which one is entitled to one's reputation, indeed the basis on which one is entitled to be treated as the person one is and not as some personality constructed by hostile or indifferent people." So, even lies that do not directly cause harm to another or made to persons not entitled to the truth are wrong, according to Finnis. In addition, lying often does do harm to others, because it violates their rights. One has a right—not merely a legal right, but a natural right—"not to be defeated in litigation by the lies of witnesses or other parties or their legal representatives," and such cases of lying are "not merely wrong but seriously wrong." And, finally, lying fails properly to respect the common good in that it undermines the rules necessary for social cooperation applicable to communities of all kinds. Finnis points particularly to the need for cooperation within a political community with respect to its enforcing the criminal law. The various actors in the criminal justice system—judges, jurors, prosecutors, defense counsel, and witnesses—must properly perform their functions in order for the truth to be revealed and justice achieved. Every participant in the process must accord proper respect for the system adopted by the particular political community, because "respect for [the] system of fair cooperation is required by the common good." Thus, someone who falsely represents himself as qualified to practice law or a lawyer who fails to reveal to the court controlling authority adverse to his client's position not only violates a rule of positive law; he fails to respect the common good, because he undermines the conditions necessary for cooperation within the community.

But Finnis denies that the duty to promote the common good

imposes on the attorney any responsibility for ensuring that the litigation is ultimately resolved properly.

It is one thing to respect the common good of the parties to litigation by not cheating on discovery and not contriving delays by
applications known to be groundless. It is quite another thing to
hold oneself responsible for securing litigation's proper outcome—
a judgment in line with law, truth, and justice—by taking on the
role of the litigation's director, the judge, forming one's own judgment about the truth of the story one's client asserts—or about the
negative effects likely to result, for one's client or for others or for
"society's best interests," if one's client prevails—and, on the basis
of that private judgment, declining to make submissions which
could properly be made to put one's client's own case before the
court—could properly be made because they do not include one's
making any assertion one does not believe to be true, or assisting
one's client to make any assertion one knows—as distinct from suspects—to be false, or failing to admit "any fact that cannot properly
be disputed." To engage in this kind of perfectionist lawyering is
wrong, Finnis says, both because it denies to the client his legal
rights and because it subverts the common good by "undermining
the system of administering civil or criminal justice...."

Finnis' position is an intriguing one, in part because it harnesses
natural law principles in service of the standard conception of the
lawyer's obligation. But critics may find fault with several aspects of
his view. First, many will object to Finnis's claim that the duty to tell
the truth is an absolute and exceptionless one. Finnis places himself
among a long line of, predominantly though not exclusively religious, thinkers who maintain that it is never permissible to lie. Perhaps most famously, Immanuel Kant held that "[t]o be truthful
(honest) in all declarations, therefore, is a sacred and absolutely
commanding decree of reason, limited by no expediency."[14]

But most of those who have considered the morality of lying
have rejected any absolute duty to tell the truth. Without disputing
that truthfulness is an important obligation, they maintain that
telling a lie may be justified in exceptional circumstances, as where
some extraordinary harm can be avoided through deception or
where the falsehood is trivial and harmless or where telling a lie
may be necessary to discharge a duty to preserve another's secrets.

Of course, Kant himself discussed the standard example of the first kind. Suppose your friend is fleeing from a would-be murderer and tells you where he is going to hide. The murderer comes to you and asks if you know where your friend has gone. You believe that if you tell the truth the murderer will seek out your friend and kill him. Should you tell the truth? Finnis apparently would agree with Kant and answer affirmatively; but this view certainly conflicts with our ordinary moral intuitions, and it is not widely shared. The opposing view holds that lying is morally justified where doing so will avert some great harm, in this case, the loss of innocent life. Finnis claims that to lie is "profoundly disrespectful to oneself," but opponents will say that truthfully to answer the murderer amounts to a betrayal of a friend and knowingly to assist in the commission of a grave wrong, whereas to lie produces but slight (if any) harm. The trade-off required by this kind of moral absolutism—preserving one's own dignity at the expense of another's life—seems implausible to most.

In the crisis examples, where telling the truth puts innocent persons at the mercy of wrongdoers, the exceptionless opposition to lying is counterintuitive because it is indifferent to consequences. But quite apart from the harm resulting to innocent third persons, Finnis' argument does not entail his absolutist stance in these cases. Even taken on its own terms, his view ought to admit exceptions to the rule against lying. He maintains that lying is wrong, even when it causes others no harm, because it divides the self into a counterfeit projection and the hidden true one and thereby "denies the basis on which one is entitled to one's reputation. . . ." But, in the extreme cases where catastrophic injuries can be averted by deception, it is difficult to see how telling the truth does not project an even more profoundly false image of one's self than would telling the lie. If one is committed to the values of human life and well-being and if these commitments are constitutive of one's identity as a wholly integrated personality, then to adhere inflexibly to telling the truth even when doing so imperils the life or welfare of others also compromises one's true self; it falsely presents to the world a picture of one indifferent to human life and suffering. Finnis could avoid committing himself to an absolutist prohibition against lying by saying that where telling the truth projects a counterfeit image of the convictions one holds most deeply or the values one holds most dear—especially commitments to genuine human goods, as opposed to mere individual preferences—then in those cases telling the truth "denies the basis on which one is entitled to one's reputation, indeed the basis on which one is entitled to be treated as the person one is"[15] even more seriously than does a single instance of misrepresenting one's belief about a matter of relatively trivial fact. At least in those limited cases, Finnis could allow an exception to the rule against lying.

In addition, Finnis' claim that "[t]he right not to be defeated in litigation by the lies of witnesses or other parties or their legal representatives is a human right, not simply the product of some specific legal system's positing" is a puzzling one. It is not clear whether Finnis means that one has a natural right not to be defeated by lies both in cases where one has no legal right to prevail and in cases where one has a legal right to prevail, but the legal right does not comprehend or protect some natural right; or whether he means that being defeated by lies in litigation is a human rights violation only where the lie deprives one of a legal entitlement correlated with a natural right. But the basis for his view is uncertain in each case.

First, take the case where the opposing party deploys a lie against a party who has no legal right to prevail in the litigation. Imagine, for example, a plaintiff who brings a personal injury claim against a defendant, even though the claim is utterly unmeritorious. Defendant's lawyer knowingly uses perjured testimony to persuade the jury to return a verdict for defendant. One need not deny the wrongfulness of the lawyer's conduct to question what human rights violation has occurred here. A human right is one that we have simply because we are human beings. In Finnis' conception of human rights, a human right is "constituted by reasons for action which are intrinsic to the human situation. . . ." But what reason for action intrinsic to the situation does the lie defeat when it is deployed against a litigant who has no legal right to prevail?

Finnis may mean that lying in litigation is a human rights violation only where it deprives the victim of his legal rights. One might imagine two different situations. First, the legal right of which the victim is deprived corresponds with a natural right, as, for example, where the legal right is one that protects a natural right. Assume, for example, a natural right to be compensated for personal injury resulting from another's negligence. Now, to deny a litigant his legal right is also to deny him his natural right. A defendant in a personal injury action who commits perjury or his lawyer who knowingly uses the perjured testimony to defeat the plaintiff's right to recover not only deprives the plaintiff of his legal entitlement, but also deprives him of a natural right. But we have no need to refer to the lie to explain the wrong that takes place in this situation; depriving the plaintiff of his natural right to compensation for his injuries presumably constitutes a moral wrong regardless of the technique employed to do so. That the denial of the natural right was accomplished by means of perjured testimony adds nothing to the moral offense perpetrated against the plaintiff.

Second, we might imagine the case where the lie deprives the defeated litigant of a legal entitlement that is exclusively a positive right with no corresponding natural right. Assume, for example, that the plaintiff brings a statutory action for a right to recover damages predicated on the notion of a "private attorney general" to vindicate some instrumental public policy with no corresponding individual natural right. In what respect does the use of perjury to defeat the plaintiff deny him his natural rights if the only right denied is entirely the creation of positive law? Finnis might claim that denying a person his legal rights just is a denial of human rights, but that move again makes recourse to the lie unnecessary to explain the wrong done to the defeated litigant. If deprivations of legal rights amount to deprivations of natural rights, then again it hardly matters whether the deprivation is accomplished honestly or dishonestly. On the other hand, if denying a legal right does not in and of itself constitute denying a human right, then we need some account of what it is about the lie itself that violates one's natural rights. What is it about the falsehood that infringes some intrinsic human good independently of the violation to that good?

But none of these objections rules out Finnis' absolutist objection to lying in court, although that proposition is as readily justified by purely instrumentalist and institutional considerations as by Finnis' natural law argument. Finnis recognizes that the negative implications for lying in adjudicative proceedings are extraordinary. As Sissela Bok writes,

> The slope here is very slippery indeed. For if some lies in court to protect a client's confidences are all right, why not others? If the lawyer is sole judge of what is a tolerable lie, what criteria will he use? Will there not be pressure to include other lies, ostensibly also to protect the client's confidence? And if lawyers become used to accepting certain lies, how will this affect their integrity in other areas?[16]

Concern for such adverse consequences for the legal profession, the system of justice, and society at large militate in favor of an exceptionless prohibition against lying in court. To take but one illustration, suppose it were widely known (or believed) that lawyers may use perjured testimony. What impact would this belief have on jurors and other fact-finders? Jurors would come to mistrust all testimony and would be led to decide matters put before them on the basis of considerations other than the evidence adduced at trial. They would become (more) mistrustful of the legal profession generally and of all judicial procedures as well. Moreover, they would come to suspect not only the testimony adduced by the lawyers at trial but also every other procedure taken by them. The efficacy of the justice system depends upon the assumption that the participants must tell the truth. Jurors will know that sometimes some people will lie and must use their ordinary powers of human discernment to distinguish honest from dishonest witnesses. But this process collapses if jurors suspect that lawyers habitually introduce testimony known to be perjured. Instrumentalist considerations like these concerning the good public institutions produce for the common advantage suggest an absolute prohibition against lying in court without acknowledging a general rule against all lies in all contexts.

Perfectionist View: Robert J. Araujo

In "The Lawyer's Duty to Promote the Common Good: The Virtuous Law Student and Teacher,"[17] Robert Araujo reveals his perfectionist commitments when he claims that a lawyer must both serve his client's interests and the public interest at the same time: the lawyer "serves two constituencies. Every lawyer shares in the responsibility to see that justice is brought to the parties as well as to society at large." Araujo invokes the distinction between the Victorious Lawyer—the lawyer who "has a solitary goal: to win regardless of the cost and regardless of the compromises made with norms which lawyers and lay people alike regard as the requirements of participating in civil and courteous society"—and the Virtuous Lawyer—one "who sees the correlation between the law and the legal system it produces on the one hand, and the fashion in which members of society live in right relationships with one another on the other." For Araujo, legal educators have a special obligation to help inculcate and foster the development of the characteristics associated with the Virtuous Lawyer who will promote the common good.

Araujo understands the common good to be found in the mutually supportive and reciprocal relationship between the good of the individual and the good of the community. He seeks to avoid the extremes of radical individualism, on the one hand, conceiving the common good as nothing more than the aggregation of individual goods, and totalitarianism, on the other hand, conceiving the common good as concern merely for the social collectivity which subjugates the interests of individual persons. For Araujo, the common good is the good of individuals, but not individuals in isolation from one another; it is rather the good of individuals in right relation with one another, as well as the welfare of the social body itself. People are social beings whose existence and well-being are rooted in relationships with others, so promoting the common good entails harmonizing private interests and the public interest and creating a framework within which competing individual claims can be resolved without undermining the social relationships on which individual life is grounded.

Araujo claims that "[the] lawyer as member of the community and as professional must think, understand, and act beyond the interests of the self—whether the self is the client or the lawyer." To do so, the lawyer must appropriate human virtues into his professional life. Virtue is a trait of character which enables the achievement of human goods; its function is to guide individuals "in their moral deliberation toward right action." Araujo identifies four virtues—justice, prudence, courage, and wisdom—as being particularly relevant to the evaluation of the professional conduct of lawyers. Justice is concerned with restoring the right relationship between people. "Prudence is the virtue that helps us choose wisely;" "[c]ourage is the virtue that enables lawyers to meet the challenge of harm or danger when they attempt to take action based on the care and concern they have for individuals and communities;" and "[w]isdom provides the insight, the sagacity, by which members of the legal profession come to understand and appreciate corporate as well as individual goods, and the nexus between them." Araujo insists that legal education must reject narrow, technical training in favor of a virtue-based education that will enable lawyers who see not only a way but "a better way to resolve a case, to reconcile conflict, to seek the just end."

Araujo also seeks to show how rejecting any rigid distinctions between rules and virtues and between legal reasoning and moral reasoning fosters the development of virtuous lawyers. The right and the good are interdependent and complement one another, and legal reasoning and moral reasoning not wholly distinct enterprises. Araujo claims that the Virtuous Lawyer recognizes these insights.

Araujo's article is ambitious and wide-ranging, drawing on the contributions of natural lawyers, communitarian thinkers, and virtue theorists; and no full evaluation of his complete position is possible within the span of this brief overview. But the central role played by the ethics of virtue deserves special mention. Araujo's emphasis on the traits of character that make a person a good lawyer is undoubtedly a welcome corrective to thinking about professional ethics that so often neglects them. Professional ethics usually asks, "What is the right thing for the good lawyer to do?" Araujo reminds us also to ask, "What kind of person is the good lawyer to be?"

But Araujo's views suffer from some of the limitations that characterize virtue ethics generally. One limitation concerns whether an ethical theory that depends exclusively on character can provide a complete account of ethical practices. Some of the

earlier contemporary virtue ethicists write as if conventional, prin-
ciple-based ethics must be abandoned altogether, but there is
grave doubt whether virtues can do all the work necessary for an
ethical theory. The virtue of courage provides a standard illustration of this limitation. Is it possible to give an account of courage
that is neutral concerning other ideals? That is, is courage really
courage when it is serving an unjust or immoral cause? Would it
be appropriate, for example, to characterize as courageous a Nazi
soldier who faces extraordinary danger without shrinking and
who fights bravely in support of an evil regime? For some, it
would not; they maintain that courage cannot serve evil ends, that
courage in support of an unworthy aim is not a virtue. Indeed, this
seems to be the view Araujo takes, for he says, "The virtue of
courage fortifies the open-minded lawyer from being swayed or
prejudiced by any pressure that could promote deviation from
seeking the just end."

What is important to note is that this conception of courage is
not content-neutral; it depends upon a particular conception of
justice or of some other moral principle. Courage here is not
simply facing risks for some ideal; it is facing risks for the right
ideal. But now that conception of the right ideal, not the virtue of
courage, is doing most of the ethical work. Does the lawyer act
courageously when he steadfastly represents a woman challenging legislation limiting access to abortion services, despite
threats and intimidation from militant pro-life groups? Does he do
so when he represents a pro-life activist charged with crimes associated with an attempt to deter physicians from providing legal
abortions or to prevent access to them, even though doing so jeopardizes his personal and professional standing in the community?
Does Abner Coates act courageously when he represents the college in contesting the Blessington will in the face of community
outrage at his action and the risk of prospective clients' boycotting
his services? Under this content-laden conception of courage, it is
impossible to say until we have given an account of whether the
lawyer's cause itself is a morally worthy one, and then courage
becomes a function of that cause's value. The ethics of virtue is
therefore incomplete; it cannot stand alone. But shifting to a content-neutral conception of courage does not avoid the problem.

One might define courage as confronting risks for some ideal, not necessarily the right one. This move makes it possible to concede that the Nazi soldier who fights bravely is courageous without denying his moral blameworthiness. Within this content-neutral understanding of courage, one might say that the soldier "displays two qualities of character, one that is admirable (steadfastness in facing danger) and one that is not (a willingness to defend a despicable regime)."[18] But the virtue ethicist still owes us an account of what counts as a "despicable regime" if we are fully to appraise the individual's conduct. The analysis of the soldier's virtue does not alone provide us with a complete picture.

The virtue-centered approach to lawyer's ethics suffers from another related limitation. By making character the centerpiece of its ethics, virtue theory does little to provide guidance concerning how one should act. Many moral problems, certainly problems of a lawyer's professional responsibility, are concerned with what one should do. Araujo himself recognizes this limitation: "The virtues of justice, prudence, courage, and wisdom, when found in and practiced by lawyers, tell us little about how a lawyer will contribute to the determination [of] a specific case." This failure is surely a serious one, however, if, as Araujo maintains, "the essential function of virtues and ethical systems that rely on them is to guide people, including lawyers, in their moral deliberation toward right action. . . ." Araujo might seek to overcome this limitation by saying that virtues provide a guide for conduct when we examine the reasons underlying the virtues. If we want to know how the just lawyer would behave, we must ask what reasons there are for being just, and so on for each of the virtues. But this answer does not solve the problem for, again, the virtues themselves are not doing the ethical work; it is the underlying reasons for the virtues that are doing it.

The concern for providing practical guidance to lawyers confronting ethical decisions reveals yet another limitation of a virtue-centered ethics, for without supplementation with some other ethical principles the virtues do not tell us how to resolve cases where multiple virtues are relevant and where they have conflicting implications for how one ought to behave. Cozzens' fictional lawyers again illustrate the problem. Fuller, the lawyer asked to draft Blessington's will disinheriting his sisters, could never decide what action he should take solely by seeking to act virtuously, for what guidance the virtues can provide surely would have pointed him in different directions. A benevolent and just lawyer would have been concerned about the material welfare of Blessington's sisters and the hurtful effects Blessington's plans would have on them, but the honest and loyal lawyer would have been concerned to support his client's decisions and to inform him fully and accurately about how the law would affect his efforts to accomplish them. How should the lawyer decide which virtues should have priority? To adjudicate between the conflicting demands of benevolence and justice, on the one hand, and of loyalty and honesty, on the other, requires recourse to some other ethical principle—some principle that accords priority to the client's interests or that requires pursuit of a just end or some other ethical precept. But then that supplementary adjudicative rule serves as the fundamental ethical principle, not the virtues. In cases where the requirements of virtue tend to pull in different directions, it is difficult to see how an unsupplemented virtue theory can provide much help for the lawyer who is trying to decide what course of conduct to adopt. The virtues alone cannot do so.

*   *   *

CONCLUSION

What I hope this extended [discussion] will do is to underscore the prospects for agreement and progress on the morality of lawyers' professional conduct. The [writers discussed] represent widely divergent theoretical perspectives, but their views reflect a surprising degree of agreement despite those differences. . . . John Finnis invoke[s] the methodology and insights of natural law theory in describing the role of the lawyer in promoting the common good; yet, despite . . . broadly perfectionist theoretical commitments, . . . defend[s] conclusions largely in accord with the standard neutralist conception of the lawyer's professional duties. . . . And Robert Araujo reminds us of the place that the virtues should have in our judgment of attorney conduct, traits of character which few, if any, of us would deny.

That diverse theoretical perspectives often may converge toward similar practical proposals should be reassuring for the lawyer who must make decisions that affect his own professional identity and standing as well as the lives of others with whom he deals. In *The Just and the Unjust*, after Abner Coates has decided to represent Peck College in challenging the will, he says to his father, the judge: "It isn't what the law should do; it's what I should do."[19] His observation echoes the Socratic dictum that morality concerns how we ought to live. This concern with putting principle into practice is at least as urgent for lawyers in their professional capacities as it is for any of us in our personal lives. . . .

NOTES

1. James Gould Cozzens, *The Just and the Unjust* (New York: Harcourt Brace Jovanovich, 1970).

2. See William A. Simon, "The Ideology of Advocacy: Procedural Justice and Professional Ethics," *Wisconsin Law Review* (1978): 36.

3. Monroe H. Freedman, *Understanding Lawyer's Ethics* (New York: Mathew Bender, 1990), p. 50.

4. See Susan Wolf, "Ethics, Legal Ethics, and the Ethics of Law," *The Good Lawyer: Lawyers' Roles and Lawyers' Ethics*, ed. David Luban (Totowa, NJ: Rowman and Allenheld, 1984), p. 48.

5. Charles Fried, "The Lawyer as Friend: The Moral Foundations of the Lawyer-Client Relation," *Yale Law Journal* 85 (1976): 1071.

6. Richard Wasserstrom, "Lawyers as Professionals: Some Moral Issues," *Human Rights* 5 (1975). Wasserstrom has expanded his views in "Roles and Morality," in Luban, ed., *The Good Lawyer*, pp. 25–37.

7. Wasserstrom, "Lawyers as Professionals," p. 3.

8. Ibid., pp. 7–8.

9. Cozzens, *The Just and the Unjust*, pp. 258–59.

10. See Wolf, "Ethics, Legal Ethics, and the Ethics of Law," p. 47.

11. Wasserstrom, "Lawyers as Professionals," p. 12. Wasserstrom concedes that the moral neutrality associated with the lawyer's role-differentiated behavior is justified for criminal defense lawyers and excuses them from this broader obligation.

12. David Luban, *Lawyers and Justice: An Ethical Study* (Princeton, NJ: Princeton University Press, 1988), p. 171.

13. John Finnis, "What Is the Common Good, and Why Does It Concern the Client's Lawyer?" South Texas Law Review 40 (1999): 41.

14. Immanuel Kant, "On a Supposed Right to Lie from Altruistic Motives," in Critique of Practical Reason and Other Writings in Moral Philosophy, ed. and trans. Lewis White Beck (Chicago: University of Chicago Press, 1949).

15. Finnis, "What Is the Common Good," p. 46.

16. See Sissela Bok, *Lying: Moral Choice in Public and Private Life* (New York: Vintage, 1989), pp. 162–63.

17. South Texas Law Review 40 (1999): 83.

18. James Rachels, *The Elements of Moral Philosophy* (New York: McGraw-Hill, 1993), p. 164.

19. Cozzens, *The Just and the Unjust*, p. 432.

BETWEEN REASON AND POWER

EXPERIENCING LEGAL TRUTH

Linda Meyer

"How can you lawyers defend the guilty?" asks the layperson of the lawyer at a cocktail party. The lawyer takes a deep breath, flushes, and launches into a well-practiced description of the value of the adversary system, or begins to cite statistics of mistaken convictions, or describes a difficult case. The layperson swirls the ice in his glass and scans the room over the lawyer's shoulder, waiting for the lawyer to finish. Then, he replies in a somewhat superior tone, "Well, I could never do it."

We as a culture think, naively, one side (at most) in a legal dispute is right; the other is wrong. Only one lawyer may be speaking the truth, though perhaps both are misleading and manipulating. Lawyers are sharks, snakes, liars, word-twisters, hair-splitters, crowd-panderers, flashy adepts at the art of fanning the flames of passion. Our profession has been vilified since Plato as a mere

University of Cincinnati Law Review (Spring, 1999) copyright © 1999 University of Cincinnati; Linda Meyer.

"trick" of making people believe and act on falsehoods. And Dean Anthony Kronman identifies the problem: either rhetoric is a sugar-coating for the truth at which we arrive through moral and political philosophy or scientific knowledge (because we think science alone can tell us truths without emotion and uncertainty about our political and social lives) or, worse, there is no truth or right, and rhetoric is just cotton-candy-sheer manipulation with no substance, serving those with the most power. Either way, rhetoric is no way to discover the truth.

The difficulty is that neither philosophic truth nor scientific truth seems to be adequate to describe or evaluate the world of law and politics, either. Though we have theorized utopias for thousands of years, human nature in its perverse unpredictability (or human reason in its limitation to generalities and probabilities) refuses even thinkers like Plato or Marx power to design human institutions from the top down. Philosophy provides us with some general principles and important distinctions, science with some behavioral generalizations, but neither can tell us what to do in a particular case, predict the human trajectory, or even keep us from arguing about basic political premises. At times, the only alternative seems to be a nihilistic skepticism that portrays law and politics as sheer power and rhetoric as manipulation. Perhaps, however, a possibility remains for another kind of truth that does not collapse into either utopian illusions or nihilism, but which is more compatible with the nature of a finite human mind and world. And perhaps there is room for, as Kronman puts it, a "sympathetic" study of rhetoric as a way to know this special truth that lies between naked desire and opaque reason.[1] Rhetoric might just be something besides the cotton-candy of manipulation or the sugar-coating of theoretical or scientific knowledge, and there might be some point to our impassioned lawerly debates over questions that lie "between reason and power."[2] If so, who are we humans that we can make truth claims about matters which are arguable and not certain, and what is this kind of truth that seems to require the alchemy of passion?

Dean Kronman asks us to begin with Plato's Gorgias and to rethink rhetoric in light of the orator Gorgias's attempt to defend it against Socrates's charge that it is a mere tool for manipulation rather than a path to truth. Gorgias defines rhetoric as the art of persuasion. The Greek words for rhetoric and for persuasion have curious, but telling, roots. The words for rhetoric and orator (ὁ ῥήτωρ) have the root of ἔρω (to say) from ῥέω, meaning flow, run, stream, gush, rain—and also glib, a flow of words. Orators, as we know, are glib and their words flow fast. But curiously, the word for love, desire, and passion—eros—shares the root. The flow of words and the flow of passion are connected somehow. And not only is this true in the root of rhetoric, but in the word for "persuade" used by Plato in the Gorgias. Our English word "persuade" is from the Latin, meaning to "sweet talk"—a spoonful of sugar helps the truth go down. Yet the Greek word relies on a different metaphor. The word in Plato is "πείθω," meaning to win over with words. The passive form of the verb means to be won over, to obey, to trust, to rely on. The connotation seems to be to render passive, to tame, or to placate. And of course, both are related to pathos, or passion and passivity, once again. Hence, emotion and passion are present in the very words of rhetoric and persuasion.

I start here because I do not think the metaphors hidden in the roots of the words are coincidental. The central difficulties that Professor Kronman identifies—the uncertainty and contestability of legal, moral, and political truth and its emotional components—are already here in the words themselves: the flow and changeability of rhetoric, the passivity and vulnerability of passion. And, as I will try to say, these same two aspects are inextricable from all human knowledge, a knowledge that is not only finite and incomplete but also aesthetic (from the senses and passions). Truth about law or politics or morality (social truths, as Kronman puts it) must be experienced; that is, only through something like rhetoric can we know them. Following in the path Kronman has pointed out, I will try here to sketch a possible "sympathetic account" of rhetoric.

First, I will pause over the most prevalent and, I argue, misleading understanding of rhetoric exemplified by Plato's attack on the orator Gorgias, that is, rhetoric as "sweet-talk"—a tool for manipulation rather than a way to truth. Second, I will turn to Kant's Critique of Judgment to help explain how truth for us humans can have the aesthetic (sensory) and emotional components that make rhetoric so suspect, without rendering that truth subjective or merely an illusion masking a power struggle. I here connect rhetoric with the mental ability Kant describes as "judgment," which lies somewhere between (or before) the empirical accomplishments of science and the theoretical achievements of philosophy. Third, I reconsider some of the traditional attacks on rhetoric in light of rhetoric's reconceptualization as a kind of judgment, and finally I try to say what kind of judgment rhetoric is, to distinguish it from poetry, practical reason, and other arts. I conclude that rhetoric is the articulation of practical reason, a bringing to words, and thereby experience, of practical deliberation that resists formulation as rules or facts and may even become clearest for both the speaker and the audience at times as analogy, metaphor, story, or image.

RHETORIC AS SWEET-TALK

The view of rhetoric as sweet-talk lies behind the cocktail party assumption that, at most, one lawyer is telling the truth in a legal dispute, and the other is manipulating an audience—the assumption that truth can be separated from technique. Rhetoric is just the sugarcoating, at best a necessary evil for convincing the non-philosophical audience to do the right thing.[3]

As rhetoric is only a "knack" or "sugarcoating," giving rise to, at best, right opinion but not knowledge, Plato assumes that truth is known through other methods—namely, philosophy. Like Rawls, Dworkin, Bentham, Hobbes, and some other legal theorists, Plato would create a philosopher-king, or a philosopher-judge, who would use the methodology of philosophy to discover legal truth, unmoved by the sound and fury of closing arguments. As in the myth of ideal judgment at the end of the Gorgias,[4] we seem to think that truth is attainable only by stripping away the "clothing" and other empirical, sensory qualities of the litigants and judges. Judges should subject themselves to philosophy, look to philosophical theory for methods of decision-making and for substantive moral values. . . .[5]

Yet as every "socratic" teacher knows well, the dialectical method employed by Socrates and championed (for a while) by

Plato for arriving at philosophic truth can be just as manipulative, just as hair-splitting, just as word-twisting as legal rhetoric—indeed, legal rhetoric itself includes such "techniques." . . . The Gorgias in many ways prefigures Plato's change in style from dialogue to a more didactic, top-down approach of reasoning from universal principles. Yet Plato's new brand of philosophy gives only the most general sort of guidance, and seems to have little bearing on matters of application. As I elaborate below, universal philosophical principles take us only so far, staying away from the rich tapestries of real disputes. In most moments of Dean Kronman's paper, however, he does not suggest the idea that rhetoric is mere sugarcoating on truths derived from some other source, but says instead that political truths are "embodied idea[s]" with "local coloration."[6] If political truth is not derived from philosophy, or science, or someplace outside of rhetoric, then perhaps a sympathetic account of rhetoric will show that it illuminates a special brand of truth, a truth that is "perspectival" and "controversial."[7] This is the thesis I will try to explicate below. For aid, I turn to Immanuel Kant.

I choose Kant here for two reasons. First, Kant was a humble philosopher. He did not believe that judges or even laypeople need to know philosophical principles to decide cases and act rightly. His work on moral philosophy is often wrongly understood as providing a blueprint for people to follow in order to be moral. But Kant explicitly denies this. He acknowledges that "we do not need science and philosophy to know what we should do to be honest and good, yea, even wise and virtuous," though philosophy does help keep us from rationalizing away our duties.[8] Because Kant is a humble philosopher, he does not collapse all human knowledge into philosophy, as Plato would. Instead, Kant deeply understood our peculiarly human stance between reason and power and devoted his life to exploring the special character and limits of human knowledge.

The Critique of Pure Reason sets forth the limits of "pure" reason or Platonic metaphysics, exposing the contingent and empirical and merely phenomenal nature of most of our knowledge of the world. By confining knowledge, Kant says, he makes room for faith and morality.[9] Indeed, his strictures on our incomplete knowledge of nature make possible an account of human nature as something other than the effect of natural causes—human action, language, and culture are not just a pattern of brain chemicals or survival adaptations. The physiological and psychological picture of humanity is only phenomenon, not truth. Freed from the reductionism of science, Kant can explore in his *Second Critique*, the *Critique of Practical Reason*, the rational preconditions of human action which ground the ethical demands of reason, true for all reasonable beings, not just humans, including the notion of free will necessary for responsibility.

In the *Groundwork of the Metaphysics of Morals*, a kind of prologue to the *Critique of Practical Reason*, Kant characterizes human life, much as Kronman does, as caught between the law of reason and the law of nature—between reason and power. We have our feet in two worlds, the rational and the natural, called by reason to ethical duties, duties conceived in an empirical vacuum, that, for us, are arduous and unpleasant given the friction of our natural impulses and desires (hence, morality is felt as "duty").[10] Our "freedom" as moral actors comes only in the often difficult and unpleasant service to reason; yet, to give in to our "natural selves," our emotions and desires, makes us little more than beasts, in perpetual war with each other and with ourselves, one person's power pitted against another's, one moment's passion defeating the passion of another moment. Kant clearly recognizes that to be human is to be constantly torn between the claims of reason and power.

Second, I choose Kant because in his third critique, the *Critique of Judgment*, he tries to work through the rift between reason and power in a way that is uniquely helpful in constructing a sympathetic account of rhetoric. Here, Kant is concerned precisely with *human* knowledge of the application of rational principles to this world, or, as he called it, judgment, the faculty which Kronman says lawyers are trained to develop.[11]

Judgment is a uniquely human function, not applicable to reasonable creatures generally.[12] Only humans need to bring universal principles to bear on experience, because only humans have both universal principles (mind) and experience (body). So, this work tries to span the gap between reason and power, explain the connection between reason and the senses (including the passions).

Yet what does a work on the nature of aesthetic judgment have to do with law? Hannah Arendt, for one, seized on this work as the core of Kant's political philosophy, and believed that it held the seeds of the completion of her own work, explaining why political truth indeed lies between reason and power and involves uncertainty and emotion.[13] The following is an initial attempt to bring some of the ideas of these great thinkers to bear on the questions Professor Kronman has posed, in keeping with the understanding that the "pursuit of the truth is itself an historical enterprise" involving "collaboration among the living and the dead."[14]

JUDGMENT AS THE EXPERIENCE OF TRUTH

[Editors' Note: This section is not included because of space constraints.]

HOW REASONABLE MINDS CAN DIFFER

Sources of Disagreement

Even if one agrees with Kant that we can eliminate subjectivity as the source of disagreement, from where does the obvious disagreement about law come? One source of disagreement among reasonable minds is that much of what we argue about in law is not morality or meaning, but run-of-the mill factual questions about the world. Our knowledge of the world, as Kant points out in the *Critique of Pure Reason,* is always provisional, distorted, and incomplete. Legal decision-making often requires inquiry into these uncertainties: human motives, past events, future consequences, counterfactual possibilities, etc. We argue about probabilities. Hence, "the battle of the experts" is as endemic to law as it is to science. What legal advocacy does, however, is make sure all perspectives are aired, because the only cure for errors in perception is what Kant calls "expanded experience," or looking at the question or problem from the situation or perspective of others.[15] So, we call witnesses, present evidence, sift documents, consult economists, psychologists, forensic experts, and engineers.

The ultimate questions in court, however, are not questions of fact, but questions of action. The bottom line decision to be made is: Given our uncertainty about the facts, the motives, the consequences, the causes, what should we do? Where should the burden of error fall and why? These questions are always questions of fairness not to be answered by rule or perception, but by sensibility and our best and most experienced judgment. (This may go part of the way toward explaining why we use juries instead of panels of experts to decide cases.)

A second layer of uncertainty comes from the problem explored above—there are no rules for the application of rules. Hence, even if the law and the facts are clear, there is still uncertainty about how the rule fits the facts. Often, there are questions of fairness or fit here too, questions upon which reasonable minds may differ, led different directions by the pull of different analogies or examples, or different dimensions of fit. Sometimes this uncertainty is minimal, and we call the case an "easy" one; sometimes the uncertainty is greater, and we call the case a "hard" one. Along this continuum, we often try to distinguish between cases in which courts "apply" law and cases in which courts "make" law (the core from the penumbra, etc.). However, the nature of the problem is the same. This form of uncertainty corresponds to Kant's discussion of determinant judgment.

A third layer of uncertainty may come from conflicts between rules or norms, clashes of values. This is a form of uncertainty that Kant might not recognize, but stems from the application of moral principles. Even if one grants Kant the premise that respect and responsibility are universally valid bases of ethics, the instantiation of those values in any particular culture or even in any particular setting cannot be deduced through reason alone. Nor can we be sure that there will not be conflicts. Given this possibility, a case may involve a hard or tragic choice between duties, a choice about which reasonable minds not only can, but possibly should, differ.

Finally, a fourth layer of uncertainty may come from the partiality of our temporal standpoint.[16] Even if we can gather all the evidence and take stock of all the legal precedent, even if we have the advice of all the experts and the testimony of all the witnesses, our perspective is never universal because it cannot know the future. How we hedge our view of the law against a possible future understanding of it may also make room for reasonable disagreement. Though we have to decide the case now, we may also leave some latitude for change later—allow a generous hem to let down the fabric as we grow. Here, we may even build uncertainty into the law, if we acknowledge with humility our imperfect and historical point of view.[17]

The Problem of Rhetoric as a Series of "Moves"

If these sources of disagreement are genuine, however, how is it that legal rhetoric so easily appears to be a set of stock moves and countermoves, "thrust" and "counterthrust"? We find catalogs of such strategies in the critical legal studies literature, in legal realist Karl Llewellyn's famous canons on statutes, and even as far back as Aristotle's *Rhetoric*.[18] As law students, we learn the standard arguments: the "slippery slope" argument ("the court cannot give relief in this case because dumber judges in the future won't know where to stop"); the "floodgates of litigation" argument ("the court cannot give relief in this case because then everybody and his brother will sue"); the "plain language" argument ("but it didn't say children couldn't feed the giraffes, it just said "No Feeding Giraffes with Children"[19]); the "deterrence" argument; ("if the court gave unseatbelted plaintiffs relief in this case, then everyone would quit wearing seatbelts"); the "counter-majoritarian argument" ("judges should refrain from dictating policy to mental institutions because judges are not elected by the people; legislatures are more representative and therefore better at making law"); and the "framer's intent" argument ("if the framers had intended the First Amendment to apply to the Internet, they would have said so"). By themselves, these arguments seem empty if not ridiculous, and can be paired with another standard opposing argument. Any of them can generate both good and bad judgments, they often conflict, and there is no overarching theory about when and how to use them. They seem to be moves in a manipulative game.

All of these arguments, stock or not, however, state general values that may be applicable to the case. It is only good judgment, based on that mysterious sense of fit, that can discern when such arguments illuminate and when they simply sound ridiculous (as I made them sound in the circumstances above).[20] We have lots of "rules" (via statute, principle, or common law) in our bags, but it takes an expert to know when to use a 7-iron and when to use a 9-iron. Both the lawyer choosing the argument and the judge responding to it need to have a feel for what rule fits the facts. Two good lawyers will certainly use opposing arguments, often even stock arguments, but, if they are good lawyers, both arguments will, in the circumstances of the case, uncover genuine difficulties about which reasonable people can disagree. And, as every lawyer knows, coming up with "boilerplate" by using such arguments thoughtlessly or mechanically is obvious and unpersuasive. Bad lawyers, like bad poets, write in clichés, clichés which dull the attention of the audience rather than sharpening it, and fail to set before us justice or truth as it seems to be already at work in the facts.

The Importance of Character

Aristotle asserts that rhetoric persuades through fact and argument, emotion, and character.[21] This last is troubling. If someone tells the truth, why should it matter who he or she is? Why should we be persuaded by someone's character? We might as well be persuaded by socio-economic status.

Again, the answer seems to lie in the space between rule and application. As Kant says, it takes experience and the ineffable something known as "good judgment" to apply a rule properly to the facts. We all know people whose judgment we respect, and others whose judgment we do not respect. Kant, that most humble of all philosophers, acknowledged that good judgment is not tied to intellectual acuity or philosophical sophistication. Hence, character matters because experience and sensibility allow some of us to see the fulcrum of a dispute or the undercurrents of a case or the situation of the litigants or the nuances of a witness's testimony more keenly than others. We trust those who have shown such discernment in the past.

We also look for sincerity. This is a tougher one for lawyers, who are called upon to take positions their clients want, not necessarily positions they think to be right. How does a lawyer satisfy this claim without sacrificing his client?

One phenomenon that we have all seen is that, when one is called upon to find the best possible light in which to present a case, one convinces oneself. Every semester I have students write briefs, assigning them their positions without regard to their views. Every semester, most report that by the time they have finished writing their briefs, they have convinced themselves. Is this selling one's soul? Not necessarily. The world is a complicated place and truth is rarely unidimensional. And, as I pointed out above, most law cases involve probabilities, not certainties. There is usually something right in both sides of a case, and the lawyer's job is to find that something and share it with the decision maker. As Aristotle puts it, rhetoric's function "is not simply to succeed in persuading, but rather to discover the persuasive facts in each case . . . What makes a man a sophist is not his abilities but his choices."[22]

The Evil Lawyer

All of this so far assumes that the advocate acts in good faith. What of the evil lawyer, who perverts the mechanics of rhetoric not to evoke truth, but to make untruths seem true? Is rhetoric that is used to manipulate still rhetoric? Is there any guarantee within the practice of rhetoric that it will present truth?

Here, my answer is threefold. First, I have given a "sympathetic" account of rhetoric—not a descriptive account of everything we usually call rhetoric. I have also acknowledged that some lawyers will be bad, in the sense of not having the good judgment or the ability to evoke legal and political truth in their speech or writing. So, this paper is not meant to apply to everything that we might normally call rhetoric, like cheap advertising, propaganda, inflammatory speeches to mobs, etc. These forms of speech are to good rhetoric what motel watercolors are to great art. I also acknowledge that speakers often manipulate their audiences. Yet one can try to move one's hearers without perverting their judgment or lying to them. Good rhetoric and manipulation resemble each other in some ways, but good rhetoric appeals to universal and unself-interested judgments of beauty and respect for others, not greed, hatred, or xenophobia.

Second, we should not make the mistake of thinking that

because some speakers manipulate audiences, all attempts to persuade lead us to falsehoods. As in any field of knowledge, we cannot guarantee that we are not under the influence of the Cartesian "evil demon," so that everything we think true or right is really false or wrong. Skepticism at this level is just barely possible intellectually, but none of us can live as though we were skeptics in this way, doubting our very eyes and minds.

Third, the way we decide whether a lawyer, or any other rhetorician, is lying is by the same process of judgment that I have tried to sketch above: We look at the "fit" or coherence of her arguments, we compare with other facts we know, we experience her vision with our own sensibilities and emotional responses, and we look at her past words and actions. From this perspective, it is hard for me to imagine a way to make falsehoods look true, at least over the long run, unless we doubt our basic capacity for thought and understanding. As the saying goes, you can fool some of the people some of the time, but you can't fool all of the people all of the time. In part, this is due to the fact that rhetoric is not just a set of techniques, but involves character, invites the thought and judgment of its audience, invokes universal and unself-interested emotions, and rests on public understandings, metaphors, and connections. The very publicity of the practice is some guarantee of good faith—few would will evil as a universal law, to put it as Kant would. Because of the public nature of rhetoric, the more common cases of bad faith are easier: We will eventually see through the lawyers who argue from self-interest, egotism, or greed, because their very motivations will lead them to be inconsistent and confused, as Socrates knew so well.

A HOME OF ITS OWN

This sympathetic account of rhetoric still needs to answer the question of the Gorgias: What is special about the domain of rhetoric that sets it apart from science or art or even cookery? Indeed, Kant's discussion of judgment applies to any intellectual endeavor that needs to fit universals to particulars and vice versa. All of rhetoric may involve judgment, but not all judgment is rhetoric.

I would give rhetoric a "home of its own" in only a qualified sense. First, I would not restrict it to political and legal forums, because the need to call forth a "concrete universal" for others to see occurs in almost any decision-making process involving others: families need to figure out what school to send their children to, scientific consortiums have to figure out what to study and how much to spend, businesses need to decide what to sell and whom to sell it to, churches need to decide on carpet as on creed. These forms of decision-making are all practical, institution building, uncertain, involve conflicts of duties and trade-offs, and involve discussions of justice, fairness, and even precedent.

These discussions differ from scientific investigation in that they are practical—about what to do, not just about how to describe the world. They also differ from science and math in that they do not aspire to the discovery of universal laws, but to factual application (judgment, in Kant's sense, not understanding). They differ from religion, contemplation, or poetry, which also seek to bring to experience a concrete universal, but with no need to act. Finally, they differ from pure practical reason, because they involve groups who must work together. Hence, these truths must be shared, unlike one's own moral duties and spontaneous right actions. Public deliberation is not necessary to practical reason— most right action is unreflective like expertise—a matter of feel and practice and good habit. Try asking a pilot how she flies a plane, or a tennis player how he swings a racquet!

Rhetoric may share features with practical wisdom—that is, its emphasis on action—but rhetoric requires the experiencing of practical wisdom *with others*. It also shares features with poetry— that is, its expression of a concrete universal—but rhetoric needs to act. The closest I can come, then, to carving out a domain for rhetoric is to say that rhetoric is something like the experience of practical wisdom. Lawyers' arguments and judicial opinions are attempts to share truths of practical wisdom publicly, allowing that truth to be experienced, seen and felt. This bringing to language of practical wisdom also allows the artist or judge herself to see it—it is not as though the rhetorician is expressing a truth she already knows in her head, but instead the necessity for trying to articulate it makes it concrete for her, too. Solomonic judgment may be perfect as practical reason, but it is veiled, even to the judge, as political or legal truth.

When we try to bring this truth to experience, to share it, we build communities. Rhetoric, in this sense, does not manipulate us into cooperation, it embodies cooperation. It is the common ground; it is our attempt to create democracy in Montesquieu's sense of a community of virtue-seekers. Of course, we can never hope to focus our vision with perfect clarity any more than we can paint or carve perfect beauty, but, as Plato says, "if such a clear image of wisdom were granted as would come through sight, it would arouse terrible love."[23]

NOTES

1. Anthony Kronman, "Rhetoric," *University of Cincinnati Law Review* 67 (Spring 1999): 709.

2. Ibid., p. 691.

3. Immanuel Kant, too, seems to take this view of rhetoric; see Immanuel Kant, *Critique of Judgment*, trans. J. H. Bernard (New York: Hafner, 1951), but insofar as rhetoric approximates poetry, it is rescued from its philosophical slanderers. See ibid., pp. 165, 170 (praising poetry over rhetoric). I have chosen here to make little of Kant's explicit and brief comments on rhetoric, which differ little from the philosophical canon and seem quite tangential to his train of thought, though he also seems to acknowledge the possibility of a more sympathetic account of rhetoric exemplified by "[t]he man who, along with a clear insight into things, has in his power a wealth of pure speech, and who with a fruitful imagination capable of presenting his ideas unites a lively sympathy with what is truly good" (ibid., p. 172, n. 50).

4. See Plato, *Gorgias*, ed. G. P. Goold, trans. W. R. M. Lamb (Harvard University Press, 1975), pp. 523–25.

5. See Ernest Weinrib, "Law as Myth: Reflections on Plato's Gorgias," *Iowa Law Review* 74 (1989): 787.

6. Kronman, "Rhetoric," p. 699.

7. Ibid.

8. Immanuel Kant, *Fundamental Principles of the Metaphysics of Morals*, trans. Thomas K. Abbott (New York: Prentice Hall, 1949), pp. 21–22.

9. Immanuel Kant, *Critique of Pure Reason*, trans. Norman Kemp

Smith (London: Macmillan, 1929), p. 29: "[E]ven the assumption—as made on behalf of the necessary practical employment of my reason—of God, freedom, and immortality is not permissible unless at the same time speculative reason be deprived of its pretensions to transcendent insight. For in order to arrive at such insight it must make use of principles which, in fact, extend only to objects of possible experience, and which, if also applied to what cannot be an object of experience, always really change this into an appearance, thus rendering all practical extension of pure reason impossible. I have therefore found it necessary to deny knowledge, in order to make room for faith. The dogmatism of metaphysics, that is, the preconception that it is possible to make headway in metaphysics without a previous criticism of pure reason, is the source of all that unbelief, always very dogmatic, which wars against morality."

10. See Kant, *Fundamental Principles of the Metaphysics of Morals*, pp. 69–72.

11. See Kronman, *The Lost Lawyer: Failing Ideals of the Legal Profession* (Cambridge, MA: Harvard University Press, 1993), pp. 113–16.

12. See Hannah Arendt, *Lectures on Kant's Political Philosophy*, ed. Ronald Beiner (Chicago: University of Chicago Press, 1982), pp. 13, 26–27; Kant, *Critique of Judgment*, p. 44.

13. See Arendt, *Lectures on Kant's Political Philosophy*, p. 4. Kronman takes note of the *Critique of Judgment* but doesn't find it relevant. See Kronman, at *The Lost Lawyer*, pp. 45–46. Indeed, its relevance is not patent, but I will try to make the connection here.

14. Kronman, "Rhetoric," p. 704.

15. See Kant, *Critique of Judgment*, pp. 135–38; Arendt, *Lectures on Kant's Political Philosophy*, pp. 42–44, 58–77; Arendt, *The Life of the Mind* (New York: Harcourt, 1978), pp. 38, 50.

16. See Kronman, "Rhetoric," p. 699: "But because laws and institutions are mortal composites, existing in time and subject like every other finite being to the forces of decay, their good can never be as clear or perfect as the good of things that exist outside of time, like the objects of mathematics. Because every regime is an embodied idea, its values must always have some local coloration. They must always have an element of particularity, of historicity, associated with the peculiar circumstances of their career in time."

17. See, for example, H. L. A. Hart, *The Concept of Law* (Oxford: Clarendon Press, 1961), pp. 126–27; Ronald Dworkin, *Taking Rights Seriously* (Cambridge, MA: Harvard University Press, 1978), p. 133: "The 'vague' standards [in the Constitution] were chosen deliberately, by the

men who drafted and adopted them, in place of the more specific and limited rules that they might have enacted."

18. See appendix C in Karl N. Llewellyn, *The Common Law Tradition: Deciding Appeals* (Boston: Little Brown and Company, 1960). See Aristotle, *Rhetoric*, in *The Complete Works of Aristotle: Revised Oxford Translation*, ed. Jonathon Barnes, trans. W. Rhys Roberts (Princeton, NJ: Princeton University Press, 1984) 2:1375a–1377b: "If you have already sworn an oath that contradicts your present one, you must argue that it is not perjury, since perjury is a crime, and a crime must be a voluntary action, whereas actions due to the force or fraud of others are involuntary. You must further reason from this that perjury depends on the intention and not on the spoken words. But if it is your opponent who has already sworn an oath that contradicts his present one, you must say that if he does not abide by his oaths he is the enemy of society, and that this is the reason why men take an oath before administering the laws. 'Do my opponents insist that you, the judges, must abide by the oath you have sworn, and yet will not abide by their own oaths?' And there are other arguments which may be used to magnify the importance of the oath" (ibid., pp. 1377b, 5–10). Sound familiar?

19. I thank Brian Bix for this example.

20. See Karen L. Llewellyn, *The Common Law Tradition: Deciding Appeals* (London: Little, Brown, 1960), p. 521.

21. See Aristotle, *Rhetoric*, p. 1358a. Kronman also recognizes that good lawyering is the development of character, not just mental facility. See Kronman, pp. 109–62.

22. Aristotle, *Rhetoric*, pp. 1355b, 10, 15.

23. See Plato, *Phaedrus*, ed. G.P. Goold, trans. Harold North Fowler (Cambridge: Harvard University Press, 1977), p. 250d.

BEYOND JUSTIFICATIONS

SEEKING MOTIVATIONS TO SUSTAIN PUBLIC DEFENDERS

Charles J. Ogletree Jr.

M ost scholarship on the professional role of the criminal defense attorney focuses on a search for the appropriate philosophical or moral justifications for the attorney's zealous advocacy. In this Article, Professor Ogletree argues that this focus is misplaced. Nearly all lawyers and legal scholars agree that the criminal defense lawyer's role is justified, and that public defenders are necessary to the constitutional and moral legitimacy of the criminal justice system. However, because little attention has been paid to developing techniques that will motivate people to become and remain public defenders, many public defenders "burn out." The result is that conduct most lawyers believe is both justified and necessary fails to occur. Professor Ogletree argues that legal scholars should move beyond abstract justifications of criminal defense work and should instead explore and develop

Harvard Law Review (April, 1993) copyright © 1993 The Harvard Law Review Association; Charles J. Ogletree.

motivations for lawyers to represent the indigent. Drawing on his personal experiences as a public defender, he identifies two factors—empathy and heroism—that motivated him to continue in the face of a tragedy that shook his faith in the system. . . .

INTRODUCTION

Many public defenders tell a familiar tale about their experiences representing indigents charged with criminal offenses. Their stories invariably begin with a young and idealistic law student who lands a highly sought-after job at a public defender's office and embarks on a mission to fight injustice and to help underprivileged citizens who have been charged with crimes.

After a few years (or, in some instances, a few months), the idealist discovers, to her chagrin, that even the noblest of efforts falls short in the face of those constraints endemic to most public defender services: staggering caseloads, tremendous time pressure, limited resources, and inadequate training. More importantly, the crusader is saddled with ever-growing doubts about the sanctity of her original mission. The story, all too often, ends with the crusader becoming jaded, disillusioned, or cynical, usually leaving the public defender's office for another career or, alternatively, settling for a routine existence of administering plea-bargained justice with little fervor for the cases or the clients. This image of the failed idealist is deeply embedded in our popular culture, and it forms the story line of myriad novels and movies. . . .

This article attempts to bridge the gap between justification and motivation in public defender work and proposes that a symbiotic relationship exists between the two concepts. Part I of this article examines some of the common justifications for being a public defender and for engaging in zealous advocacy on behalf of guilty clients. The conclusion of this analysis is that these justifications are quite convincing. In Part II, however, I illustrate the shortcomings of justification arguments by describing an event in my life that led me to question my commitment to being a public defender. Through an examination of some of my own experiences as a public defender, I show that theoretical justifications do not go far enough because they fail to offer sufficient motivation to do indigent defense work. In Part III, I reflect on the factors that made it possible for me to continue public defense advocacy. I argue that a sustaining motivation for criminal defense advocacy can stem from two factors. The first of these is empathy for the client. By "empathy," I do not mean merely that defense lawyers should have greater understanding of their clients' plight. Although empathy at its most basic level does indeed involve compassion for the accused, I refer more specifically to a particular style of representation, a degree of involvement in the client's life that transcends the conventional scope of criminal representation. By seeing the client as more than a criminal defendant and by understanding the adverse conditions he endures and the bleak future he may well face, the public defender perceives a shared humanity. The result is a perspective that allows the defender to relate to the client more closely and that affects the defender's performance in a myriad of ways. The second of the sustaining motivations I explore in this Article is a feeling of "heroism." I define "heroism" as the desire to take on "the system" and prevail, even in the face of overwhelming odds.

Examining the factors that motivated me to become a defender and shaped my style of representation, I conclude that, because I both empathized with my clients and saw myself as a hero taking on a powerful system, I was able to maintain my motivation even when events in my personal life exposed the limitations of traditional justifications. Finally, in Part IV, I try to draw from my own experiences concrete measures that lawyers and law schools can take to instill the motivations that are central to effective and sustained indigent criminal defense work, as well as to other forms of legal practice.

A significant portion of this article is in narrative form. As others have recognized, personal narratives are uniquely suited to exploring human motivations, and this article ultimately is about what moves people. The formalized, doctrinal style of argument that characterizes much contemporary legal writing can too easily elude the realities of human experience. My use of narrative stems from my firm conviction that individual experience must be considered more carefully, analyzed more critically, and elevated in importance. Thus, my narrative is a "call to context."[1] In particular, I hope that through my narrative I can trigger the empathic responses of others.

TRADITIONAL JUSTIFICATIONS FOR CRIMINAL DEFENSE ADVOCACY

This part will explore the theories commonly asserted to justify public defenders' work. As my argument concerns the relationship of justifications to motivations, it is necessary first to distinguish between the two concepts. A justification, as used in this article, is a morally or legally acceptable reason for taking action. It answers the question "why should it be done?" By contrast, a motivation persuades a particular person to take a certain action and answers the question "why should I do it?" To place this discussion within the context of the defense of indigents, a justification tells us why criminal defendants too poor to afford a lawyer should be provided with one; for example, one justification is the constitutional mandate that all individuals be provided with assistance of counsel. A motivation, by contrast, inspires me to be such a lawyer. For example, I might be motivated by a desire to gain the litigation experience that public defender work provides.

The distinction between motivation and justification cannot always be clearly drawn. Indeed, a justification may also serve as an effective motivation. A person may find the existence of police justified by the need for public safety and order. Because she values these goals, that justification may also be sufficient to motivate her to become a police officer. Conversely, a person may find the task of serving as the executioner in capital cases justified, but not find the justification personally motivating. The problem in indigent defense is that the conventional justifications for doing the work often do not correspond with effective or sustaining motivations.

This article is not an attempt to analyze all of the arguments that have been asserted to justify public defender work. Others have adequately performed this task. My project is a different one, focused on the realities of public defender practice. My concern is with the lack of sustaining motivations to do indigent defense work. Accordingly, I begin by examining the commonly asserted justifications in order to explore their limitations.

Many theorists have considered the role of the criminal defense attorney. Although they identify different and often competing conceptions of that role, most agree that zealous advocacy is necessary and justified. Theorists discuss these justifications in the context of criminal defense generally, but they are fully applicable to indigent defense work. As an initial step in my analysis, the justifications merit scrutiny.

All justifications for the work of defense counsel generally (and for the public defender in particular) must be considered in the context of the Sixth Amendment right to counsel, which creates a duty on the part of the state to provide representation to the indigent accused. The Sixth Amendment provides that "[i]n all criminal prosecutions, the accused shall enjoy the right . . . to have the Assistance of Counsel for his defence." This right has been interpreted as an absolute right, independent of guilt or innocence, to appointed counsel in criminal proceedings. . . .

Once one accepts the constitutional right to counsel for criminal defendants, one must determine the character and scope of the legal assistance this right entails. The American Bar Association (ABA) Model Code of Professional Responsibility instructs the lawyer, in both civil and criminal proceedings, to "represent a client zealously within the bounds of the law." Indeed, a lawyer may be subject to disciplinary action for "intentionally . . . failing to seek the lawful objectives of his client. . . ." The Model Code and its successor, the ABA Model Rules of Professional Conduct, further define conduct which is outside "the bounds of the law" to include the knowing use of perjured testimony, false statements of law or fact, the fabrication of evidence, and the knowing assistance in fraudulent or illegal conduct. Despite such definitions, the parameters of the ABA mandate remain quite vague.

A predominant conception of the criminal defense attorney's role has developed to fill this void. In its simplest form, the defense attorney is a "hired gun," a professional who takes her clients' ends as her own, and may do anything short of breaking the law to attain these ends.[2] "Provided that the end sought is not illegal," explains one theorist, "the lawyer is, in essence, an amoral technician whose peculiar skills and knowledge in respect to the law are available to those with whom the relationship of client is established." Indeed, the criminal lawyer has great leeway in the defense of his client. As Justice White noted in *United States v. Wade*:

> [D]efense counsel has no . . . obligation to ascertain or present the truth. . . . If he can confuse a witness, even a truthful one, or make him appear at a disadvantage, unsure or indecisive, that will be his normal course. Our interest in not convicting the innocent permits counsel to put the State to its proof, to put the State's case in the worst possible light, regardless of what he thinks or knows to be the truth.

But what are the ethical ramifications of this role? Often, in attaining a client's end—typically that of avoiding conviction—public defenders do many things that would commonly be considered immoral. Public defenders defend clients who they know are guilty, seek to suppress relevant evidence, fail to reveal incriminating facts, and make truthful witnesses appear to be liars. If defenders do their jobs well, their work undoubtedly achieves results in the courtroom that may or may not reflect the truth.

Theorists of the ethical dimension of lawyering have struggled to endow this form of representation with moral coherence. One response to the charge of immorality in public defender work suggests that there is a "role morality" attending criminal defense work that gives a defense attorney certain unique moral responsibilities and absolves her of others. The Model Rules expressly note the distinction between acts of representation and acts of individual moral choice: "A lawyer's representation of a client, including representation by appointment, does not constitute an endorsement of the client's political, economic, social or moral views or activities." This absence of direct moral responsibility, or "role differentiation," provides the basis for the argument that "where the attorney-client relationship exists, it is often appropriate and many times even obligatory for the attorney to do things that, all other things being equal, an ordinary person need not, and should not do."[3] Ultimately, as part of the advocate's role, a principle of non-accountability ensures that "when acting as an advocate for a client according to the Principle of Professionalism, a lawyer is neither legally, professionally, nor morally accountable for the means used or the ends achieved."[4]

Accordingly, some theorists conclude that, in her role as public defender, a lawyer is not implicated in the guilt or immorality of her clients. Provided that she acts within the bounds of the law, she bears no responsibility for the choices and actions of her clients. The guilt or innocence of the client and the nature of the crime are extraneous.

In addition to "role-morality," two other theories have been advanced to justify zealous advocacy on the part of the public defender: "client-centered" and "systemic" justifications.

Commentators who espouse "client-centered justifications" maintain that zealous advocacy is necessary to promote the social and moral good of the client. "Systemic justifications" focus not on the interests of the various actors within the adversary system, but on the adversary system itself. I will treat each of these in turn below.

Client-Centered Justifications

Client-centered justifications are premised on a vision of the lawyer as a facilitator for the client's interaction with an otherwise impenetrable legal system. This argument generally rests on the premise that "first-class citizenship is dependent upon access to the law."[5] In this view, the overriding moral obligation of the lawyer is to provide unobstructed access to the legal system. Given that such access is crucial to citizenship, and thus to autonomy and equality, theorists argue that the lawyer impedes autonomy and equality by erecting moral barriers between her client and full access to the tools of the legal system. If we were to hold a lawyer morally responsible for the client's ends that she facilitates through her legal assistance, her moral predilections would inter-fere with her client's autonomy. In order to counteract this danger, "the values of autonomy and equality suggest that . . . the client's conscience should be superior to the lawyer's."[6]

Critics have charged that the client autonomy argument fails to note "the crucial distinction between the desirability of people acting autonomously and the desirability of their autonomous act."[7] Proponents of absolute client autonomy privilege such autonomy above all other moral inquiries. They appear to believe that because client autonomy is desirable as a general proposition, facilitation of such autonomy is always desirable, irrespective of the client's goals. Unfortunately, proponents of the client autonomy argument fail to consider the force of the view that because "doing bad things is bad, helping people do bad things is bad."[8] The advantage attained by facilitating morally justified autonomy must be balanced against the detriment incurred by facilitating an immoral act, to determine ultimately if the lawyer's conduct is moral or immoral.

Professor Charles Fried provides a client-centered justification that builds upon and refines the personal autonomy argument. Fried argues that "[t]he lawyer acts morally because he helps to preserve and express the autonomy of his client vis-a-vis the legal system."[9] Fried analogizes the lawyer-client relationship to the relationship between friends. "Like a friend, the lawyer acts in your interests, not his own; or rather he adopts your interests as his own."[10] Just as a person appropriately treats friends with partiality, a lawyer justifiably favors the interests of her client over those of other actors in the legal system, including the opposing party, adverse witnesses, police, and the state.

Many critics have faulted Fried's "Lawyer as Friend" justification as resting on an empirically and normatively problematic analogy. Critics have questioned whether "friendship really involves adopting the friend's interests as one's own, even when the friend defines her interest as requiring the commission of a moral wrong."[11] In addition, critics have challenged Fried's friendship analogy itself. Noting the lack of reciprocity and sacrifice in the typical lawyer-client relationship, critics charge that "friendship" explains virtually nothing about the interaction between lawyers and clients. These critics contend that Fried fails to address adequately the implications of the fact that, unlike friendship, the lawyer-client relationship is not a bond of mutual interest and affection. Rather, the relationship is premised on the client's willingness to pay. The lawyer's loyalty to her client stems entirely from this fiduciary relationship, and is thus one-sided and transitory. Similarly, under the traditional model of the lawyer-client relationship, the lawyer does not act like a friend when representing the client; she behaves more like a mercenary, using her specialized skill and training to battle her client's opponents and achieve her client's objectives.

Yet it is Fried himself who, by pointing to the difference in moral accountability between the lawyer and friend, presents perhaps the strongest critique of the analogy. The lawyer's acts are imputed to the legal system that mandates them rather than to the lawyer herself; thus, the lawyer bears no personal responsibility for her actions. In the pure friendship context, no such exonerating mechanism exists. In response to these criticisms, Fried has modified his analogy and has asserted that it is merely intended to illustrate the discretion that both lawyers and friends enjoy in allocating their efforts and loyalty. However, the question remains: even if lawyers are justified in devoting themselves wholeheartedly to clients, shouldn't they be morally accountable for their choice of clients? Fried's response rests on his faith in the lawyer's inherent rights to personal liberty. Because Fried's justifications are independent of client characteristics, and the choice of where to allocate one's resources is a fundamental personal liberty, the lawyer need not explain her choice of clients at all.

Systemic Justifications

Systemic justifications of zealous advocacy are premised on the underlying structure of the adversary system. This structure requires an advocate for each of the parties, an impartial judge, and in the criminal context, the right to have a jury determine, after hearing all evidence, where the "truth" lies. In this vein, some commentators have argued that it is impossible for a lawyer to do anything "untruthful"—even when presenting a false defense, or placing a perjurious witness on the stand—because she can never know the absolute truth. These commentators rely on the assertion that the "truth," in the adversary system, "is what the trier of fact determines it to be."[12] Ultimately, proponents of this systemic justification argue that when two adversarial parties each present their strongest case, "the truth will emerge through a dialectical process, in which the vigorous advocacy of thesis and antithesis will equip the neutral arbiter to synthesize the data and reach a conclusion."[13]

This "truth-centered" justification suffers from several flaws. Most important, it fails to draw a distinction between legal and factual truth. Certainly, an attorney is capable of knowing the "factual" (as opposed to the "legal") truth of the matter. For example, an attorney can know whether or not his client pulled the trigger of the murder weapon. But the "legal" truth—whether or not the client's act constituted murder—can be determined only by the trier of fact.

This distinction between factual and legal conclusions exposes the central problem with this justification. The argument remains circular; the adversary system determines legal truth, and therefore legal truth can be determined only by the adversary system. If a singular truth will ultimately be discovered, why cannot an attorney apply the same standards as those of the trier of fact and determine legal truth as well? . . .

A second, more persuasive, systemic justification stems from the unique aspects of criminal defense practice. Proponents of this justification argue that the disparity in strength and resources of the parties in criminal cases—the weak individual against the powerful state—requires heightened protection for the defendant. Consequently, the criminal defendant's lawyer is entitled to broader moral leeway in the representation of her client than that granted to lawyers in civil cases.

This argument directly responds to the truth-centered justifications. The claim that the adversary system is incapable of finding the truth is unpersuasive in the criminal context because truth is not the only goal of the system. The adversary system functions not only to find truth, but also, perhaps more fundamentally, to protect individuals from the tyranny of a powerful government. Within this framework, zealous advocacy serves as an effective constraint on the power of the state.

In the context of the adversary system, the criminal defense attorney must vigorously challenge evidence presented by prosecutors and put forth the strongest possible defense. Only by taking this approach can the attorney ensure that the state meets its burden of proof. The defense attorney who fails to defend her clients vigorously jeopardizes the protection of individual rights in our society.

A variation of this systemic justification focuses on the disempowered status of individuals represented by public defenders. Indigent defendants, many of whom lack both legal sophistication and the funds to hire an attorney, particularly need and deserve protection against state overreaching:

> Most people who commit crimes are themselves the victims of horrible injustice. This statement is true generally because most of those accused of rape, robbery and murder are oppressed minorities. . . . A lawyer performs good work when he helps to prevent the imprisonment of the poor, the outcast, and minorities in shameful conditions.[14]

This approach to criminal defense work represents the strongest of the theories offered to justify zealous advocacy. This argument does have weaknesses, however. Indigent defense work cannot be justified solely as a means of protecting individuals from overreaching by the state. If this were the exclusive goal of the criminal justice system, "a more direct method would be just to stop prosecuting altogether."[15] Our justice system does not focus solely on defendants' rights. As one theorist notes, "surely there cannot be a right to gain an acquittal whenever the imagination of one's attorney is good enough to produce one."[16]

Thus, although theorists do not necessarily agree on which justification most persuasively supports the role of the public defender, nearly all theorists and practitioners agree that the defender's role is morally justified. Whether we find persuasive the client-centered justifications, the systemic justifications, or some combination of the two, we all essentially agree that some justification exists.

My goal in this article, however, is to move beyond defending and attacking these justifications. I seek to show that even the most compelling justification fails to motivate public defenders to do their jobs with energy and enthusiasm. Regardless of their theoretical or logical merits, these abstract justifications simply do not

inspire or excite; and, for the public defender who has become disillusioned or dispirited, they do not offer a source of renewed
vitality or commitment.

In the next part, I describe a personal tragedy that forced me to
reexamine my role as a public defender. That experience led me to
appreciate the importance of seeking personal motivation over
and above the traditional justifications for criminal defense work.

RECONCILING A PERSONAL TRAGEDY WITH A COMMITMENT TO PUBLIC DEFENSE ADVOCACY

Seeing the System From a Victim's Perspective

Barbara was my younger sister, one of six Ogletree children. We
grew up in Merced, California, a small agricultural community in
the San Joaquin Valley. I remember that when we were young, Barbara assumed an almost maternal role toward the youngest child,
our sister Rose. Even then, it was clear to me that regardless of
what Barbara would ultimately choose to do professionally, she
would be successful.

I left California after college to attend law school, and after
graduation I took a job with the District of Columbia Public
Defender Service (PDS). While I chose a career defending criminals, Barbara became a police officer, dedicated to catching,
arresting, and helping to prosecute the criminals I fought so zealously to free. Barbara remained in our hometown and was one of
the first black women hired by the Merced County Sheriff's
Department.

Even though we were thousands of miles apart, Barbara and I
maintained a close relationship. It is interesting that, despite our
similar experiences growing up, my sister and I chose to work on
opposite sides of the criminal justice system. At heart, we
respected each other's work and often teased each other about our
opposing roles. Moreover, there was a striking similarity in the
ways in which we treated criminal defendants. My sister always
treated the detainees with dignity, even breaking rules to help

them. She would sneak them cigarettes, let them call home, and do other small favors to bring a little comfort into an otherwise impersonal system. Despite the difficulties and risks of her career, Barbara was the person in our family whom we worried about least, the one who seemed safe and in control at home in Merced.

In August of 1982, I received a phone call from my mother that I will never forget. The words exploded in my head as my mother said: "Barbara's dead." A still unknown assailant had entered my sister's home and stabbed her to death in her living room. I felt alternating sensations of numbness and pain. Why Barbara? Why now? I wanted to know who was responsible for her death, and I wanted that person brought to justice. I questioned my mother with clinical precision, trying to ascertain every conceivable detail of the event. I pressed her for information: the time of death, the murder weapon, evidence of forced entry, and a list of possible enemies. I knew that my mother could not answer these questions, yet I persisted. It was the only way I could deal with the pain.

That night, I called the Merced Police Department to see if they had any leads. Still reeling from the initial shock, I pressed the police as I had my mother, and sought out every detail that they possibly could provide about the murder. I requested the autopsy report, the police report, photographs, and other documents that typically make up a case file. As a public defender I had been trained to approach cases by conceptualizing how the prosecutor would present evidence at trial. In my quest for answers, I pursued my sister's murder in the only way I knew how—as a lawyer trying to solve a problem.

I left for California early the next morning to help with the funeral arrangements, and while I was there I continued to investigate the case. By this time, my shock at the news of Barbara's murder had developed into an obsession with solving the case. I spent hours talking to police officers, pacing through Barbara's house, looking through her things for any possible clues. I wanted to see photographs and diagrams of the crime scene, witness statements, telephone logs, work schedules, a diary, credit card receipts. Rumors of the murderer's identity were rampant in the community. While suspicious of a number of people, I had little evidence. Based upon my experience in defending similar homicides, the facts of the case suggested that someone Barbara knew had killed her. The scene of the crime supported this conclusion. There was no evidence of forced entry into her home. Her son had been present at the time of the murder and was left uninjured. Nothing was stolen. Furthermore, the medical examiner found no evidence of defensive wounds of the type that would be expected if Barbara, a police officer, had been confronted in her home by an intruder. Unfortunately, this meager evidence failed to point to any particular suspect. The police actually made one arrest, hoping the suspect would confess. When he did not, they were forced to release him. When all else had failed, desperate for clues, I surveyed the crowd during the funeral, looking for suspicious conduct by Barbara's friends or colleagues.

My investigative efforts brought me into close contact with members of the Merced police department. The officers, some of whom had been my classmates in high school, showed sympathy and cooperated with me. Up to that time, my relations with the police had always been adversarial. Although I had often contacted the police to report personal experiences of police harassment or to help people who had been arrested, on those occasions my posture toward the police had necessarily been aggressive. Now, for the first time, I felt that the police were on my side, working with me to find and punish my sister's murderer.

My determination to track down my sister's murderer and secure his conviction led me to adopt an outlook that was in many ways incompatible with the justifications I had consistently used to defend my profession. As a public defender, I firmly believed in the necessity of putting the state to the test at trial, and just as importantly, of severely constraining the behavior of police in pursuit of criminal suspects. I now saw only the harm that could result from constitutional restrictions on a police officer's ability to search for evidence and suspects. When it came to my sister's murder, I did not want any procedural safeguards for the criminal. I wanted the state to use all evidence, obtained by any means whatsoever, to convict her attacker. I wanted the satisfaction of knowing that the person responsible for her death would be brought to justice. I wanted retribution.

As I experienced this unsettling contradiction between my

abstract beliefs and my reaction to Barbara's murder, I began to reconsider my role as a public defender. I imagined the assailant's trial and contemplated the posture that his defense lawyer might take. I began to fear that the killer's attorney might be someone like me, zealously committed to challenging the state's case— someone intent on acquittal, regardless of the crime with which his client is charged and the strength of the evidence against his client. I feared that such a defense lawyer might expose a previously unknown dark side of Barbara's life, or through obfuscation, innuendo, and distortion, create a dark side to her life.

Imagining the role the defense attorney would play at the trial of Barbara's killer forced me to face squarely the real consequences suffered by victims and their families as a direct result of the zealous advocacy of clever defense lawyers. I had to consider how victims feel about lawyers like myself, lawyers who secure dismissals on technicalities, or who seek to raise sufficient doubt for a jury to find the client not guilty, even in the face of strong evidence against the accused. I also imagined the impact on my mother of a defense strategy that would present Barbara's life in a negative light. I agonized over the possibility that the person responsible for my sister's death might walk away.

Reconsidering My Professional Role

My grief over my sister's death, coupled with my frustration at being unable to solve her murder, shook my faith in the criminal justice system and my commitment to criminal defense work. I had dedicated my life to defending people charged with a wide range of criminal offenses. In return for my efforts and sacrifices, I had to live through the horror of burying my younger sister, who had died a violent death.

This experience made me wonder whether I could return to PDS. I discussed my misgivings with my colleagues, who were genuinely concerned for my welfare. My colleagues uniformly indicated that they would understand if I wanted to resign. After reflecting for some time, I concluded that I could still approach my work with the same conviction that I had always brought to it. In reaching this decision, I asked myself what Barbara would have done in a similar situation. I tried to imagine how Barbara would have responded if a police officer had killed me without cause. I knew she would have been angry, devastated, and hurt, and she would have expected the officer to be punished. Yet Barbara's commitment to victims in the criminal justice system probably would have led her to continue her work with the same pride and professionalism as before. Ultimately, I decided to return to PDS.

Shortly thereafter, the Deputy Director of the Criminal Justice Act Office requested that I take a case. He asked me to represent a defendant charged with felony murder, with an underlying felony of rape. The facts of the case struck a resonant chord. A young black woman had been found dead; she had been raped and then strangled with her own stockings. About twenty feet from the victim's body, the police had discovered a man's wallet containing the identification of the defendant, Craig Strong.[17] Strong had recently been paroled from prison, where he had been serving a life sentence for rape. Prior to his conviction he had been acquitted of two previous rape charges; all three of the earlier rapes had occurred in the same area as the crime scene, a mere two blocks from Strong's house.

Following the lead of the wallet, the police had arrested Strong in his house at 5:00 a.m. without having obtained an arrest warrant. They found twigs in his hair, pubic hair on his clothing, and dirt on his knees. The lab tests showed that this evidence matched samples taken from the crime scene and the victim's body. When the police questioned Strong about his whereabouts that night, he responded that he had been out with friends and had returned home at about 1:00 a.m. Unfortunately for Strong, however, his statement was consistent with his presence in the area at the time of the victim's death: without knowing that the body had been discovered at 1:00 a.m., the medical examiner had placed the time of death between 12:30 a.m. and 1:30 a.m.

After learning these background facts, I went to visit Strong. When I saw him in the cell block, it was clear to me that he was frightened. He did not know what would happen to him that day or thereafter. In telling me about his life, his family, and his fears, Strong revealed that his father had been murdered when Strong was young, and that he had no positive male role models as he grew up. He did not know whether anyone would represent him, or how his family would react to his arrest. As awful as his crime was, I could see that he wanted someone—anyone—to say, "I'm on your side."

The abundant physical evidence clearly indicated that the case would be difficult for Strong's defense team. However, the conduct of the police in the case raised troubling Fourth Amendment issues. Like most PDS attorneys, I found cases like this to be the most challenging.

Despite my sister's recent murder, I accepted the case. Though I had made my decision, I continued to reexamine my commitment to zealous representation of indigent defendants in general, and of Craig Strong in particular. I was concerned that my feelings about my sister's murder might interfere somehow with my ability to represent Strong, especially in light of the fact that her assailant had not been caught. Might I subconsciously harbor unacknowledged resentments that would lead me to be under zealous in Strong's defense? Might I over-identify with the victim's family, and therefore be unworthy of my client's trust? I examined the Model Code and reviewed some of the cases cited therein, seeking some guidance for a situation of this sort. I found discussions of various ethical issues, including conflict of interest cases and cases referring to the appearance of impropriety. In my own experience, I was aware of instances in which lawyers decided not to represent clients for undisclosed personal reasons. Nothing in the Model Code, however, explicitly addressed potential internal conflicts of the sort I was confronting.

I decided to tell Strong about Barbara's murder. I described the potential conflict and explained that he had the right to seek new counsel if he doubted my ability to represent him. We went before the judge, who also knew of my sister's murder, and the judge offered Strong the opportunity to seek new counsel. Strong confirmed that he wanted me to represent him, and the judge expressed no misgivings about that decision.

In preparing for Strong's trial, my first move was to seek suppression of the physical evidence taken from his person and his statement placing him in the vicinity of the crime. We thus filed a suppression motion, contending that the evidence was inadmissible because the police had failed to obtain an arrest warrant before they entered Strong's house. We argued that the police had had enough time to obtain a warrant, considering the delay between the discovery of Strong's wallet and his arrest. If the police could spare four hours to collect evidence at the crime scene, we argued, they had plenty of time to obtain a warrant. In spite of our strong constitutional argument, I realized that judges rarely grant suppression motions in murder cases. Judges, like other public officials, are not immune to public criticism, and, in close cases, may deny such a motion and leave the issue for appellate review. To my surprise, the judge ruled in our favor, concluding that the evidence obtained during the arrest was tainted by the failure to obtain a warrant and would therefore be suppressed.

Although pleased with this early victory, I began to think about the real possibility that we might win. Would this victory at the suppression hearing ultimately allow a murderer and rapist to walk away unpunished? I thought about what Craig Strong might do if released. This was his fourth rape charge; it was reasonable to believe that Strong might commit another rape if he escaped conviction. Although these thoughts troubled me even more than they had before, I still felt an obligation to fight vigorously for his release.

The government appealed the suppression ruling, and the District of Columbia Court of Appeals reversed the district court's order. At trial, the government would be permitted to introduce the wallet found at the scene, Strong's statement, and all the evidence seized at the time of Strong's arrest.

I spent an exceptional amount of time preparing Strong's case for trial. I visited him regularly in jail, talked to him on the phone almost every day, and took pains to keep him apprised of our efforts. I sent him letters and copies of all motions and briefs filed on his behalf. I also visited his family. Strong lived with his mother, his sister, a niece, and a nephew. His mother was a proud woman who tried to hide her pain upon hearing that her son had again been arrested. She wanted the best for her son, and she could not bring herself to believe that he had again been accused of rape, let alone that he may have killed his victim.

At trial, the government presented a powerful case. We did all we could to challenge their witnesses. We pointed out weaknesses in the experts' qualifications and errors in their reports, but there was little that we could do to rebut the powerful evidence: the presence of Strong's wallet near the victim's body and the testimony of witnesses who saw him with his wallet one hour before the crime. As I watched the jurors listen intently to the testimony and study the physical evidence, I realized the tremendous precariousness of our position. Our hostility and aggressiveness toward the government's witnesses during cross-examination had been a risky move. Despite the powerful evidence against Strong, however, I thought that we had raised enough questions about the government's case to create a reasonable doubt.

The jury was out for almost a week. With each passing hour, my expectation that Strong would be acquitted increased. While we awaited the verdict, my co-counsel also sensed the possibility of acquittal and expressed her misgivings about our role. "What happens if he is acquitted and released?" she asked. I responded, almost mechanically, that we could not allow our apprehensions about his possible future conduct to affect the zealousness of our advocacy on his behalf. Our role, I insisted, was to work wholeheartedly for his acquittal. "How can you feel that way after what happened to your sister?" she demanded. I responded, as I had in previous conversations, that I could not allow what happened to my sister to interfere with my ability to represent my clients zealously. But this pat answer, the standard response of the "professional," did not ease my inner discomfort. I thought about how I would respond to an acquittal. I was in the paradoxical position, common to defense counsel, of feeling genuine concern for someone who had probably committed a horrible crime; Strong was a person whom I had come to know as more than the sum of his criminal acts. From this position, I was able to look beyond the crimes to care for the person.

Finally, the jury reached a verdict. We gathered in the courtroom. When the judge requested the verdict, the foreman stood up and announced "guilty" on every count. I was devastated. I genuinely felt for Craig Strong and his family. Given Strong's record, there was no hope that the judge would consider any sentence short of life imprisonment. The best we could hope for was that the judge would permit Strong to serve his sentence at a prison close to Washington, DC, because his family could not afford to travel any distance to visit him.

I had worked hard on Strong's behalf, perhaps harder than on any other case I had handled while at PDS. What was I trying to prove? With hindsight, I have come to realize that I was testing whether I would be able, ethically and emotionally, to continue criminal defense work in the aftermath of my sister's death.

Until this point, the abstract, traditional principles had adequately motivated me. I have understood my job as both morally justified and constitutionally mandated, and this had been sufficient. After my sister's death, however, these justifications were inadequate to motivate me to continue with my work. Although I remained convinced that the traditional justifications morally condoned representing Strong, neither the Model Code nor any existing theory or ethic compelled me to defend him. Friends and acquaintances often asked me, "How can you defend those people?" "With pleasure," I invariably responded. But after experiencing the tragedy of a murder in my family, I became personally aware that special procedural protections afforded to criminals in our system often impose painful consequences on victims and their families.

This realization, of course, is not unique to my experience. One need not experience personally the pain of violent crime to need a sustaining motivation in order to continue working as a public defender. Virtually all public defenders fight a daily battle against burnout and the creeping erosion of confidence that inevitably accompany defending acts we cannot condone and protecting those who are the source of so much harm and grief. This slow, daily erosion differs from my own personal motivational crisis only in that mine was more sudden and sharp in its onslaught. Whether the process unfolds subtly or suddenly, all defenders must confront the disturbing consequences of their zealous representation of guilty clients. All public defenders face the problem of remaining motivated to represent clients with zeal. Thus, in a certain sense, the personal and professional tragedy I experienced is universal.

SEEKING A SUFFICIENT MOTIVATION

The phenomenon of burnout is one of the most powerful and widely experienced forces that causes public defenders to lose interest in their work, or to abandon criminal defense practice altogether. Former public defenders typically attribute burnout to the psychological impact of confronting hundreds of crimes, victims, and criminals on a daily basis. Moreover, the better the defender is, the more frequently she must face the consequences of getting favorable results, even for guilty clients.

I describe burnout as the failure of one's moral justification for undertaking indigent defense work to provide a day-to-day motivation for getting up each morning, putting on a suit, and going to the office or to court. Thus, although we saw in part I that there are many well-articulated justifications for criminal defense advocacy, a key challenge for those who write about or teach criminal defense practice is to develop psychological motivations that will sustain the attorney through the virtually inevitable deterioration of morale that leads eventually to burnout.

In this part, I explore how, in the aftermath of my sister's murder, I overcame the burnout that afflicts so many public defenders. My ultimate goal is to propose a framework for identifying and evaluating the motivations necessary to sustain public defenders and lawyers generally. I first examine the interplay between the justifications explored in part I and motivations for indigent defense work. I highlight the two motivations that were central to resolving my own feelings of burnout: heroism and empathy. What I loosely call "heroism" is a desire to take on "the system" and win, while empathy is an identification with another person in distress. I show how these two motivations, especially when operating together, are likely to be more sustaining than abstract justifications. Both of the motivations I identify have their dangers, however, and these are explored in this part as well.

Justifications as Motivations

Public defenders typically explain their choice of vocation in terms of abstract justifications like those discussed in part I. As noted above, justifications are external moral criteria that provide a reason to take a certain action. Often, justifications will provide an individual with an impetus to take action—a motivation. For example, many public defenders will be motivated by their ardent belief in the constitutional values that the public defender upholds.

At some point, however, abstract theoretical justifications fall short in the face of reality. For example, defenders who are motivated by a belief that no individual is guilty until proven so, soon find that such moral indeterminacy does not comport with their daily experiences. Public defenders know that frequently their clients are guilty beyond any reasonable doubt. In the face of this reality, many public defenders who continue to believe strongly that indigent defense is both necessary and justified decide that it is time for someone else to take their turn defending the guilty. . . .

Furthermore, justifications often conflict with one another when serving as motivations. Most lawyers confront real situations in which acting on the basis of one justification undermines another. For example, an attorney's pursuit of a guilty client's interests in acquittal on the basis of a belief in client autonomy may sharply conflict with a commitment to the pursuit of truth. As these instances add up, the resulting cognitive dissonance will detract from her ability to derive motivation from abstract justifications. Even if she can develop an orderly system for ranking her justifications, she is left with feelings of anxiety and dissatisfaction because she knows that her actions are morally questionable. . . .

Empathy as a Sustaining Motivation

In looking back on my experience with Craig Strong, I believe that my empathy for Strong became one of the primary sustaining motivations for continuing zealously to defend him in spite of the pain of my sister's murder. I viewed Strong as a person and as a friend, and thus I was able to disassociate him from the person who had murdered my sister. I did not blame him, nor did I resent him because I had been victimized by crime. Instead, I viewed Strong as a victim as well. However, my sense of his victimization differed from traditional justifications for criminal defense practice in that it was not based on generalizations about criminals or pity for him. Instead, my empathy was based on my ability to relate to him as a person and to develop a friendship with him. I viewed Strong as a man whom the police had surprised in a warrantless arrest; someone from whom the police had seized incriminating evidence without a search warrant. I did not think about what he had done, nor did I feel responsible for what he might do if released. I knew that at that moment I was my client's only friend, and that my friend wanted to go home.

Although the term "empathy" has been used in numerous contexts, with various meanings, it is a seriously undervalued element of legal practice. Empathy has been broadly defined as "understanding the experiences, behavior and feelings of others as they experience them. It means that lawyers must to the best of their abilities, put aside their own biases, prejudices and points of view in order to understand as clearly as possible the points of view of their clients."[18] I use the term to capture two different concepts: first, to require the listener not simply to hear her clients, but to understand their problems, and, second, to have compassion for her clients. . . .

My view of empathy has significant implications for the character of the lawyer-client relationship. My relationships with clients were rarely limited to the provision of conventional legal services. I did not draw rigid lines between my professional practice and my private life. My relationship with my clients approximated a true friendship. I did for my clients all that I would do for a friend. I took phone calls at all hours, helped clients find jobs, and even interceded in domestic conflicts. I attended my clients' weddings and their funerals. When clients were sent to prison, I maintained contact with their families. Because I viewed my clients as friends, I did not merely feel justified in doing all I could for them; I felt a strong desire to do so.

Fried's conception of "Lawyer as Friend" might be perceived as similar to my own vision of the lawyer-client relationship. However, my relationships with clients differed from the relationship Fried posits. To Fried, " a lawyer is a friend in regard to the legal system. . . . To be sure, the lawyer's range of assistance is 'sharply limited.' But within that limited domain the intensity of identification with the client's interests is the same."[19] Thus, under Fried's model, the lawyer is justified in doing all that he would for a friend in trouble, but only within the context of the legal system. My relationships with clients were not similarly bounded.

The idea that empathy helps to forestall burnout may appear counterintuitive because of a popular conception among professionals of all persuasions that the attorney must distance herself from the personal problems of her client in order to maintain perspective and avoid exhaustion and frustration. In the case of indigent defense, however, the distanced perspective is perhaps the most difficult to maintain. Viewed dispassionately, most defendants are simply criminals. Thus, it is critical to look beyond the crime with which the client is charged, to gain insight into the often difficult, impoverished, and painful life that preceded the commission of the crime. If a public defender maintains distance, she might overlook the humanity of her client—his positive attributes, the background which may have led him to commit crimes, and the multiple needs that transcend his current criminal case. Had I seen Craig Strong only as a rapist and murderer, it would have been difficult to spend hours each day researching his case, talking to him on the telephone, and fighting for his interests. Because I fully appreciated the pain Strong's family experienced from seeing him once again charged with a violent crime, and because I allowed myself to imagine his fears, I could find the energy to work for his acquittal.

Until now, I have focused on the value of empathy as a sustaining motivation. But before moving on, I want to emphasize that the quality of a lawyer's representation often will improve when she takes an empathic view of her client. Empathizing with a client necessarily means caring more deeply for the client. The attorney with a deeper understanding of and sensitivity to the client wants to help him, and this desire directly affects both her will to represent the client and the form that the representation itself takes. When she cares about the client as an individual, not only does she want to assist him through the complex maze of our legal system, but she also wants him to succeed; as a result, her defense is zealous.

Additionally, empathy provides defenders with the ability to hear "complex, multivocal conversations."[20] As a result, empathy enhances a lawyer's ability to interview and counsel clients, to negotiate with opposing counsel, and to engage in the numerous other types of communication that are demanded of lawyers. Empathy also improves a lawyer's problem-solving skills, for she is better able to assess the client's goals and to integrate them into an evaluation of potential solutions. This client contact may in turn have positive effects on one's motivation to do the work, for when an attorney sees her success rate in terms of improvements in the overall quality of her clients' lives, she may come to realize that she does much more good on a daily basis than the record of her "wins" and "losses" might indicate.

The Heroic Public Defender

As I reflect upon my experiences as a public defender, I realize that empathy alone did not sustain me. I also felt various motivations that centered around how I envisioned myself and my task. I describe these motivations under the rubric of "heroism." I saw myself as a kind of "hero" of the oppressed, the one who fights against all odds, a sort of Robin Hood figure who can conquer what others cannot and who does not always have to conform to the moral rules society reserves for others. One element of this "hero" mentality, of course, is the thrill of winning. Certainly, many public defenders are driven in part by a desire to win; at PDS, for example, lawyers with excellent track records of acquittals were regarded with awe. For the public defender, there is glory in the "David versus Goliath" challenge of fighting the state, and the battle of wits that characterizes the courtroom drama only adds to the thrill of the trial. Even the phrase we commonly used to describe a successful defense—"stealing" the case from the prosecution—invoked the image of Robin Hood stealing from the rich and powerful to give to the helpless and weak. Indeed, "some people become criminal defenders because they love the challenge, are competitive by nature, and have unusual personal curiosity. They like the idea of representing the underdog, where the scales are tipped against them, the prosecutor has all the resources, and they have virtually none."[21]

This heroic motivation may also have its less benign aspects. James Doyle asserts, for example, that criminal defense attorneys are often drawn to their work by a kind of voyeuristic desire to experience the "darker side" of society—to interact with criminals and to learn about their exploits. More importantly, feminist literature points out that many of our heroic images are male or embody male traits, and that an appeal to heroism thus may tend to exclude certain groups.

Nonetheless, if a lawyer keeps these qualifications in mind and maintains a proper perspective, the heroic ideal may play a valuable role as a motivating force. In reflecting on my experience in the Strong case, I came to realize that this conception of heroism was an important factor in my decision to represent Strong and to fight zealously on his behalf. Because there was a client who needed me, I was willing to put aside my own feelings and needs. Indeed, I thought that only a truly committed public defender could represent faithfully an accused murderer so soon after the murder of his own sister.

Earlier I noted that empathy, in addition to serving as a motivation, can render a lawyer's performance more effective. The same is true of heroism, albeit to a lesser extent. If a lawyer is convinced of the heroic nature of her role, she may be able to argue more forcefully and persuasively for a certain result in trials, negotiations, and other contexts. Moreover, by extending the definition of heroism to encompass the listener, the lawyer may be able to convince the jury to adopt the course of action that will produce the noblest and most just result.

The Limitations and Dangers of Heroism and Empathy

Having outlined two motivations that sustained me through the difficult challenge of impending burnout, I now turn to an evaluation of their practical and moral strengths and weaknesses. To be effective, a motivation for indigent defense must do two things. First, it must provide a sustaining reason to do the job, and second, it must not conflict with or undermine the moral justifications for indigent defense. Reconsidering empathy and heroism in light of these criteria reveals that each motivation has its weaknesses. Neither empathy nor heroism is, by itself, sufficient to sustain public defenders. Moreover, when taken to extremes, empathy and

heroism can lead to overzealousness, over-identification, or irra-
tional allocation of the public defender's limited resources. In the
paragraphs below, I explore some of these problems.

The daily realities of the PDS office pose challenges to both
empathy and heroism as motivations. Even the most empathetic
public defender will find her commitment sorely challenged by the
persistence of defendants who commit violent crimes repeatedly.

Moreover, as an empathetic person, she may find that she has
empathy for not just the defendant but also for the victim, and perhaps even for future victims whose safety would be threatened by
the defendant's release. In the face of such feelings, empathy for
one's client may prove difficult to sustain. Likewise, while the
Robin Hood ideal will add a certain thrill to the job of public
defender, the luster soon fades as the defender confronts the practical realities of the job—the daily drudgery of paperwork and the
less-than-glamorous settings of the public defender's office, the
criminal court, and the jail.

Empathy and heroism also may prove counterproductive
when taken to the extreme. They may cause the public defender to
lose sight of the external moral limitations on her conduct.
Empathic feelings, for example, can result in over-identification
with the client. Without the benefit of critical distance, a defender
may be tempted to overstep ethical boundaries in her zeal to help
her client. The same result can occur when a lawyer becomes
overly enamored of the "heroic" role—the hero of the oppressed,
after all, does not have to play by society's rules. For example, an
overly empathetic or heroic attorney may be inclined to present a
perjurious witness if this course of action is likely to win the case.

Another potential danger of empathy is that it can lead to problematic allocation of resources. The empathic role I have described
demands that the public defender devote substantial time and
effort to every client. In a situation of extremely limited attorney
resources, hours spent in the service of one client necessarily come
at the expense of another equally needy criminal defendant. The
motivation of empathy does not tell the defense lawyer toward
whom she should direct her empathy. The time that I spend getting
to know my clients, listening to their stories, helping them find jobs,
is time that I could spend representing others.

Heroism can lead to similar problems. The heroic defender views herself as the champion of her client against the oppressive system. To her, each case is an epic battle against an inhumane established order. As a result, the defender will necessarily focus on winning each battle rather than on the total number of battles she wins. And, like empathetic representation, attainment of the heroic ideal is time-consuming. To beat the system when the odds are stacked against her, the attorney must pour an inordinate amount of scarce resources into each case. Again, this is time that she could spend representing others.

Of course, the resource allocation problems I have identified cannot be attributed solely to the use of empathy and heroism as motivations. These problems arise in all public interest work, and no satisfactory answer is readily apparent. In a society where access to legal representation is largely dependent on wealth, the poor inevitably have restricted access to attorney services. One solution to the problem I have posed would be to increase the aggregate amount of time available to indigent clients by providing more attorneys and a wider distribution of subsidized legal services. Unfortunately, this solution is as unrealistic as it is obvious; an increase in the availability of legal services is precluded by a lack of funding and compounded by a shortage of attorneys interested in legal aid. In addition, the character of the demand for legal services creates a situation in which the demand always rises to meet the supply.

As the above discussion has shown, the motivations of empathy and heroism have significant limitations and present certain risks. To some extent, each of the motivations can compensate for the short-comings of the other. When empathy for the client fades as a motivation—either because of frustration with the client's persistent recidivism or empathy for the client's victims—heroism can kick in to "jump start" the attorney's commitment and interest. Likewise, when the thrill of battle begins to wane, empathy for one's client generates renewed energy to continue.

More importantly, when taken together, empathy and heroism may counter some of each other's dangers. In a given case, empathy and heroism usually combine to propel the lawyer toward a more zealous defense. In the case of Craig Strong, for example, my empathy for his situation, together with my desire to win, inspired me to seek acquittal. But because empathy and heroism are based on different rationales, each will cause the attorney to reexamine her conduct when it approaches the ethical line, restraining the tendency to cross over that line. For example, a defender's desire to bask in the glory of victory may find itself checked by her empathy with a client who is better served by a plea bargain.

Yet the motivations of empathy and heroism also may conflict with each other. This is particularly likely to happen in situations in which the client has a goal or interest that conflicts with—and, in the client's view, trumps—the winning strategy. For example, the client may be unwilling to call a relative or friend to the witness stand, even though the witness has exculpatory information to offer, because the experience of testifying would cause too much anguish for the relative or friend. Similarly, a defendant in a rape case may be unwilling to use a meritorious consent defense, and may be inclined to resort to less meritorious defenses because he is afraid to tell his wife that he engaged in consensual intercourse with another woman. A defendant at first may be unwilling to invoke the insanity defense even though he probably would prevail, because he is reluctant to suffer the stigma of being labeled mentally ill and spending time in a mental hospital. In situations such as these, the empathetic defender will understand the client's motivations and be inclined to respect his priorities. The heroic defender, on the other hand, driven by the goal of winning, is likely to give short shrift to the client's views. If ethical rules designate the decision at issue as a strategic judgment left to the lawyer, the "heroic" defender may simply disregard the client's wishes; if the decision is one that must be left to the client, the defender may try to override the client's will and coerce him into following the lawyer's advice.

As these examples suggest, the tensions between empathy and heroism go to the very core of one's conception of the proper roles of lawyer and client. The empathetic lawyer quite naturally embraces the client-centered approach to representation. . . . She is likely to bring the client into decision making and to respect the client's decisions, even on strategic matters that have been traditionally allocated to the lawyer. By contrast, the "heroic" public defender tends to accord a much less central role to the client. Narrowly focused on the goal of winning the case, she is likely to limit client autonomy and input to the minimum required by ethical rules, for fear that the client will make the "wrong" decisions.

In my view (and in my experience), the clash of these contrasting conceptions produces a model of the lawyer-client relationship that incorporates the best elements of each. Empathy enables the "heroic" defender to broaden her understanding of what "winning the case" really means, so that she works to attain the client's ends as defined by the client, not the lawyer. At the same time, the heroism model helps to keep the empathetic lawyer focused on the goal of winning the case when she otherwise might be tempted to devote too much time or attention to other problems or needs of the client. . . .

CONCLUSION

In this article, I have argued that theoretical justifications are insufficient to ensure that people will become and remain public defenders. Although most of us agree with at least one of these justifications, they fail to motivate many people to enter indigent defense work, and rarely can they motivate anyone forever. At some point, a defender will face either a single event or a steady accumulation of daily experiences that tests her faith in the system. Unless she has a sustaining motivation which does not rely on the theoretical justifications, the defender will cease to be an effective advocate on behalf of the indigent accused. . . .

If we are truly committed to ensuring that indigents receive adequate representation, we must turn our attention to developing motivations that will sustain public defenders through trying times.

I have attempted to build on the two forces that motivated me after my sister's murder—empathy and heroism—in order to develop a model that can provide sustaining motivations for other public defenders. Although these motivations have their drawbacks and limitations, together they can effectively move people to enter and remain in the public defense sector. . . .

NOTES

1. Toni M. Massaro, "Empathy, Legal Storytelling, and the Rule of Law: New Words, Old Wounds?" *Michigan Law Review* 87 (1989): 2099, 2105. Professor Massaro's words express particularly well my purpose here: "Academics, judges, and lawyers often juggle concepts and spar with abstractions, without consulting the human concerns actually at issue in their deliberations. Stories can shock them back into sensation, into life as it is versus how we talk about it. Stories are one way to bring law down to life, to the people, 'to the ground.'" Ibid.

2. For a detailed analysis of this metaphor and its implications, see Joseph Allegretti, "Have Briefcase Will Travel: An Essay on the Lawyer as Hired Gun," *Creighton Law Review* 24 (1991): 747–51.

3. Richard Wasserstrom, "Lawyers as Professionals: Some Moral Issues," *Human Rights* 5 (1975): 1, 5. Wasserstrom concludes that "the amoral behavior of the criminal defense lawyer is justifiable" due to the threat posed by the state to a defendant whose counsel is hobbled. Ibid., p. 12. However, "[o]nce we leave the peculiar situation of the criminal defense lawyer . . . it [is] quite likely that the role-differentiated amorality of the lawyer is almost certainly excessive and at times inappropriate." Ibid.

4. Murray L. Schwartz, "The Professionalism and Accountability of Lawyers," *California Law Review* 66 (1978): 669, 673. As Schwartz explains: "I represent [the criminal defendant] because the system demands that I do so. Moreover, I must cross-examine and try to impeach truthful witnesses, make arguments with which I personally disagree, decline to introduce probative, adverse evidence against my client, and attempt to present matter in ways I think personally are inaccurate, because the system demands that. You may not hold me substantively, professionally, or morally accountable for that behavior" (ibid., 673–74 [footnote omitted]).

5. See Stephen L. Pepper, "The Lawyer's Amoral Ethical Role: A Defense, A Problem, and Some Possibilities," *American Bar Foundation Research Journal* (1986): 613, 617.

6. Ibid. In propounding this view, Pepper does not distinguish between criminal and noncriminal lawyers, or between litigation and non-litigation contexts, except to note that the impact upon client autonomy may appear more dramatic in litigation contexts. See ibid., p. 623.

7. David Luban, "The Lysistratian Prerogative: A Response to Stephen Pepper," *American Bar Foundation Research Journal* (1986): 637, 639.

8. Ibid. Luban uses a particularly salient analogy to illustrate this

point: "The automobile, by making it easier to get around, increases human autonomy; hence, other things being equal, it is morally good to repair the car of someone who is unable by himself to get it to run. But such considerations can hardly be invoked to defend the morality of fixing the getaway car of an armed robber, assuming that you know in advance what the purpose of the car is." Ibid.

9. Charles Fried, "The Lawyer as Friend: The Moral Foundations of the Lawyer-Client Relation," *Yale Legal Journal* 85 (1976): 1060, 1074.

10. Ibid., p. 1071.

11. Michael K. McChrystal, "Lawyers and Loyalty," *William & Mary Law Review* 33 (1992): 367, 392.

12. Harry I. Subin, "The Criminal Lawyer's 'Different Mission': Reflections on the 'Right' to Present a False Case," *Georgetown Journal of Legal Ethics* 1 (1987): 125, 136.

13. Subin, "The Criminal Lawyer's 'Different Mission,'" p. 136 (citations omitted).

14. Barbara A. Babcock, "Defending the Guilty," *Cleveland State Law Review* 32 (1983): 175, 178. Barbara Babcock describes this justification as "The Political Activist's Reason." Ibid.

15. Stephen Ellmann, "Lawyering for Justice in a Flawed Democracy," *Columbia Law Review* 90 (1990): 116, 142, n.51 (reviewing David Luban, *Lawyers and Justice: An Ethical Study* [Princeton, NJ: Princeton University Press, 1988]).

16. Subin, "The Criminal Lawyer's 'Different Mission,'" p. 147. Subin proposes a system in which the advocacy of defense counsel is restricted under the following standard: "It shall be improper for an attorney who knows beyond a reasonable doubt the truth of a fact established in the state's case to attempt to refute that fact through the introduction of evidence, impeachment of evidence, or argument." Ibid., p. 149.

17. Client names were changed to protect privacy.

18. David Binder, Paul Bergman, and Susan Price, *Lawyers as Counselors: A Client-Centered Approach*, 1st ed. (St. Paul, MN: West, 1991), p. 40 (citing Gerard Egan, *The Skilled Helper*, 3rd ed. [Belmont, CA: Thomson Wadsworth, 1986], p. 87).

19. Fried, "The Lawyer as Friend," pp. 1071–72.

20. Lucie E. White, "Revaluing Politics: A Reply to Professor Strauss," *UCLA Law Review* 39 (1992): 1331, 1338.

21. Philip B. Heymann and Lance Liebman, *The Social Responsibilities of Lawyers: Case Studies* (Thomson West, 1988), pp. 69, 103 (summarizing my views on why lawyers go into criminal defense work).

RELIGIOUS LAWYERING IN A LIBERAL DEMOCRACY

A CHALLENGE AND AN INVITATION

Russell G. Pearce and Amelia J. Uelmen

. . . .

AMY UELMEN: A BIG FIRM LITIGATOR BRIDGES RELIGIOUS AND PROFESSIONAL LIFE

In response to the invitation of a Muslim friend on the New York organizing team, I attended Fordham's December 1998 Conference, and was impressed by the openness, depth and sincerity of the conversation it generated. Throughout my education and career I had tried to integrate my Roman Catholic values and perspective into my approach to law and legal practice, but in conversations with professors and colleagues I often felt as though I was speaking

Case Western Reserve Law Review (Fall, 2004) copyright © 2004 Case Western Reserve Law Review; Russell G. Pearce, Amelia J. Uelmen.

a foreign language. In the course of my work as a junior litigator in a large law firm, I worked hard to "translate" these values into a language that my colleagues and friends could understand.

At the 1998 Fordham Conference, I realized that many lawyers were working to bridge their professional lives with their religious perspectives. In order to connect with and encourage others in their efforts, I wrote an essay describing some of the challenges I faced in weaving religious values and perspectives into my work as a "big firm" litigator representing mostly large corporations. . . .

When Fordham Law School's own efforts to provide in-depth and consistent support to the national and local dialogue on how religious faith, teachings, and traditions may be a resource for the practice culminated in the January 2001 opening of its Institute on Religion, Law & Lawyer's Work, I came aboard as its first director.

So What's New?

Associations of Catholic lawyers and Jewish lawyers, as well as chapters of the Christian Legal Society, have been gathering for decades. Many religious traditions include illustrious examples of lawyers who have integrated their religious values into their professional decisions. And certainly the ties between religious values and the legal profession's goals of public service, civility, and honesty were evident long before the 1990s. Thus, considering the more recent development in religious lawyering one might ask, "so what's new?"

In one sense, the religious lawyering movement builds upon and strengthens these long-standing community organizations and commitments. For example, it would be interesting to trace the extent to which efforts to integrate religious values into professional life have contributed to the growth of faith-based pro bono legal services to the poor. Religious lawyering may also strengthen lawyers in their resolve to set aside the necessary time for religious observance, even in the midst of the profession's pressing demands on their time.

But we would posit that the religious lawyering project which has been germinating over the past decade asks for more—and presents a much deeper challenge for the legal profession. . . .

Unlike many previous "law and religion" discussions, the religious laywering movement focuses less on the conceptual relationships and tensions between law and religion and how these play out in a democracy, and more on ways in which religious values and perspectives may provide a completely different structural framework for an approach to professional life.

As anthropologist Clifford Geertz has described, the core of religious perspective is not so much to posit the theory of an invisible world beyond the visible; nor the doctrine of a divine presence; nor that there are "things in heaven and earth undreamt of in our philosophies."[1] Rather, the heart of the religious perspective is:

> [T]he conviction that the values one holds are grounded in the inherent structure of reality, that between the way one ought to live and the way things really are there is an unbreakable inner connection. What sacred symbols do for those to whom they are sacred is to formulate an image of the world's construction and a program for human conduct that are mere reflexes of one another.[2]

Religious lawyering draws out the "unbreakable inner connection" between "the way things really are" and "the way one ought to live"—not only in a private "non-work" sphere, but also in professional life. On this basis religious lawyering insists that there should be room in the profession for such convictions about the "inherent structure of reality," and for lawyers then to integrate this perspective and to apply its substantive critiques and contributions to the issues which arise not just at the margins, but in the heart of ordinary day-to-day legal practice.

Finally, the religious lawyering movement suggests that this is a step to be taken not just within one's heart or the quiet of one's individual conscience. It insists that this is an appropriate topic for open conversation, dialogue, and debate in law offices, in judges' chambers, in legislatures, and even in law schools.

RELIGIOUS LAWYERING'S CHALLENGES TO PROFESSIONALISM

In the eyes of many, the religious lawyering movement's insistence that religious worldviews and the substantive content of religious perspectives could and should be brought to bear on approaches to work as a lawyer is—to put it bluntly—unprofessional. As Sanford Levinson explains, professionalism posits that the lawyer's role requires lawyers to "bleach out" the "merely contingent aspects of the self, including the residue of particularistic socialization that we refer to as our 'conscience.'"[3] The exclusion of these "aspects of the self" derives from professional role morality—the conception that the professional's conduct is governed by the morality dictated by the profession and not from outside the profession.

Bolstering this concept is the notion that rule of law depends upon lawyers' neutrality. The adversarial understanding of the legal system posits that the clash of opposing views before a neutral fact finder is the best way to ascertain truth and justice. To function properly, the argument goes, the adversarial system requires that all parties receive equal representation and that lawyers function as extreme partisans who should not bring their own moral or religious sensibility to bear on their representation. In this model, "[r]ule of law implies that the quality of lawyering and of justice an individual receives does not depend on the group identity of the lawyer or judge."[4] A lawyer's religion, morality, race, gender, or other personal attributes should be irrelevant.

A Tennessee ethics case illustrates the approach. A Tennessee lawyer who was a devout Catholic opposed to abortion asked the Tennessee Supreme Court's Board of Professional Responsibility for permission to decline a court appointment to represent a female minor seeking to waive the statutory prohibition of abortion without parental consent. In a stark illustration of the "bleaching out" approach to professionalism, the Board, while recognizing that the attorney's religious and moral beliefs were "clearly and fervently held," concluded that they were not "compelling reasons" for withdrawing from the appointment. Although commentators have generally concluded that the Board was wrong from the perspective of legal ethics, the case demonstrates the power of the "bleaching out" concept.

The problem with the argument that personal attributes such as religion are irrelevant to the practice of law is that it runs counter to experience. Lawyers are neither fungible nor neutral. They differ in their abilities, as well as in the ways that their identities and experiences influence their conduct. The religious lawyering movement insists that we should not ignore this reality. While it acknowledges that as a community lawyers must seek to improve our system so that all people receive impartial treatment, it nonetheless insists that this must occur within a framework that respects that lawyers are not "neutral" interchangeable parts. It emphasizes that it is important for lawyers to honestly acknowledge their differences and to strive together to manage those differences in service of the shared goal of rule of law.

RELIGIOUS LAWYERING AS A RESPONSE TO THE CRISIS IN PROFESSIONALISM

If religious lawyering is "unprofessional," what explains its growing popularity? At least part of the answer lies in what is commonly called the "crisis" of professionalism. The first major public acknowledgement of this crisis was Chief Justice Warren Burger's 1984 Report to the American Bar Association on the State of Justice in which he complained that lawyers were betraying their responsibilities as professionals. Since that time leaders of the bench, bar, and legal academy have described lawyers, their ethics, and their professionalism in the most dismal terms: "lost" and "betrayed," in "decline" and in "crisis," even to the point of facing "demise" and "death," and most certainly in need of "redemption."[5]

What these commentators often lament is the collapse of the careful distinction at the heart of professionalism's ideology: the divide between business and the legal profession. The Business-Profession dichotomy dates back to the Federalist Papers, which argued that only an elite governing class could ensure that a system of majority rule would promote the public good, preserve rule of law, and protect minority rights.

According to Federalist 35, the elite would consist of "learned professionals" who would pursue the public good, in contrast to merchants and business people who tend to pursue their own selfish interests. It soon became clear that lawyers would serve this governing class role. In formal government, they controlled the judicial branch and led the legislative and executive branches. As they advised clients on the law, structured personal and business relationships, advocated before courts and juries, and participated in civic life, they served informally as the primary intermediaries between the government and the people. In Alexis de Tocqueville's words, lawyers were the de facto aristocracy of America.

A minority of lawyers argued for a "hired gun" conception of the lawyer's role—evoking the notion that lawyers should exclusively represent the self-interest of their clients—but the elite soundly rejected it. Although lawyers were advocates for their clients, the governing class role bounded their advocacy.

In the late 1800s, the governing class conception faced a crisis. Lawyers and non-lawyers complained that "law had become a business, with lawyers placing self-interest above the public good."[6] In response, lawyers turned to professionalism's emphasis on self-regulation. Bar Associations, led by the "best men," would decide who could practice law, articulate ethical standards, and discipline violators.

Professionalism had three interdependent elements that hinged on the distinction between business and the legal profession. First, lawyers had expertise that was not accessible to non-lawyers. Second, in contrast to business people, most lawyers worked for the common good, and not to maximize self-interest. Finally, given their expertise and their governing class role in the service of the common good, lawyers, unlike business people, could be trusted to regulate themselves.

Professionalism remained dominant until the 1960s. For example, when sociologist Erwin Smigel interviewed Wall Street lawyers, they frequently described themselves as "guardians of the public good."[7] Through the 1960s, most lawyers believed in professionalism, and looked to professionalism to give meaning to their work.

Toward the end of the 1960s, lawyers began to question their status as part of a governing class, precipitating what has been termed a "crisis" in professionalism. Commentators declared that lawyers were just as selfish and greedy as everyone else—and many lawyers agreed. Gradually the "hired gun" image replaced the governing class as the dominant conception of the lawyer's role. Nonetheless, the bar continued to use the rhetoric of professionalism, especially when it came to protecting lawyers' privileges from the incursions of accounting firms and others seeking to enter the legal services market.

The result of this shift has been quite unsatisfying for lawyers in a number of ways. First, in contrast to the grandeur of the governing class ideal, the hired gun is a mercenary for selfish interests who cares nothing for moral values. The only way to justify this conduct is procedural—the adversarial system demands that each client have the opportunity to have a hired gun champion their interests. For those lawyers who possess or desire a conception of substantive justice, the hired gun ideal is inadequate. Second, even for those whose conception of justice is exclusively procedural, the adversarial system is a disappointment. Widespread inequality of access to legal services ensures that there will not be equal justice under law. Third, the hired gun ideal offers lawyers no guidance for dealing with the increasingly harsh demands of the market for legal services. If lawyers are no longer an altruistic governing class, what are they? The hired gun paradigm offers no answers. To make matters worse, continued reliance on the rhetoric of professionalism makes many lawyers feel ashamed of their business conduct.

It is not surprising, therefore, that many lawyers find the combination of the hired gun ideal and professionalism rhetoric disheartening. Surveys indicate that lawyers are far less satisfied with their work than people in other occupations. Many say that if they could do it over, they would not choose to become lawyers and they would advise people they care about not to become lawyers. Of any occupation in the United States, lawyers have the highest incidence of depression, and are fifteen times more likely than the general population to suffer other forms of emotional distress. Moreover, alcohol abuse among lawyers is significantly higher than the national average.

The recent growth of the religious lawyering movement is, at least in part, a response to the legal profession's failure to offer lawyers a satisfactory way to understand their role and responsibilities. With the decline in the ideology of professionalism, lawyers are looking elsewhere. And for those who are religious people, their religion is a natural place to look for guidance in reconciling their personal aspirations with their work as lawyers.

Religion offers religious lawyers a constructive framework within which they can respond to a host of questions that the professionalism rhetoric leaves unanswered. It not only offers answers to the more practical question of how to be a good lawyer and a good person, but also responds to deeper and more existential questions such as why try to be a good person in the first place. For many religious people, this larger overarching framework provides a moral anchor that enables them not only to resist temptations of greed and abuse of power, but also to situate their legal work within a sense of responsibility and service to the larger community. Although the answers will differ depending on the religion and the individual, there will be answers.

Religion also offers religious lawyers a way to transcend the dichotomy between the noble professional and the selfish business person. The notion of a calling or vocation, common to many religions, can make all work meaningful. As Martin Luther King, Jr. taught:

If it falls your lot to be a street sweeper, sweep streets like Michelangelo painted pictures, like Shakespeare wrote poetry, like Beethoven composed music; sweep streets so well that all the host of Heaven and earth will have to pause and say, "Here lived a great street sweeper, who swept his job well."[8]

What is true of street sweepers is equally true of lawyers.

By providing inspiration to individual lawyers, religious lawyering also makes an important contribution to society. Even if lawyers describe their role with the image of the hired gun, they nonetheless continue to serve as a governing class. They still control the judicial branch and lead the legislative and executive branches. In representing clients, they still serve as the primary intermediaries between the government and private parties. Following the collapse of the Business-Profession dichotomy, religious lawyering brings to the profession a much needed and persuasive explanation for why lawyers are individually and collectively responsible for the quality of justice and the stability of society.

Religious lawyering provides a robust framework for lawyers to explain why they are morally accountable for their service as the governing class and why they must incorporate personal integrity and consideration of the public good into client representation. This does not mean lawyers must abandon client advocacy. It does require, however, that lawyers recognize that their own decisions regarding client goals are always morally laden, thus pushing them to engage clients in conversation regarding the morality of their conduct.

OBJECTIONS TO RELIGIOUS LAWYERING

Despite these benefits, religious lawyering faces three types of objections related to its effectiveness, fairness, and compatibility with liberal democracy.

Does religious lawyering really make a difference?

The first objection is quite simple. Religious people are no more moral than anyone else. After all, recent headlines recount many examples of religiously devout business people and professionals who nonetheless have been caught in corporate scandals and other illegal conduct.

Our claim is not that religious people are inherently more moral. Rather, we argue that religious lawyering offers lawyers a reason to behave ethically at a time when persuasive reasons to accept moral accountability are hard to find. While no guarantee, it does offer religious lawyers a way to draw a substantial and consistent connection between their religious values and their professional decisions. People who find religion a compelling source of moral authority may find it an equally compelling source in their work as lawyers.

The second form of this objection asks whether religious lawyering adds anything to secular values such as honesty, civility, moral counsel, and service to the poor. The answer to this objection hinges on the premise that identity and perspective do make a difference. For those working within a religious framework, religious values often have additional—and perhaps decisive—pull which allows them to situate their professional decisions within an integral, coherent, and transcendent framework. Paraphrasing Geertz, religious lawyering will help religious lawyers make an "unbreakable inner connection" between "the way things really are" and "the way one ought to live" one's professional life. For religious people, religious lawyering makes a difference because it offers an often more compelling reason to adopt these values. Granted not all people necessarily see the "unbreakable inner connection," but there should be room in the profession for those who do to draw on their deepest and most compelling resources for an integrated approach to their professional lives.

Is religious lawyering unfair to clients?

Another objection arises from the fear that religious lawyers will impose their religious discourse and worldviews on clients. This brings to mind an incident in which an American Airlines pilot asked Christian passengers to raise their hands and suggested that the other passengers might want to speak to the Christians about their faith during the flight. Many thought that the pilot's suggestion was completely inappropriate and that it was extremely unfair for the pilot to proselytize his captive passengers.

Is a religious lawyer like that American Airlines pilot? The 1996 Tennessee ethics opinion discussed above would probably say yes. In that case, the Board concluded that the Catholic lawyer should not discuss with his minor client either potential alternatives to abortion or the virtues of her consulting with her parents or legal guardian.

As legal ethics scholars have noted, this conclusion is contrary to the legal ethics rules. Model Rule 2.1 provides that "[i]n rendering advice, a lawyer may refer not only to law but to other considerations, such as moral, economic, social and political factors, that may be relevant to the client's situation." The comment to the rule makes clear that "[i]t is proper for a lawyer to refer to relevant moral and ethical considerations in giving advice." If the religious lawyer explains to the client the full range of options, including the moral implications of each, that seems to fall squarely within the rule and not to present a problem.

But what if the lawyer refers specifically to religion and not just to morality? Although Rule 2.1 does not expressly mention religion, it does refer generally to "other [non-legal] factors." This broad language would include religious considerations so long as they are "relevant to the client's situation."[9]

What the rule does not expressly authorize is an action analogous to that of the American Airlines pilot who introduced religious discourse that was not relevant to his work. But would that conduct be forbidden? Most agree that a lawyer should not charge for that time. Beyond that, it does not appear to be forbidden. . . .

Even while permitted, discussion of religion with clients is often inappropriate. What is most bothersome about the American Airlines example is the pilot's abuse of his power in imposing his views on a literally captive audience of buckled-in passengers. While perhaps not captive to the same degree, in many practice contexts clients are often more vulnerable than their trusted lawyers. For this reason some ethics authorities advocate prohibition of otherwise permitted behavior between lawyer and client, including the giving of gifts as well as consensual sexual relationships. But it is important to emphasize that these concerns go to a professional's coercive abuse of power, and not the discussion of religion.

In light of these concerns, some have suggested that a lawyer must disclose her commitment to religious lawyering to each client at the start of the representation. Here, the legal ethics rules provide the proper framework for balancing lawyer beliefs and client vulnerability. Rule 1.7(a)(2) requires a lawyer to disclose a personal interest only when there is a "significant risk" that it will "materially" limit the representation. Unless such a material limit exists, as in the rare case where a religious lawyer would refuse to seek a particular remedy that would ordinarily be available, the rules do not and should not require disclosure. Religion should be treated no differently than other attitudes or opinions that could be conceivably relevant but pose no significant risk of a material limitation.

Nevertheless, when a lawyer introduces irrelevant personal comments, whether religious, political, or moral, disclosure may be appropriate as a matter of prudence and respect. Like those American Airlines passengers who felt that the pilot was disrespectful, clients who wish to avoid proselytizing of any kind in their professional relationships should be able to do so.

Is religious lawyering dangerous for democracy?

The third challenge to religious lawyering is the argument that it poses a danger to liberal democracy—our system of majority rule that protects individual and minority rights. As some initial reactions to religious lawyering indicate, this objection carries a lot of intuitive punch. For example, at a Fordham conference, when a distinguished lawyer proclaimed the importance of his relationship with Jesus Christ, a prominent judge walked out and angrily told one of us, "You have created a nightmare." Some law school faculty and legal scholars have expressed similar concerns.

These fears appear to arise from two sources. First, in a country that is more than 75 percent Christian, Jews, Muslims, and people of other minority religions might very well worry that they will suffer unequal and unfair treatment if actors in our legal system make decisions based on religious identity. Moreover, nonbelievers may have an even greater fear of discrimination given that close to 87 percent of Americans identify themselves as believers. A second and related worry is that allowing more room for religion in the public square will inevitably lead to divisiveness and intolerance, adding further fuel to the fires of polarizing culture wars.

Despite these fears, religious lawyering does not offend our system of liberal democracy. The United States Constitution promotes liberal democracy by prohibiting the establishment of religion and protecting free exercise. While disagreeing about the particular contours of these provisions, most political theorists agree that in a liberal democracy, citizens should have the freedom to make political decisions based on religious convictions. Whether and how to express religious convictions in the public square, especially when one serves a public role, is of course the subject of intense controversy. But even assuming the disputed point that the lawyer-client relationship is part of the public square, this debate implicates how religious lawyers discuss their religion with their clients, not whether they can appropriately ground their approach to lawyering in their religion.

Even when religious lawyering is placed against the backdrop of American liberal democracy's protections and constraints, some may still fear discrimination and intolerance. It is understandable that minority groups fear majorities, whether religious or not. Nonetheless, as a practical matter, the United States continues as a liberal democracy only because the vast majority of religious Americans find liberal democratic values consonant with their religious values.

Fears about religious lawyering may also stem from misperceptions and stereotypes about religion and religious people. The assumption that religion leads to divisiveness and cultural polarization is often based on a perception of religious traditions as monolithic. In reality, religious perspectives both within and among different religious traditions run the cultural gamut, and intersect with secular perspectives at many points along the spectrum. Similarly, the assumption that religious people are intolerant and incapable of complex interactions in a pluralistic society is a stereotype. Beyond stereotypes, of course, neither religious nor non-religious people have monopolized small-mindedness or generosity of spirit.

If a lawyer's religious approaches to lawyering generate discrimination and intolerance, the lawyer's conduct should be subject to professional and social critique, and discipline where appropriate, just as any other approach that is less than respectful of others. To the extent that religious approaches and perspectives are difficult for others to understand, religious lawyers should work harder to make themselves understood—as would be reasonable to ask of any attorney who fails to communicate her views effectively.

At its core, religious lawyering is an invitation to appreciate the ways that liberal democracy leaves room for a variety of approaches and perspectives to enrich the practice of law without detracting from its essential values. Indeed, we will better promote the rule of law by honestly acknowledging our differences and managing them rather than denying that they exist. As Martha Minow has observed, "You cannot avoid trouble by ignoring difference. You cannot find a solution in neutrality."[10]

CONCLUSION

At a time when many believe that law is no longer a noble profession, many lawyers see no reason to devote time and energy to promoting the public good. Religious lawyering may offer a powerful antidote: a robust framework for lawyers to integrate into their professional lives their most deeply rooted values, perspectives and critiques, and persuasive reasons to improve the quality of justice and work for the common good. At its best, religious lawyering echoes Martin Luther King's advice to the street sweeper. How wonderful it would be, indeed, if we practiced law so well that the host of heaven and earth would pause to say, here lived great lawyers who did their job well.

NOTES

1. Clifford Geertz, "The Struggle for the Real," *Islam Observed: Religious Developments in Morocco and Indonesia* 97 (New Haven, CT: Yale University Press, 1968).

2. Ibid. We are deeply indebted to Howard Lesnick for identifying Geertz's perspective as a literary key for religious lawyering, and for sharing his treasure trove of many other extraordinarily rich texts which have nourished our scholarship and work. See generally Howard Lesnick, *Listening for God: Religion and Moral Discernment* (Bronx, NY: Fordham University Press, 1998).

3. Sanford Levinson, "Identifying the Jewish Lawyer: Reflections on the Construction of Professional Identity," *Cardozo Law Review* 14 (1993): 1577, 1578.

4. See Russell G. Pearce, "Jewish Lawyering in a Multicultural Society: A Midrash on Levinson," *Cardozo Law Review* 14 (1993): 1613, 1629.

5. See Russell G. Pearce, "The Professionalism Paradigm Shift: Why Discarding Professional Ideology Will Improve the Conduct and Reputation of the Bar," *New York University Law Review* 70 (1995): 1229, 1257.

6. See generally Russell G. Pearce, "Retreat of the Elite: How Public Interest and Pro Bono Undermine Business Lawyers' Commitment to the Public Good," *American Lawyer* (July 16, 2001): 79, 80.

7. See ibid.

8. "Facing the Challenge of a New Age." Address delivered at the First Annual Institute on Nonviolence and Social Change, December 3, 1956, in Clayborne Carson, et al., ed., *Papers of Martin Luther King, Jr.* 3 (Berkeley, CA: University of California Press, 1992).

9. *Model Rules of Professional Conduct Review* 2.1 (American Bar Association, 2004).

10. Martha Minow, *Making all the Difference: Inclusion, Exclusion, and American Law* (Ithaca, NY: Cornell University Press, 1990), pp. 374–75.

REFLECTIONS ON THE PRACTICE OF LAW AS A RELIGIOUS CALLING, FROM A PERSPECTIVE OF JEWISH LAW AND ETHICS

Samuel J. Levine

INTRODUCTION: LIFE AS A RELIGIOUS CALLING

I n thinking about the practice of law as a religious calling, it might be helpful to first consider the broader issue of the general relevance of religion to various areas of life, including work. From a perspective of Jewish law and ethics, moral conduct comprises an imperative at home and at the workplace no less than at the house of worship.[1] Starting with the biblical text and spanning thousands of years of legal interpretation and philosophy, Jewish religious thought has addressed not only the apparently sacred, but also the seemingly mundane aspects of human behavior. Indeed, the range of halacha, Jewish legal and ethical thought, encompasses all facets of the human experience, emphasizing the

---

Pepperdine Law Review 32 (2005): 411.

importance of an ethically unified life and demonstrating that every area of life has moral significance.[2]

The Biblical verse that may best articulate this concept commands "[i]n all your ways acknowledge [God]."[3] As noted in the Talmud and elaborated upon in many of the foundational works of Jewish ethical literature, this concise formulation powerfully captures a basic *ethos* of Jewish thought.[4] Maimonides understands this verse to teach that all of one's activities, pursued with proper motivation, may and should be performed in service to God.[5] Likewise, a classic ethical tract delineating an aspirational path toward "holiness" concludes with a citation to this verse, to support the notion of the individual's unique means of achieving piety, corresponding to the unique circumstances and experiences encountered in life.[6]

Indeed, Rabbi Joseph Soloveitchik has explained that "[t]he idea of holiness according to the hala[c]hic world view does not signify a transcendent realm completely separate and removed from reality."[7] Rather, "[h]oliness, according to the outlook of Hala[c]ha, denotes the appearance of a mysterious transcendence in the midst of our concrete world. . . . appear[ing] in our actual, very real lives."[8] Thus, "[t]ranscendence becomes embodied in [a person's] deeds, deeds that are shaped by the lawful physical order of which [humans are] a part."[9] In short, "[t]he true sanctuary is the sphere of our daily, mundane activities, for it is there that the realization of the Hala[c]ha takes place."[10]

WORK AS A RELIGIOUS CALLING

Of all of life's activities, a person's work demands an arguably disproportionate amount of time and energy. Regardless of the particular form it takes, nearly every job occupies a substantial portion of an individual's most productive hours. In addition, depending on the nature of a job, a person may be required to expend considerable physical and/or psychic energy in order to perform an often mundane set of responsibilities. Thus, it would seem that a person's work may present a significant challenge to, and, therefore, perhaps should be central to a discussion of, the goal of imbuing daily activities with moral and spiritual meaning.

Responses to this challenge are based in various conceptions and applications of the moral and spiritual potential latent in the performance of occupational tasks. For example, some jobs, such as that of the Biblical shepherd,[11] may allow for contemplation of and concentration on more profound matters unrelated to the often mundane nature of the work. Alternatively, Jewish thought recognizes ethical and religious value in the fulfillment of obligations owed to a customer or an employer.[12]

These two approaches are expressed in differing explanations of the Biblical narrative stating that "Enoch walked with God."[13] A midrashic interpretation of this verse posits that Enoch was a shoemaker who worshipped God with every stitch.[14] The apparent meaning of this interpretation suggests that, while physically involved in the mundane work of shoemaking, Enoch directed his attention toward overtly spiritual pursuits such as prayer.[15] However, some commentators were concerned that such an understanding attributes to Enoch thoughts that might have distracted him and detracted from his work, thereby leading to a violation of his duty to focus all of his energies on the task for which he was employed.[16] Therefore, others instead explained the midrash as teaching that Enoch worshipped and served God in the measure of honesty and integrity with which he performed his job.[17] Through the virtue of such conduct, Enoch merited the Biblical praise of having walked with God.[18]

On another level, many jobs may provide an avenue for the service of God through the opportunities they present to help others and to contribute to society. Thus, Rabbi Yitzchak Hutner responded with encouragement to a student who expressed concern that his choice of a secular profession was inappropriate as potentially leading him to live a "double life."[19] Citing the example of the conduct of a doctor, Rabbi Hutner explained that, through his work, the student was instead engaging in a "broad life," incorporating professional activities consistent with his religious values.[20]

THE PRACTICE OF LAW AS A RELIGIOUS CALLING

In addition to general issues that confront many other occupations as well, lawyers may be presented with unique challenges to and, perhaps, corresponding opportunities for, aspirations of spiritual and religious expression and growth. In considering the relevance of religion to the work of lawyers, it may be helpful to employ a framework that is familiar in legal thought, looking at what might be termed "substantive" and "procedural" areas of legal practice.

"Substantive" issues might include the clients a lawyer chooses to represent and the goals or causes a lawyer chooses to advocate. Although similar questions undoubtedly apply to many professions, they may be of distinct significance in the practice of law because lawyers may be—or may, at least, be perceived as—particularly prominent and influential members of society.[21] Moreover, although scholars have debated and offered numerous characterizations of the precise nature of the attorney-client relationship,[22] it often may be necessary for lawyers to become—or, again, lawyers may be perceived as—closely associated with the clients and causes they represent.[23]

Challenges and opportunities for the expression and fulfillment of spiritual and moral values may arise in a variety of areas of legal practice, including representation of low-income clients, vindicating clients' civil rights, family law, and even corporate law.[24] In addition, opposing lawyers in the same arena may encounter respective avenues for religious and ethical growth. Thus, in the area of criminal law, the prosecutor may find that the obligation to serve justice[25] is consistent with concepts in Jewish law and tradition emphasizing the importance of the human role in bringing justice to God's world.[26] At the same time, however, the criminal defense attorney may embrace the role of counseling, comforting, and guiding those who are in many ways often among the most vulnerable in society, consistent with religious imperatives to assist the needy and the downtrodden.[27]

"Procedural" aspects of legal practice may likewise present challenges to and, perhaps, opportunities for, spiritual expression and growth, relating to the manner in which lawyers conduct their professional obligations. The work of lawyers may often encourage or even require behavior that, in other contexts, might be considered less than ideal, if not downright improper. Indeed, a brief look at just a few of the tactics central to a lawyer's work demonstrates the potentially detrimental impact the practice of law may have on an individual's spiritual, moral, and ethical character.

Perhaps the most fundamental element of the lawyer's conduct is the obligation to argue on behalf of a client, which is behavior that, in other contexts, may lead a lawyer to develop an overly contentious personality.[28] Moreover, it is not uncommon for a lawyer to advocate an argument that, although not frivolous, does not comport with the lawyer's own assessment of the issue, thus requiring that the lawyer sacrifice intellectual honesty in favor of supporting the client's position.[29] Likewise, commercial and transactional lawyers, among others, may find themselves involved in a difficult bargaining process that calls for tough and unpleasant, if not morally questionable, negotiation tactics.[30] In the courtroom, upon cross-examination, lawyers may have to treat opposing witnesses in a way that, at the very least, may be considered hostile and may result in insult and embarrassment.[31] Indeed, the prevailing basic norm of lawyering, providing a zealous representation of a client's interests, though open to some degree of interpretation, undeniably elevates the interests of the client as paramount, generally disregarding potential detriment to others.[32]

Attempts to confront these challenges and possibly transform them into opportunities for spirituality may prove even more difficult than responding to challenges arising out of substantive aspects of the practice of law. The very nature of the procedural questions, relating largely to internal issues of character, seems to defy general prescription. Perhaps resolution of these matters requires even greater attention to individual circumstances and conditions. Ultimately, then, it may be particularly appropriate for the lawyer's religious and personal values to provide moral and ethical guidance in these areas.

CONCLUSION

Numerous scholars have documented a growing ethical, psychic, and spiritual crisis in the legal profession, resulting in the emergence of various responses and movements.[33] One of the most promising developments in this area, the "religious lawyering movement," examines the relevance of religion to the practice of law, in the interest of demonstrating that religion may serve to provide lawyers a valuable source of moral and ethical values.[34] In recent years, through the emergence of conferences, symposia, and law school institutes, the movement has gained considerable prominence and many adherents.[35] The establishment of the Pepperdine Institute on Law, Religion, and Ethics represents an important step forward, not only for Pepperdine University and the religious lawyering movement, but also, more broadly, for the exploration of an increasingly significant area of legal ethics.

NOTES

1. As Rabbi Joseph Soloveitchik has explained, Jewish thought "does not differentiate between the [person] who stands in [the] house of worship, engaged in ritual activities, and the mortal who must wage the arduous battle of life." Rabbi Joseph B. Soloveitchik, *Halakhic Man* 93, trans. Lawrence Kaplan (Jewish Publication Society of America, 1983). (Originally published in Hebrew as *Ish ha-halakhah*, in 1 *Talpiot* 3-4 [1944]). Instead, Jewish law "declares that [a person] stands before God not only in the synagogue but also in the public domain, in [one's] house, while on a journey, while lying down and rising up." Ibid. In short, "[t]he marketplace, the street, the factory, the house, the meeting place, the banquet hall, all constitute the backdrop for the religious life." Ibid., p. 94.

2. It may be instructive to quote at length from the eloquent words of a leading contemporary scholar of Jewish law and ethics: "On the one hand, there may be a dualistic conception that would set up a rigid barrier between [religious and secular life], a conception that conceives of [a person's] purely natural life as intrinsically corrupt, that sees the religious as established not upon the secular but despite it. . . . On the other hand, we have a unified conception that stems from a deep-seated belief that life is basically one, that the secular and religious aspects of human experience

are in fundamental harmony. . . . I think that the attitude of [the] Torah is clearly aligned with the latter view. . . . Our whole *Weltanschauung*, from eschatology to ethics, is firmly grounded upon the profound conviction that the physical, the natural, the secular, is not to be destroyed but to be sanctified. The Hala[c]ha stresses not rejection but inclusion, not segregation but transmutation. . . . The Torah is neither world-accepting nor world-rejecting. It is world-redeeming." See Rabbi Aharon Lichtenstein, *Leaves of Faith: The World of Jewish Learning* 1 (Ktav Publishing House, 2003), p. 103 [hereinafter Lichtenstein, *Leaves of Faith*]. See also Samuel J. Levine, "Introductory Note: Symposium on Lawyering and Personal Values: Responding to the Problems of Ethical Schizophrenia," *Catholic Lawyer* 38 (1998): 145; and Thomas L. Shaffer, "On Living One Way in Town and Another Way at Home," *Valparaiso University Law Review* 31 (1997): 879.

3. Proverbs 3:6. A literal translation of the quoted phrase might read, "in all your ways know him." I have chosen the term "acknowledge," however, because, as is often true of translations, this substitution for literalism may in fact provide a more accurate and meaningful translation of the original into modern English. See generally Aryeh Kaplan, *Translator's Introduction to Rabbi Aryeh Kaplan, The Living Torah: The Five Books of Moses* v-vii (Moznaim Publishing Corporation, 1981), describing the perils of a literal translation of the Talmud. See also *The Holy Scriptures* 1763 2 (Jewish Publication Society of America, 1955) regarding using the term "acknowledge" in translating this verse.

Nevertheless, there is clear significance to the use of the Biblical term for "knowledge" in the original Hebrew verse, connoting a close form of intimate connection, which is applied here to an individual's relationship with God. See, e.g., Genesis 4:1; see also Yitzchak Hutner, *Pachad Yitzchak, Purim* (1998), pp. 77–78; "Iggeres Ha-Kodesh," in *Kisvei Ramban* 2, ed. Chaim Dov Chavel (Mosad HaRav Kook, 1994), p. 334; Rabbi Joseph B. Soloveitchik, *Family Redeemed: Essays on Family Relationships*, eds. David Shatz and Joel B. Wolowelsky (Toras HoRav Foundation, 2000), pp. 94–95. Finally, the last word in the quoted phrase is actually the pronoun "him," to which the antecedent is clearly "God." See Proverbs 3:6.

For an analysis of some of the more technical legal applications of this verse, see Samuel J. Levine, "Taking Prosecutorial Ethics Seriously: A Consideration of the Prosecutor's Ethical Obligation to 'Seek Justice' in a Comparative Analytical Framework," *Houston Law Review* 41 (2004): 1337 [hereinafter Levine, "Taking Prosecutorial Ethics Seriously"].

4. See Talmud Bavli, *Berachoth*, p. 63a.

5. See Maimonides, *Mishne Torah, Laws of De'oth* 3:2–3; Maimonides,

Shemona Perakim, ch. 5; see also Rabbi Yosef Karo, *Shulchan Aruch* 231; Rabbi Aharon Lichtenstein, address in *By His Light: Character and Values in the Service of God*, ed. Rabbi Reuven Ziegler (Ktav Publishing House, 2003) [hereinafter Lichtenstein, *By His Light*]. See generally Samuel J. Levine, "Professionalism without Parochialism: Julius Henry Cohen, Rabbi Nachman of Breslov, and the Stories of Two Sons," *Fordham Law Review* 71 (2003): 1339 [hereinafter Levine, "Professionalism without Parochialism"]; and Samuel J. Levine, "The Broad Life of the Jewish Lawyer: Integrating Spirituality, Scholarship and Profession," *Texas Tech Law Review* 27 (1996): 1199 [hereinafter Levine, "Broad Life"].

For further explication of this verse in support of the proposition that, when conducted with the proper intention, seemingly optional and mundane activities may be infused with holiness, see Rabbi Yitzchak Hutner, *Pachad Yitzchak: Pesach* (1999): 123–26; Rabbi Aryeh Kaplan, *The Light Beyond: Adventures in Hassidic Thought* 2 (Moznaim Publication Corporation, 1981); Lichtenstein, "By His Light," ch. 2; Lichtenstein, *Leaves of Faith* 2: 327–29; Rabbi Menachem Mendel Schneerson, *Igroth-Kodesh* 23 (1994): 450. In fact, Nachmanides understands the command to "be holy" as referring specifically to activities not otherwise regulated under enumerated biblical commands. See Ramban (Nachmanides), *Commentary on the Torah* 3, trans. Charles B. Chavel (New York: Shilo Publishing House, Inc., 1971) [explicating Leviticus 19:2]. See also Rabbi Mordechai Yoseph of Izhbitz, *Mei Ha-Shiloach* (Jason Aronson, 2001) [explicating Numbers 30:3]. See generally Samuel J. Levine, "Taking Ethics Codes Seriously: Broad Ethics Provisions and Unenumerated Ethical Obligations in a Comparative Hermeneutic Framework," *Tulane Law Review* 77 (2003): 527; Samuel J. Levine, "Unenumerated Constitutional Rights and Unenumerated Biblical Obligations: A Preliminary Study in Comparative Hermeneutics," *Constitutional Commentary* 15 (1998): 511.

6. See Rabbi Moshe Chaim Luzzatto, *Mesillat Yesharim*, trans. Shraga Silverstein (Jewish Publication Society of America, 1966), pp. 336–39. The notion that each individual has a unique role and potential to fulfill is captured in the statement of the Chassidic master Rebbe Zusia who declared, shortly before his death: "When I shall face the celestial tribunal, I shall not be asked why I was not Abraham, Jacob or Moses. I shall be asked why I was not Zusia." Elie Wiesel, *Souls on Fire: Portraits and Legends of Hasidic Masters,* trans. Marion Wiesel (New York: Random House, 1972), p. 120. See also Rabbi Hershel Schachter, *Nefesh Harav* (1994), pp. 63–68; and Rabbi Joseph B. Soloveitchik, *Yemei Zikaron*, ed. Moshe Krone (Jerusalem: World Zionist Organization, 1986), pp. 9–27.

7. Soloveitchik, *Halakhic Man*, p. 45.

8. Ibid., p. 46. For further discussion of the concept in Jewish thought that holiness is manifested specifically when spirituality and morality are applied to the physical aspects of human behavior, see Rabbi Chaim Yaakov Goldvicht, *Arba'a Ma'amrim B'Aggada* (1984), pp. 21–31; Rabbenu Bachya ben Asher, "Kad Ha-kemach," *Kisvei Rabbenu Bachya*, ed. Chaim Dov Chavel (1995): 350–54. See also Schachter, *Nefesh Harav*, pp. 285–86; Rabbi Mordechai I. Willig, *Am Mordechai on Tractate Berakhot* (1992), pp. 13–14; Rabbenu Bachya ben Asher, "Shulchan Shel Arba," *Kisvei Rabbenu Bachya*, 453.

9. Soloveitchik, *Halakhic Man*, p. 45.

10. Ibid., pp. 94–95.

11. See, e.g., Malbim, *Commentary on Psalms* (explicating Psalms 23:1 and describing David's days as a shepherd as a uniquely spiritual time in David's life).

12. A Biblical model for this virtue may be found in Jacob's description of his meticulous and selfless service in behalf of Laban. See Genesis 31:6, 38–40; see also Maimonides, *Mishne Torah, Laws of Sechiruth* 13:7; Lichtenstein, "By His Light," p. 41. See also Lichtenstein, "By His Light," p. 42 (stating that "[i]t is entirely conceivable that a person may be more spiritually engaged in a less inherently spiritual activity, than a person who is engaged in an inherently spiritual activity but performs it in a very lackadaisical manner").

13. Genesis 5:22.

14. Levine, "Professionalism without Parochialism," p. 1344 n. 31 (citing Eliyahu Dessler, *Michtav M'Eliyahu* 1, eds. Aryeh Carmell and Alter Halpern [1954], p. 34).

15. A similar lesson is expressed in a famous Chassidic tale: A teamster in Berdichov was saying his morning prayers, and at the same time, was greasing the wheels of his wagon. He was indeed an interesting sight, praying with his grease-covered hands, and townspeople snickered, "Look at this ignoramus. He doesn't know better than to grease his wagon wheels while he is praying." The great Rabbi Levi Yitchok then came along and said, "Master of the universe, look at Your servant, the teamster. Even while he is greasing his wagon wheels he is still praising Your great and holy Name." Kaplan, *The Light Beyond: Adventures in Hassidic Thought*, p. 5.

16. Levine, "Professionalism without Parochialism": p. 1344 n. 31.

17. Ibid. (citing Dessler, *Michtav M'Eliyahu*, pp. 34–35).

18. See ibid.; see also Dessler, *Michtav M'Eliyahu*, pp. 34–35.

19. Levine, "The Broad Life of the Jewish Lawyer: Integrating Spirituality, Scholarship and Profession," p. 1204 (citing Yitzchak Hutner, *Pachad Yitchak, Letters*, no. 94 [1991]).

20. Ibid.

21. See, e.g., Charles W. Wolfram, *Modern Legal Ethics* (St. Paul, MN: West Publishing Company, 1986): ch. 1.

22. See, e.g., Monroe H. Freedman and Abbe Smith, *Understanding Lawyers' Ethics*, 2nd ed. (Matthew Bender, 2002), pp. 7–9, 56–62; Thomas L. Shaffer and Robert F. Cochran Jr., *Lawyers, Clients, and Moral Responsibility* (West Publishing Company, 1994); Wolfram, *Modern Legal Ethics*, pp. 76–78; Edward A. Dauer and Arthur Allen Leff, "Correspondence: The Lawyer as Friend," *Yale Law Journal* 86 (1977): 573; Charles Fried, "The Lawyer as Friend: The Moral Foundations of the Lawyer-Client Relation," *Yale Law Journal* 85 (1976): 1060.

23. Indeed, a perception that a lawyer's representation of a client or a cause reflects the lawyer's personal approval of the client or cause was the apparent impetus behind the somewhat anomalous Model Rule stating that "a lawyer's representation of a client . . . does not constitute an endorsement of the client's political, economic, social or moral views or activities." *Model Rules of Professional Conduct Review* (1983): sec. 1.2 (b) [hereinafter *Model Rules*].

24. Of course, a more complete list would extend to many other areas of legal practice providing a potential means for spiritual growth. The enumeration in the text corresponds to those areas of practice addressed at the Conference.

25. See *Model Code of Professional Responsibility*, EC 7–13 [hereinafter *Model Code*]. ("The responsibility of a public prosecutor differs from that of the usual advocate; his duty is to seek justice, not merely to convict.") See also *Model Rules*, R. 3.8, Comment [1] ("A prosecutor has the responsibility of a minister of justice and not simply that of an advocate"). See generally Levine, "Taking Prosecutorial Ethics Seriously," p. 1337.

26. See Levine, "The Broad Life," pp. 1206–10.

27. There are countless enumerations and expositions of these imperatives in sources of Jewish law and ethics, from the Torah to contemporary works. Moreover, the criminal defense attorney might point to Elie Wiesel's characterization of the approach espoused by the Chassidic master Rabbi Nachman of Breslov: "Miscreants need redemption more than saints." Wiesel, *Souls on Fire: Portraits and Legends of Hasidic Masters*, p. 189. See ibid. (explaining, according to Rabbi Nachman, that "[t]o pull [others] out of the mud, [a righteous person] must set foot into that mud";

that "[t]o bring back lost souls, [a righteous person] must leave the comfort of home and seek them wherever they might be"; and that "[a] Messiah who would seek to save only the Just, would not be the Messiah"). For further discussion of the thought and works of Rabbi Nachman of Breslov, see Levine, "Professionalism without Parochialism."

For perspectives of contemporary American legal ethics scholars applying many of these concepts to their work as criminal defense attorneys, see Monroe H. Freedman, "Legal Ethics from a Jewish Perspective," *Texas Tech Law Review* 27 (1996): 1131; Abbe Smith and William Montross, "The Calling of Criminal Defense," *Mercer Law Review* 50 (1999): 443, 451–452.

28. It may be instructive that although Jewish thought acknowledges the necessity of argument as an element of legal dispute, the Talmud suggests that, with the proper attitude toward the resolution of legal analysis and dispute, the process has the potential to bring individuals closer rather than perpetuating personal contentiousness. See Talmud Bavli, *Kiddushin*, 30b; see also Lichtenstein, *Leaves of Faith*, pp. 14, 90–91.

29. See, e.g., Marvin E. Frankel, *Partisan Justice* (New York: Hill and Wang, 1980); David Luban, "The Adversary System Excuse," in *The Good Lawyer: Lawyers' Roles and Lawyers' Ethics*, ed. David Luban (Totowa, NJ: Rowman and Allenheld, 1983).

30. See, e.g., Alvin B. Rubin, "A Causerie on Lawyers' Ethics in Negotiation," *Louisiana Law Review* 35 (1975): 577; Gerald B. Wetlaufer, "The Ethics of Lying in Negotiations," *Iowa Law Review* 75 (1990): 1219.

31. See, e.g., Stephen Gillers, *Regulation of Lawyers: Problems of Law and Ethics*, 6th ed. (New York: Aspen Publishers, 2002), pp. 465–69 (describing the debate over the tactics of Max Steuer's cross-examination of truthful witnesses in the criminal trial connected with the Triangle Shirtwaist Company fire).

32. See *Model Code*, Canon 7 ("A lawyer should represent a client zealously within the bounds of the law"); *Model Rules*, R. 1.3, Comment [1] ("A lawyer should also act with commitment and dedication to the interests of the client and with zeal in advocacy upon the client's behalf"). See also Freedman and Smith, *Understanding Lawyers' Ethics*, pp. 79–125; Fred C. Zacharias, "Reconciling Professionalism and Client Interests," *William and Mary Law Review* 36 (1995): 1303, 1340. When the codes authorize lawyers to choose between emphasizing partisanship and important third party or societal interests, lawyers' natural [personal and economic] incentives encourage them to select partisanship. Lawyers who make that choice can readily justify their conduct as mandated by

the code by claiming adherence to the code provisions that call for zeal. Ibid. But see William H. Simon, *The Practice of Justice: A Theory of Lawyers' Ethics* (Cambridge, MA: Harvard University Press, 1998). See generally Samuel J. Levine, "Taking Ethical Discretion Seriously: Ethical Deliberation as Ethical Obligation," *Indiana Law Review* 37 (2003): 21.

33. See, e.g., Samuel J. Levine, "Faith in Legal Professionalism: Believers and Heretics," *Maryland Law Review* 61 (2002): 217; Russell G. Pearce, "The Professionalism Paradigm Shift: Why Discarding Professional Ideology Will Improve the Conduct and Reputation of the Bar," *New York University Law Review* 70 (1995): 1229.

34. See, e.g., Russell G. Pearce, "Foreword: The Religious Lawyering Movement: An Emerging Force in Legal Ethics and Professionalism," *Fordham Law Review* 66 (1998): 1075.

35. See generally Russell G. Pearce and Amelia J. Uelmen, "Religious Lawyering in a Liberal Democracy: A Challenge and an Invitation," *Case Western Reserve Law Review* 55 (2004): 127. See, e.g., Symposium, "Faith and the Law," *Texas Tech Law Review* 27 (1996): 911; Symposium, "Lawyering and Personal Values," *Catholic Lawyer* 38 (1998): 145; Symposium, "Rediscovering the Role of Religion in the Lives of Lawyers and Those They Represent," *Fordham Urban Law Journal* 26 (1999): 821; Symposium, "The Relevance of Religion to a Lawyer's Work: An Interfaith Conference," *Fordham Law Review* 66 (1998): 1075; Rose Kent, "What's Faith Got to Do with It?" *Fordham Law Review* 6 (2001): 11 (describing Fordham University School of Law's Institute on Religion, Law and Lawyer's Work).

ON BEING A RELIGIOUS PROFESSIONAL

THE RELIGIOUS TURN IN PROFESSIONAL ETHICS*

Martha Minow

W hat divides Senator Joseph Lieberman and Chief Justice
William Rehnquist? I assume many things, such as the
street between the Capitol building and the Supreme Court, but it
strikes me as surprising that Democratic and Jewish Senator
Lieberman has argued that individuals' religious beliefs and practices should guide their professional conduct while Republican
and Lutheran Rehnquist has disagreed. Attorney General John
Ashcroft may represent the bridging example: he certainly thought
his religious views should animate his role as a legislator, but
recently indicated that professional duties at the Department of
Justice would require him to enforce laws with which he has had
religious objections.

These are not simply isolated individuals. The growing atten-

University of Pennsylvania Law Review (December, 2001) copyright © 2001 University of Pennsylvania; Martha Minow

*Editors' Note: Virtually all footnotes have been omitted.

tion to what it means to be a Catholic lawyer, a Jewish judge, or a Christian doctor occupies not only pages in academic journals but also bulletin boards and panel discussions at professional schools and, increasingly, broad public debate. (There is almost nothing, by the way, about Moslems, Hindus, or members of other religions, and my remarks, unfortunately, will do little to remedy this lack.)

Why is there a turn to religion now in discussions of professional conduct? What are the benefits and worries that this turn signals? And what paths can individuals and institutions use to navigate the emerging debate over the place of religion in professional life? These are the questions that I will explore here.

WHY NOW?

It is not obvious what to use as a baseline, and I do not pretend to offer scientific assessment, but even a casual observation detects surging interest in the specific relevance of particular religions to professional practices and the general pertinence of religion to public debates. Take the law review literature. Attention to religion and professional practice always occupied specialized religious journals, such as *The Catholic Lawyer*, but now mainstream journals are in the business. . . . [It] is not unusual now to see religious sources—ranging from the Talmud to papal teachings—cited in law review footnotes. . . . Some observers have noted that critics, since time immemorial, have decried the ethical crisis of the legal profession, but the cries became louder and more widespread after the Watergate scandals. The thinness of professional ethics, uninformed by religion, is another repeated theme. Many endorse Sandy Levinson's critique of professionalization as "bleach[ing]" out important aspects of the individual, such as religion and ethnicity. Others join Stephen Carter in criticizing the trivialization of religion in contemporary life and disdain for religion in the academy. . . .

Whatever your qualms about President Bush's proposals to increase government support for faith-based initiatives, candidate Gore endorsed very similar initiatives. Both have personal convictions leading them in this direction, but they also have sophisticated pollsters. Their pollsters no doubt found trends similar to those documented most recently in a study entitled, "For Goodness' Sake: Why So Many Want Religion to Play a Greater Role in American Life." Produced for the nonprofit Public Agenda group and funded by the Pew Charitable Trusts, this study summarized findings from 1,507 half-hour telephone interviews of adults in the general public conducted in November 2000, and a mail survey of religious leaders, public officials, and journalists. The study found that a large proportion of respondents believe that religion helps improve individual behavior and conduct. . . .

Behind these survey results, I suspect, are two short-term and one longer-term phenomenon. First, it is no small matter, I think, that the baby-boomers are getting older. As boomers age, they—we—have looked for ways to raise children in a violent and commercial world, and also looked for meaning and support in dealing with both material success and personal challenges, such as illness and the deaths of friends and family members. Coincidentally, boomers largely control mass media, private institutions, and public debate. This enables us to project our own concerns onto the public stage even more directly than when we tried to steer the political and cultural agenda through activism in the '60s.

Second, in the recent decade, wide perceptions of national and global problems have led many people of all generations into spiritual and religious searches. Local scandals can have this effect. Remember how President Clinton turned to ministers not only for forgiveness but also for their public relations effect? More profoundly, drug and alcohol abuse, related crime, and the persistent poverty of many, alongside the raging and at times conspicuous consumption of others, lead many to seek grounds for critique and reform. Internationally, inter-ethnic violence and genocide, and the international versions of widespread suffering alongside remarkable bounty, generate similar searches for intellectual, political, and moral critique, resulting in mobilization and response. After the terrorist attacks of September 11, churches, synagogues, and mosques became filled with people searching for reassurance, community, and belief.

But a deeper, longer trend across longer time spans is also vital to this transition. The past two centuries mark a period of secularization followed by recent expressions of religious reaction. After the religious wars in Europe, political thinkers such as John Locke argued for separating church and state, and political actors such as Thomas Jefferson tried to institutionalize such ideas. Yet from our vantage point, even such people assumed far greater scope and influence for religion as a feature of public life than we see in today's society. If separation of church and state served as a norm at all in the eighteenth and nineteenth centuries, it applied only to the federal government, not states or localities. . . . The debate over prayer in public schools often turns into contests over history, but no responsible historian would deny that publicly funded schools throughout the nineteenth and early twentieth centuries taught the Bible and presided over prayers without much opposition— that is, without much mainstream opposition, for the integration of religion and public life in the United States largely meant Protestantism. The common school movement in particular confirmed a Protestant culture.

In contrast, Catholic leaders in the nineteenth century saw public schools as failing to serve their community; as the century wore on, anti-Catholic movements pushed for compulsory school laws in order to block the development of parochial, Catholic schools. It took a Supreme Court decision that rejected compulsory public schooling as a violation of parents' abilities to influence their children's upbringing to put such laws to rest. But during the same period, Protestant leaders inspired the social gospel movement that influenced the shape of Progressive era reforms, including the encouragement of evangelical missions that at times conflicted with the religious commitments of increasing waves of Catholic and Jewish immigrants. Many of these immigrant Jews held onto Orthodox practices, surprising both well-established German reform Jews and other Americans. The Catholic leadership decided to hold onto the ethnic and national traditions of its new immigrants, and as a result, structured parishes and imported priests to reinforce religious and ethnic practices rather than allow them to melt into America. Struggles between these groups and the Protestant majority generated political battles and federal and state court decisions that increasingly challenged the view of the country as a Protestant nation. Combined with pragmatic cooperation among religious groups during World War I, these political and legal developments challenged the implicit hegemony of Protestantism.

Between the 1920s and the 1980s, the emerging public solution involved greater secularization. This pattern is exhibited partially in court decisions during the period. Courts approved school instruction about evolution, recognized nonreligious conscientious objection to military service, rejected instruction in "creation science" by public schools, prohibited prayer in public schools, and legalized abortion. These decisions supported not only secularization but also pluralism, and stimulated intense reactions by religious groups. The Christian "religious right" rose, in part, in reaction to these secularizing legal decisions. Religious academics, public intellectuals, and lawsuits criticized secular humanism as an established religion. And the general commitment to tolerance, as well as the dominance of a particular Protestant conception of the private realm as the proper domain of religion, seemed to tell even devout people to treat religion as a once-a-week, private activity—in tension with the view that religion affords a complete way of life.

Reacting to the long-term trend of secularization, many religious people have engaged in "culture wars" over values in the United States. Leaders of the religious right interestingly have taken advantage of the emerging multicultural framework. That made respect for diverse identities a foundation in public settings and labeled the treatment of any group different from others to be di[s]crimination—enabling arguments for equality and accommodation for groups that had been excluded in the past. An obvious example is the Equal Access movement, which convinced Congress and the Supreme Court to ensure to religious student groups the same rights to hold meetings and events accorded to any student organization. This development on the one hand seemed a compromise or middle position between those who would ban religion from public places and those who would integrate it fully. . . .

[B]y the 1990s, the growing search for religious values and "God-talk" in many settings reflected both the resurgence of an evangelical, Christian religious right and the prevalence of a tolerant, equal respect framework welcoming to all kinds of identity politics. . . .

Increasing American materialism and secularization also prompted the revival of religious reflection. From the 1980s onward, members of a variety of religious faiths—and people from both the right and left of the political spectrum—criticized commercialism and greed. Tipper Gore found support first among the religious right but later among secular left-leaning parents in her campaign for labeling pop music. It was not only conservative religious figures but also post-hippy left-leaning parents who began to condemn the commercial glorification of violence, racism, sexual abuse, and greed in popular culture. These left-leaning parents also forged alliances with clergy and organized religious groups. Religious groups have also developed arguments for forgiving international debt by developing nations.

It is against this complex backdrop that we should understand the growing interest in discussing the religious identity and values of lawyers, judges [and other professionals].

Two kinds of persistent questions emerge for professionals. When there is a conflict between religious and professional norms, which should an individual professional follow, or are compromises possible? For it is not only religion that one may profess. A profession itself encompasses beliefs, practices, and commitments; the two sources can conflict. And in the absence of such a conflict, what are the benefits and what are the dangers—for those they serve and for the larger society—if professionals rely on their religions to guide their conduct? For both questions, analysis must prominently point to respect for the client or patient, who may have different views on religion. But also relevant are the norms and practices that should govern private professional institutions, such as law firms and hospitals. And vital as well are potential effects on the larger civil society, if more emphasis on religion occupies professional training and practice. Lawyers play a disproportionate role in this country's public life. Health care provided by medical doctors is salient to everyone's quality of life. The ground rules for religion, equality, and freedom, set by law for private and public enterprises, may be reshaped if religion plays a different role in professional identity and practice than it has in the past.

Thus, there are three dimensions that matter. First, there are the effects on the professional-client relationship. Second, there are effects on civil society. Third, there are consequences for the nation's ground rules. On each dimension, I find (and I confess, I feel) ambivalence about a growing salience of religious identity and practice. After sketching such ambivalence, I will return to the persistent questions for professionals and the search for paths through this thicket.

AMBIVALENT RESPONSES

One way to describe the Constitution's use of two phrases governing state and religion is ambivalence. The guarantee of individuals' free exercise of religion and the prohibition of governmental establishment of religion seem to express simultaneous attraction toward and repulsion from religion. The apparent tension can be resolved by emphasizing the Constitution's concern for protecting individual freedoms in a diverse society. When individuals are involved in diverse, mutually inconsistent, and sometimes antagonistic religions, government will more readily guard individual freedoms by providing an across-the-board commitment not to prefer one kind of religion over others. But the combination of the Free Exercise and Establishment Clauses also expresses a simultaneous respect for the significance of religion and a profound worry about what happens when government supports religion.

The historical origins and continuing purposes of the Establishment Clause reflect concerns about governmental intrusions into religion as much as worries about religion moving into the governmental realm. Both concerns argue against public preference for any one religion, or for religion over nonreligion, even as individuals' religious views and practices warrant deep respect and protection. And both concerns caution against any activities that would lead members of different religions to bring theological and institutional conflicts into the public sphere, or invite government to monitor or regulate religious belief or practice.

The ambivalence—or high-wire act—embodied in the Constitution's treatment of religion matches my personal ambivalence. As a student of ethnic and religious conflict in this country and around the globe, I have become deeply worried about the incendiary effects of governments and political actors mobilizing people around religious differences in places such as Bosnia, Israel, and Northern Ireland. As a member of a religious minority group, I am reminded of the risk of second-class status, exclusion, and worse. Even mild expressions of majority religious belief by governmental officials (such as President Bush's repeated mentioning of Jesus Christ in his Inaugural Address) can have painful exclusionary effects. Yet I also admire very much the many individuals who draw upon religion in their lives and their professions. I have great respect for the commitments of groups such as Catholic Charities, Lutheran Social Missions, and the Jewish Federation to serve people in great need.

More worrisome, to me, are religiously inflected arguments in the political realm, yet I acknowledge and often admire the critical and prophetic perspectives that religious groups contribute to democratic debate. Religious teachings inspired leaders of the civil rights movement and the antiwar (as in Vietnam War) movement. These movements generated debates and policies that much improved this nation. I learned recently that Michael Harrington's book, *The Other America*, which kicked off the War on Poverty, was itself inspired by Dorothy Day's Catholic Worker movement. My colleague Lucie White is documenting the remarkable influence of Black women church leaders on Head Start legislation and practices. I embrace these ready examples because I agree with their substantive visions. Although I disagree with the pro-life movement, and abhor violence committed at times on its behalf, I respect the sincerity of so many of its advocates and the underlying project to advance appreciation of and protection for human life regardless of utilitarian claims. I disagree with the religiously inspired absolutism, the particular elevation of early embryos, and the neglect of the circumstances that drive many women to seek abortions. But it is not the religious impetus to the pro-life effort that is troubling, any more than the religious dimensions of civil rights, anti-death penalty, and antiwar arguments that I do find compelling. Religious beliefs and practices, in each instance, give people bases for criticizing their circumstances and working, by their own light, to improve them. Religion thereby offers a wellspring of moral and political guidance that can critique and also replenish our society.

Its worth cannot be measured solely in terms of each particular position taken by religious believers. Thus, I disagree with John Rawls, who would test the contributions of religious views to political debate by asking how well they advance values recognized by reasonable liberal conceptions of justice, described as the overlapping consensus of varied comprehensive views. The very vigor and critical capacities of political argument depend, in my view, on the contributions of diverse people, drawing on diverse beliefs, traditions, and points of reference. And the shape of overlapping consensus—the very boundaries of reasonable liberal conceptions of justice—do and must change over time as people criticize, argue, and struggle with one another, each informed by life experiences and multiple sources of values and beliefs.

I do worry about the risk that some may seek to use the instruments of government to impose their views on others rather than to work for a world that can be held in common. And I also worry that the notable increase in the religious content of political argument will make communication, trust, and coalition building across different groups more difficult, and unravel our already fraying public realm. In the current climate of federal interest in supporting religious solutions to the problem of poverty, I worry about competition for governmental resources and public fights over what even is a religion. Do Scientologists count? Wiccans? Secular humanists?

Many of these issues may seem largely in the background, however, when religion is joined with professional identity and practice. Except where the professional fills a public role—such as Attorney General, Surgeon General of the United States, or Supreme Court Justice—the professional operates as a private individual whose own acts do not risk violating the Establishment Clause or the values it represents. Thus, as a theoretical matter, an entirely different set of problems arises when a judge quotes in an opinion from a Christian biblical text than when a private attorney quotes the same text while advising a client. The distinction blurs, however, if the lawyer quotes the same text in a brief to a court. . . . Moreover, the very distinction between public and private is one that I and others have questioned when it comes to application of public norms, such as antidiscrimination. Others challenge it from a different direction when they object to how privatized and removed from public discourse are expressions of religious faith. So the distinction between state and non-state action, or between public and private realms, does not resolve my ambivalence about growing expressions of religious views and practices by professionals.

Focusing specifically on the place of religion in the professional's conceptions of role, there is much to admire but also real grounds for worry. When religion shapes the institutions where law [is] practiced, people who share my ambivalence have grounds for cheering and for objecting.

Similarly, there is much to commend but also reason to worry about the use of religious perspectives to develop normative visions to animate law. I am saddened by descriptions of law as having nothing to do with justice (even as I acknowledge that we do call these places law schools, not justice schools). I disagree with those who say that "[a] lawyer's relationship to justice and wisdom . . . is on a par with a piano tuner's relationship to a concert. He neither composes the music, nor interprets it—he merely keeps the machinery running."[1] Lawyers—and law—should draw upon all sources of wisdom and guides for pursuing justice, including religious ones.

But I find much to admire in John Rawls's argument that such visions must be capable of expression in secular terms, or what he calls "public reason." This means that reasons used in political discussion must be accessible to the comprehension, scrutiny, and response of those who do not share the speaker's religious convictions. Otherwise, the prospects for open and reasoned debate diminish potentially irreparably. Speakers with some ostensibly secular views would also be disciplined by this injunction. Michael Ignatieff has written recently of the danger that human rights activists, in particular, may be developing a kind of religious attachment to their arguments. Their own beliefs may seem to insulate them from rational response. Their tone may carry the "triumphalism" associated with religious true believers, and may be capable of silencing competing views. As a sometime human rights advocate myself, I am stung, usefully, by this critique.

Similar problems arise with professionals who claim religious authority for their positions or actions. Religiously guided critics of professionals draw on traditions that others may not share. I can welcome those religious views as sources of critique meant to inspire a generally accessible debate over ends, while objecting to any effort to install the very same religious views as official policies. An example here is scholarship criticizing the work of individual judges for failing to reflect the religious teachings associated with the judge's own religious affiliation. I have been especially struck by Maria Failinger's article entitled, "The Justice Who Wouldn't Be Lutheran: Toward Borrowing the Wisdom of Faith Traditions." The article criticizes Chief Justice Rehnquist's strict constructionism and deference to government actors with apparent inattention to human hardship. Failinger further argues that the Chief Justice fails to recognize the inevitability of conflicting loyalties, loyalties to intimate relationships vis-à-vis loyalties to the larger community and state. She claims the teachings of the Chief Justice's own religion—Lutheranism—would push the balance precisely in the other direction, toward responding to human hardship and human need. She asserts that "the Lutheran position would construct a positive vision of the role of the judge, both in restraining evil and in providing for the nurture of the community." Failinger warns against Senate confirmation inquiries into a judicial candidate's religious beliefs. Such inquiries would be unduly intrusive, and whatever they could discover would also offer poor predictions of ultimate judicial performance. Yet she also cautions against policies that force judges' religions underground because, in her words, "perhaps the most important source of self-critique for a judge is his or her faith." I am not sure what Failinger has in mind. But her comments bring to my mind the willingness of even religious German judges to implement the Nazi system, South African judges to enforce Apartheid, and United States judges to enforce slavery. In light of those examples, I would agree that religious and other sources of self-critique—and external critique—are essential to check judicial subordination to unjust regimes. Failinger's own punchline is that a religiously inspired humility would better serve Chief Justice Rehnquist in working out his own commitment to respect democratic outcomes.

I enjoyed Failinger's article and learned from it, although I worry I like it mostly because it skewers Chief Justice Rehnquist in terms that he might hear better than ones posed solely from my political point of view. I have the same response to criticisms of Justice Scalia in light of his Catholicism: a guilty pleasure for one who worries about a vision of courts that urges judges to consult their religious traditions. Of course, as Justice Cardozo wrote eloquently, any judge consciously or unconsciously draws upon the entire range of experiences, training, and beliefs he or she has developed over a lifetime. But the question is whether the judge should revel in all these influences or instead try to restrain them while seeking to interpret and apply secular legal guides. The critic can challenge what the judge does in religious terms; the judge, too, can question judicial decision making through religious sources of critique. But judicial answers must be guided and expressed through secular, legal reasons. Indeed, if a judge's religious convictions make it impossible for her to enforce the law as a secular analysis would indicate, within the actual span for discretion permitted by the law, she should resign the post, not bend the post to the religious views. Similar analyses can address the qualifications of jurors and grounds for excluding individuals from a jury.

Still, what's not to like in the vision of Lutheranism offered to a Chief Justice by Failinger? That vision does not conflict with the task of the secular judge. Instead, it supports a stance for hearing facts and interpreting law to do justice while respecting democratic institutions. Yet not all interpretations of Lutheranism or other religions point to humility before democratic outcomes in a pluralist society. Decision making in light of a judge's religious tradition may be less resistant to the open argument, critique, and adversarial debate that our system expects and demands. Most troubling, religious references and guidance—however well-motivated and however universalistic in their outcome—risk signaling (or worse, implementing) the exclusion for some and inclusion for others that a democratic society committed to freedom and equality must resist.

Moving from judges to lawyers, elevating religion as the conscious guide could resolve what some call an "ethical schizophrenia" produced by a professional role conception. That professional role seems to require separation from the individual's beliefs and values. Thomas Shaffer's landmark work, *On Being a Christian and a Lawyer*, offers a powerful and admirable cure—at least for those who share his views about ways to bring conscience and care to law practice. He rejects a professional role conception that requires separation from one's beliefs and values. He also recasts certain professional commitments to render them more compatible with Christian ethics. Thus, he calls for revising the lawyer's duty of loyalty to the client and recasting it as a duty of fidelity. The duty of fidelity would support counseling the client and preserving the right to raise moral objections rather than serving as a hired gun, doing whatever the client wants, as the duty of loyalty may imply. Shaffer also argues that lawyers can and should help clients search for conciliation and reconciliation rather than search for power.

Informed by Christian beliefs, this recommendation etches a path that would help many people combine their religious and moral beliefs with the practice of law. But if all lawyers followed this search for conciliation, instead of pressing adversarial interests and adverse rights, I confess I would worry. I would worry about so truncated a range of lawyering styles for a client who seeks to vindicate a right, not reconcile with an opponent, or whose sense of violation would be compounded, not assisted, by efforts to seek reconciliation. I would worry about the lawyer who is so intent on conciliation that he or she does not explore with the client all the litigation options. I would be concerned for those who do not share the lawyer's religious views. And I would be concerned for an adversary system predicated on competitive fact-finding and argument. The system will not work if the lawyers appearing in court curtail the arguments available to them in an effort to promote reconciliation between the opposing parties.

Some others have argued that Christian lawyers can and should provide religious and moral counsel. Daniel Conkle notes with approval a lawyer's reference to the Bible to remind a client to make decisions based on the client's sense of morality. But he does caution against an aggressive evangelism, in order to respect a religiously plural society and ensure effectiveness. I would add my hope that evangelistic lawyers would give notice to clients ahead of time that religious ministry or counsel is part of their practice, either to make it less embarrassing and less expensive for the client who does not want this part of the relationship to change lawyers or to opt out of this portion of the lawyer's services. Such notice would respect pluralism, help the lawyer who wants to be effective, and also restrain the use of the attorney's power in consulting a vulnerable client.

I have not found much by United States scholars on Islamic, Hindu, or Buddhist lawyering, although I am still looking. There is, however, a growing literature on being a Jewish lawyer. I suppose it is some source of comfort for ambivalent people like me that this scholarship on Jewish lawyering is too filled with disagreements about what being Jewish offers to lawyering to provide much of a threat to the range of approaches to lawyering. As a Jew familiar with how Jews raise arguments about everything Jewish, this makes me chuckle. Sandy Levinson's articles alone include at least five alternative conceptions joining Jewishness and lawyering, and other scholars add still more. I admire Seth Kreimer's interpretation of Jewish tradition as urging lawyers to support those who are disadvantaged. This is, however, only one of many readings of what the tradition means for lawyering in America. One that Sandy Levinson discusses elevates the ethnic rather than the religious dimension and urges a kind of interest-group-politics approach to lawyering.

I am not sure what this means. But I worry about a use of ethnic pride in lawyering, whether by Jews or others, if this in any way leads to the appearance or actual practice of bias against members of other groups in the way deals are negotiated or suits are litigated. Justice Thurgood Marshall used to tell of secret signals used by lawyers to jurors, reflecting their shared membership in all-white Masonic lodges. Any direct or indirect signaling of membership and non-membership could so jeopardize the perception and fairness of the legal process; it is another reason to be scrupulous in confining religion away from the public corridors of law practice. Signaling a private language that operates by membership rather than argument threatens even the pretense of equality and transparency that allows us to criticize departures from those ideals.

The settings of private law practice—law firms, corporate

counsel departments, and public interest practices—can be influenced by the religious beliefs and affiliations of their founders and managers. Michael Kelly describes one law firm whose chief clients are Roman Catholic institutions and whose common purposes include a spirit of cooperation and earned reputations for public service, quality lawyering, and effective service. It certainly looks like an appealing place—even though (or perhaps in part because?) the attorney compensation is notably lower than at comparable firms. Kelly does not discuss how that firm—given a fictional name in his book—hires, or whether it seeks or discourages non-Catholic lawyers and staff, and I have no reason to believe that it discriminates. Surely, if a given religious institution believed it needed to employ exclusively lawyers affiliated with its tradition, it could hire such lawyers, and even build an internal law practice. Yet, historical practices of religious exclusion, informally replaced by religious "clubbiness" at other law firms, make me worry. This is why Title VII antidiscrimination norms do—and should—apply to law firms above the minimum size. Because sites of law practices are work settings like any other, the commitment to creating a society open to all should be carried out there; because law is so tied to public norms and institutions, fulfilling this commitment is, if anything, greater for law practice settings. This includes accommodating the individual lawyer's religious beliefs.

Such accommodations would include permitting the lawyer to observe religious holidays, hours of prayer, dietary restrictions, and clothing requirements. Reasonable accommodations should also allow a lawyer to refuse to work for a particular client or cause when his objection grows from religious or sincerely held conscience grounds. Similarly, neither courts nor the bar should refuse to accommodate a lawyer's religious beliefs or conscience when a court seeks to appoint a lawyer to represent a client.

Thus, I think that the Board of Professional Responsibility of the Tennessee Supreme Court wrongly concluded that a Catholic lawyer could not decline to represent a minor seeking an abortion even though the lawyer claimed that such representation violated his religious beliefs. Indeed, this might even be an instance of wrongful efforts to establish secularism and surely to constrain the free exercise of an individual's religion. The duty to ensure representation under the Sixth Amendment for indigent criminal defendants and the more general duty to represent unpopular clients does not and should not oblige individual lawyers to represent any particular client, especially in the absence of demonstration that no one else will do so. If it truly came to pass that no one could be found to represent an individual but the lawyer who has a religious objection, then my ambivalence would surface, but I think we can wait for such a moment to resolve the matter. Even where the lawyer—out of conscience or religious belief—would object to representing the pregnant minor client who seeks an abortion, professional duty should be understood to require the lawyer, consulted by that individual, to disclose the option of going to court or else to refer her to someone who would offer that kind of representation. . . .

GUIDES FOR THE AMBIVALENT

Ah, time grows near for a conclusion. I feel a little bit like Vita Sackville-West, who once commented, "I have come to the conclusion, after many years of sometimes sad experience, that you cannot come to any conclusion at all."

Yet even with my ambivalence, I have been hinting at my own conclusions about how professionals should respond to conflicts between their professional role and religious commitments. I have suggested that where there are conflicts between the professional's role and deeply held religious beliefs, the individual should seek a way to meet the needs of the client or patient—through referrals if necessary—or to shift away from work in the field of conflict, or else resign the professional role. The professional norms may be thin in some respects, but here they are thick. Failure to educate a patient or client about her options as they exist under prevailing standards of practice breaches these professional norms.

I have also suggested that where there are conflicts between a religiously governed practice setting for professionals and rights ensured by the secular state to patients and clients, responsibility shifts to those who govern the mix of institutions to ensure that patients' and clients' rights can be met. And I have indicated the vital role that religious belief and practice can play in both inspiring individual professionals to do their hard daily work and inspiring persistent but external critiques of the professional practices and institutions.

Where there is no obvious conflict between professional duty and religious commitment, it would seem that an individual could pursue the religious guidance fully. Yet here, I expressed caution about truncating the range of professional services and strategies. And I expressed my worries about signaling bias and exclusion toward any but co-religionists if a professional makes religious language and values dominant in the professional practice. The religiously guided professional should also disclose his or her reliance on religious values to avoid misleading the client and to ensure acknowledgment of alternative approaches.

Along the way, I have considered but found inadequate a range of guideposts to mark where religion should run unfettered and where it should be restrained. The distinction between public practice and private practice, at first appealing, simply fades in our world of intermingled public and private activities, funds, and institutions. I considered drawing the line between the personal, individual action and the institutional design for professional practice, but this too cannot mark the places for religious guidance from those where religion should stay out. I do find much to recommend John Rawls's view that religion can offer springboards for action but not justifications in public life. Otherwise, the prospects for communication across different groups grow very dim, and the occasions for using religious authority as a club—of both the weapon and social variety—jeopardizes equality, participation, and mutual exchange. But Rawls's own recommendation is complex and difficult to clarify. If acceptable justifications are those found in an overlapping consensus—marking the convergence between comprehensive views, like religions and ideologies—then separating springboards and justifications can be a sticky business. It is also likely as much a function of a given historical movement as anything else whether a particular argument appears accessible to people who hold a different comprehensive view.

I am humbled by the difficulty of sharply concluding what place religion should have in the lives of professionals in a pluralist society. Humility is itself, of course, often a deeply religious notion. But, so often, its opposite seems to come with the territory of religious practice and identity. Did you hear about the two Christian ministers who concluded an ecumenical conference where they had shared respectful discussions of their denominational differences? One grasped the hand of his new friend, and reported, "I now see that we both worship God; you in your way, and me in His." . . .

Pride or smugness, even in the guise of humility, is unfortunately a familiar feature or impression associated with religiosity. Some devout people I know deliberately keep their religiosity private for fear of implying a "holier than thou" attitude. That kind of restraint is admirable, but the resulting divisions of the self are unfortunate. The individual may feel torn and unable to integrate two sets of beliefs; the profession may be deprived of enriching sources of values and critique; clients and the broader society may be short-changed as well. Yet professionals who live and work in a multireligious and multicultural society must also comport with secular values and ensure equal respect for clients and patients, whatever their affiliations. So should the institutions set up to deliver professional services. I think this entails avoiding what Howard Lesnick calls "triumphalism" or even its appearance. The secular professions of law and medicine need the humility and the questions that religious sources and concerns can sustain. But resisting the implication that your religious convictions give all the answers—for you and for those you serve—may be the most critical challenge for those who would overtly combine religion and professional identity.

NOTE

1. Lucille Kallen, *Introducing C. B. Greenfield* (Ballantine Books, 1980), quoted in Rosalie Maggio, ed., *The Beacon Book of Quotations by Women* 184 (Beacon Press, 1992).

PART THREE

CIVIL DISOBEDIENCE
WHEN IS IT JUSTIFIED?

ON NOT PROSECUTING CIVIL DISOBEDIENCE*

Ronald Dworkin

How should the government deal with those who disobey
... laws out of conscience? Many people think the answer
is obvious: the government must prosecute the dissenters, and if
they are convicted it must punish them. Some people reach this
conclusion easily, because they hold the mindless view that conscientious disobedience is the same as lawlessness. They think that
the dissenters are anarchists who must be punished before their
corruption spreads. Many lawyers and intellectuals come to the
same conclusion, however, on what looks like a more sophisticated
argument. They recognize that disobedience to law may be *morally*
justified, but they insist that it cannot be *legally* justified, and they

The New York Review of Books 10, no. 11 (June 6, 1968)

*Editors' Note: This essay was written in 1968 in the midst of the Vietnam
War. Dworkin's discussion of the civil disobedience that had emerged in opposition to the draft laws then in effect became the occasion for his advancing a position concerning the punishment of those involved in such disobedience. The
essay has been significantly edited to focus on that theoretical discussion.

think that it follows from this truism that the law must be enforced. . . .

But the argument that, because the government believes a man has committed a crime, it must prosecute him is much weaker than it seems. Society "cannot endure" if it tolerates all disobedience; it does not follow, however, nor is there evidence, that it will collapse if it tolerates some. In the United States prosecutors have discretion whether to enforce criminal laws in particular cases. A prosecutor may properly decide not to press charges if the lawbreaker is young, or inexperienced, or the sole support of a family, or is repentant, or turns state's evidence, or if the law is unpopular or unworkable or generally disobeyed, or if the courts are clogged with more important cases, or for dozens of other reasons. This discretion is not license—we expect prosecutors to have good reasons for exercising it—but there are, at least *prima facie*, some good reasons for not prosecuting those who disobey . . . laws out of conscience. One is the obvious reason that they act out of better motives than those who break the law out of greed or a desire to subvert government. Another is the practical reason that our society suffers a loss if it punishes a group that includes—as the group of draft dissenters does—some of its most thoughtful and loyal citizens. Jailing such men solidifies their alienation from society, and alienates many like them who are deterred by the threat. . . .

In the United States, at least, almost any law which a significant number of people would be tempted to disobey on moral grounds would be doubtful—if not clearly invalid—on constitutional grounds as well. The Constitution makes our conventional political morality relevant to the question of validity; any statute that appears to compromise that morality raises constitutional questions, and if the compromise is serious, the constitutional doubts are serious also. . . .

What should a citizen do when the law is unclear, and when he thinks it allows what others think it does not? I do not mean to ask, of course, what it is *legally* proper for him to do, or what his *legal* rights are—that would be begging the question, because it depends upon whether he is right or they are right. I mean to ask what his proper course is as a citizen, what in other words, we would consider to be "playing the game." That is a crucial question, because it cannot be wrong not to punish him if he is acting as, given his opinions, we think he should.[1]

There is no obvious answer on which most citizens would readily agree, and that is itself significant. If we examine our legal institutions and practices, however, we shall discover some relevant underlying principles and policies. I shall set out three possible answers to the question, and then try to show which of these best fits our practices and expectations. The three possibilities I want to consider are these:

(1) If the law is doubtful, and it is therefore unclear whether it permits someone to do what he wants, he should assume the worst, and act on the assumption that it does not. He should obey the executive authorities who command him, even though he thinks they are wrong, while using the political process, if he can, to change the law.

(2) If the law is doubtful, he may follow his own judgment, that is, he may do what he wants if he believes that the case that the law permits this is stronger than the case that it does not. But he may follow his own judgment only until an authoritative institution, like a court, decides the other way in a case involving him or someone else. Once an institutional decision has been reached, he must abide by that decision, even though he thinks that it was wrong. . . .

(3) If the law is doubtful, he may follow his own judgment, even after a contrary decision by the highest competent court. Of course, he must take the contrary decision of any court into account in making his judgment of what the law requires. Otherwise the judgment would not be an honest or reasonable one, because the doctrine of precedent, which is an established part of our legal system, has the effect of allowing the decision of the courts to *change* the law. Suppose, for example, that a taxpayer believes that he is not required to pay tax on certain forms of income. If the Supreme Court decides to the contrary, he should, taking into account the practice of according great weight to the decisions of the Supreme Court on tax matters, decide that the Court's decision has itself tipped the balance, and that the law now requires him to pay the tax.

Someone might think that this qualification erases the difference between the third and the second models, but it does not. The doctrine of precedent gives different weights to the decisions of different courts, and greatest weight to the decisions of the Supreme Court, but it does not make the decision of any court conclusive. Sometimes, even after a contrary Supreme Court decision, an individual may still reasonably believe that the law is on his side; such cases are rare, but they are most likely in disputes over constitutional law when civil disobedience is involved. The Court has shown itself more likely to overrule its past decisions if these have limited important personal or political rights, and it is just these decisions that a dissenter might want to challenge. . . .

We cannot assume, in other words, that the Constitution is always what the Supreme Court says it is. Oliver Wendell Holmes, for example, did not follow such a rule in his famous dissent in the *Gitlow* case. A few years before, in *Abrams*, he had lost his battle to persuade the court that the First Amendment protected an anarchist who had been urging general strikes against the government. A similar issue was presented in *Gitlow*, and Holmes once again dissented. "It is true," he said, "that in my opinion this criterion was departed from in [Abrams] but the convictions that I expressed in that case are too deep for it to be possible for me as yet to believe that it . . . settled the law." Holmes voted for acquitting Gitlow, on the ground that what Gitlow had done was no crime, even though the Supreme Court had recently held that it was.

Here then are three possible models for the behavior of dissenters who disagree with the executive authorities when the law is doubtful. Which of them best fits our legal and social practices?

I think it plain that we do not follow the first of these models, that is, that we do not expect citizens to assume the worst. If no court has decided the issue, and a man thinks, on balance, that the law is on his side, most of our lawyers and critics think it perfectly proper for him to follow his own judgment. . . .

It is worth pausing a moment to consider what society would lose if it did follow the first model or, to put the matter the other way, what society gains when people follow their own judgment in cases like this. When the law is uncertain, in the sense that lawyers can reasonably disagree on what a court ought to decide, the reason usually is that different legal principles and policies have collided, and it is unclear how best to accommodate these conflicting principles and policies.

Our practice, in which different parties are encouraged to pursue their own understanding, provides a means of testing relevant hypotheses. If the question is whether a particular rule would have certain undesirable consequences, or whether these consequences would have limited or broad ramifications, then, before the issue is decided, it is useful to know what does in fact take place when some people proceed on that rule. (Much anti-trust and business regulation law has developed through this kind of testing.) If the question is whether and to what degree a particular solution would offend principles of justice or fair play deeply respected by the community, it is useful, again, to experiment by testing the community's response. The extent of community indifference to anti-contraception laws, for example, would never have become established had not some organizations deliberately flouted those laws in Connecticut.

If the first model were followed, we would lose the advantages of these tests. The law would suffer, particularly if this model were applied to constitutional issues. When the validity of a criminal statute is in doubt, the statute will almost always strike some people as being unfair or unjust, because it will infringe some principle of liberty or justice or fairness which they take to be built into the Constitution. If our practice were that whenever a law is doubtful on these grounds, one must act as if it were valid, then the chief vehicle we have for challenging the law on moral grounds would be lost, and over time the law we obeyed would certainly become less fair and just, and the liberty of our citizens would certainly be diminished. . . .

We must also reject the second model, that if the law is unclear a citizen may properly follow his own judgment until the highest court has ruled that he is wrong. This fails to take into account the fact that any court, including the Supreme Court, may overrule itself. In 1940 the Court decided that a West Virginia law requiring students to salute the Flag was constitutional. In 1943 it reversed itself, and decided that such a statute was unconstitutional after all. What was the duty, as citizens, of those people who in 1941 and 1942 objected to saluting the Flag on grounds of conscience, and thought that the Court's 1940 decision was wrong? We can hardly say that their duty was to follow the first decision. They believed that saluting the Flag was unconscionable, and they believed, reasonably, that no valid law required them to do so. The Supreme Court later decided that in this they were right. The Court did not simply hold that after the second decision failing to salute would not be a crime; it held (as in a case like this it almost always would) that it was no crime after the first decision either.

Some will say that the flag-salute dissenters should have obeyed the Court's first decision, while they worked in the legislatures to have the law repealed, and tried in the courts to find some way to challenge the law again without actually violating it. That would be, perhaps, a plausible recommendation if conscience were not involved, because it would then be arguable that the gain in orderly procedure was worth the personal sacrifice of patience. But conscience was involved, and if the dissenters had obeyed the law while biding their time, they would have suffered the irreparable injury of having done what their conscience forbade them to do. It is one thing to say that an individual must sometimes violate his conscience when he knows that the law commands him to do it. It is quite another to say that he must violate his conscience even when he reasonably believes that the law does not require it, because it would inconvenience his fellow citizens if he took the most direct, and perhaps the only, method of attempting to show that he is right and they are wrong.

Since a court may overrule itself, the same reasons we listed for rejecting the first model count against the second as well. If we did not have the pressure of dissent, we would not have a dramatic statement of the degree to which a court decision against the dissenter is felt to be wrong, a demonstration that is surely pertinent to the question of whether it was right. We would increase the chance of being governed by rules that offend the principles we claim to serve. . . .

Thus the third model, or something close to it, seems to be the fairest statement of a man's social duty in our community. A citizen's allegiance is to the law, not to any particular person's view of what the law is, and he does not behave improperly or unfairly so long as he proceeds on his own considered and reasonable view of what the law requires. Let me repeat (because it is crucial) that this is not the same as saying that an individual may disregard what the courts have said. The doctrine of precedent lies near the core of our legal system, and no one can make a reasonable effort to follow the law unless he grants the courts the general power to alter it by their decisions. But if the issue is one touching fundamental personal or political rights, and it is arguable that the Supreme Court has made a mistake, a man is within his social rights in refusing to accept that decision as conclusive. . . .

We can draw several tentative conclusions from the argument so far: When the law is uncertain, in the sense that a plausible case can be made on both sides, then a citizen who follows his own judgment is not behaving unfairly. Our practices permit and encourage him to follow his own judgment in such cases. For that reason, our government has a special responsibility to try to protect him, and soften his predicament, whenever it can do so without great damage to other policies. It does not follow that the government can guarantee him immunity—it cannot adopt the rule that it will prosecute no one who acts out of conscience, or convict no one who reasonably disagrees with the courts. That would paralyze the government's ability to carry out its policies; it would, moreover, throw away the most important benefit of following the third model. If the state never prosecuted, then the courts could not act on the experience and the arguments the dissent has generated. But it does follow from the government's responsibility that when the practical reasons for prosecuting are relatively weak in a particular case, or can be met in other ways, the path of fairness may lie in tolerance. The popular view that the law is the law and must always be enforced refuses to distinguish the man who acts on his own judgment of a doubtful law, and thus behaves as our practices provide, from the common criminal. I know of no reason, short of moral blindness, for not drawing a distinction in principle between the two cases.

I anticipate a philosophical objection to these conclusions: that I am treating law as a "brooding omnipresence in the sky." I have spoken of people making judgments about what the law requires, even in cases in which the law is unclear and undemonstrable. I have spoken of cases in which a man might think that the law requires one thing, even though the Supreme Court has said that it requires another, and even when it was not likely that the Supreme

Court would soon change its mind. I will therefore be charged with the view that there is always a "right answer" to a legal problem to be found in natural law or locked up in some transcendental strongbox.

The strongbox theory of law is, of course, nonsense. When I say that people hold views on the law when the law is doubtful, and that these views are not merely predictions of what the courts will hold, I intend no such metaphysics. I mean only to summarize as accurately as I can many of the practices that are part of our legal process.

Lawyers and judges make statements of legal right and duty, even when they know these are not demonstrable, and support them with arguments even when they know that these arguments will not appeal to everyone. They make these arguments to one another, in the professional journals, in the classroom, and in the courts. They respond to these arguments, when others make them, by judging them good or bad or mediocre. In so doing they assume that some arguments for a given doubtful position are better than others. They also assume that the case on one side of a doubtful proposition may be stronger than the case on the other, which is what I take a claim of law in a doubtful case to mean. They distinguish, without too much difficulty, these arguments from predictions of what the courts will decide.

These practices are poorly represented by the theory that judgments of law on doubtful issues are nonsense, or are merely predictions of what the courts will do. Those who hold such theories cannot deny the fact of these practices; perhaps these theorists mean that the practices are not sensible, because they are based on suppositions that do not hold, or for some other reason. But this makes their objection mysterious, because they never specify what they take the purposes underlying these practices to be; and unless these goals are specified, one cannot decide whether the practices are sensible. I understand these underlying purposes to be those I described earlier: the development and testing of the law through experimentation by citizens and through the adversary process.

Our legal system pursues these goals by inviting citizens to decide the strengths and weaknesses of legal arguments for themselves, or through their own counsel, and to act on these judgments, although that permission is qualified by the limited threat that they may suffer if the courts do not agree. Success in this strategy depends on whether there is sufficient agreement within the community on what counts as a good or bad argument, so that, although different people will reach different judgments, these differences will be neither so profound nor so frequent as to make the system unworkable, or dangerous for those who act by their own lights. I believe there is sufficient agreement on the criteria of the argument to avoid these traps, although one of the main tasks of legal philosophy is to exhibit and clarify these criteria. In any event, the practices I have described have not yet been shown to be misguided; they therefore must count in determining whether it is just and fair to be lenient to those who break what others think is the law. . . .

[T]he government has a special responsibility to those who act on a reasonable judgment that a law is invalid. It should make accommodation for them as far as possible, when this is consistent with other policies. It may be difficult to decide what the government ought to do, in the name of that responsibility, in particular cases. The decision will be a matter of balance, and flat rules will not help. . . .

Some lawyers will be shocked by my general conclusion that we have a responsibility toward those who disobey . . . laws out of conscience, and that we may be required not to prosecute them, but rather to change our laws or adjust our sentencing procedures to accommodate them. The simple Draconian propositions, that crime must be punished, and that he who misjudges the law must take the consequences, have an extraordinary hold on the professional as well as the popular imagination. But the rule of law is more complex and more intelligent than that and it is important that it survive.

NOTE

1. I do not mean to imply that the government should always punish a man who deliberately breaks a law he knows is valid. There may be reasons of fairness or practicality, like those I listed in the . . . [second] paragraph, for not prosecuting such men. But cases like the draft cases present special arguments for tolerance; I want to concentrate on these arguments and therefore have isolated these cases.

CHRISTIAN DUTY AND THE RULE OF LAW

William H. Pryor Jr.

Recently officials of the judicial system of Alabama were at the center of a national drama about Christian duty and the rule of law. On August 14, 2003, Chief Justice Roy Moore announced that he would not obey an injunction of the US District Court for the Middle District of Alabama to remove a monument with a depiction of the Ten Commandments from the rotunda of the State Judicial Building. Two days earlier [as Attorney General of the State of Alabama], I had written a letter to the associate justices of the Supreme Court of Alabama urging them to exercise their authority, under the Constitution and Code of Alabama, to ensure compliance with the injunction. The day after the expiration of the deadline for compliance set by the federal district court, the eight associate justices unanimously ordered the manager of the State Judicial Building to comply with the injunction as soon as practicable. I immediately provided my support of their order,

Cumberland Law Review 34 (2003): 1. Copyright © 2003 Cumberland Law Review.

which I believe preserved the rule of law, even though I have long contended that it is constitutional to depict the Ten Commandments in a courthouse.

In the days following the removal of the monument, Chief Justice Moore and his prominent supporters advanced three arguments against those of us who complied with the federal injunction. They argued, first, that we had a legal and moral duty to acknowledge God that required us to disobey the injunction. Second, as they surrounded the State Judicial Building in hopes of preventing the removal of the monument, Chief Justice Moore's prominent supporters compared their struggle with that of the civil rights movement led by Dr. Martin Luther King Jr. In turn, they compared those of us who complied with the federal injunction with the defenders of racial segregation. Finally, Chief Justice Moore argued that we had a duty to disobey the injunction as we would, he argued, if the injunction had allowed slavery.

Now that the monument has been removed, the media and demonstrators have returned home, and the shouting has subsided, I want to take this moment at this fine law school [Cumberland School of Law], where I had the privilege to serve as an adjunct professor for several years, to state a respectful and complete response to these arguments. I believe I had a moral duty, as a Christian, to obey the federal injunction. There was no moral justification for civil disobedience. My oath to uphold the US Constitution, sworn to God with my hand on the Bible, required me, as Attorney General of Alabama, to obey the injunction without regard to whether I agreed with the basis for that injunction. My moral duty was not in conflict or even tension with my legal duty. My Christian duty instead provided the foundation for my public duty.

My duty as a Christian is explained first by reference to the Holy Bible. Out of respect for [Samford] a fine Baptist university, I will refer not to the Catholic version but to the more lyrical King James version. In chapter 22, verses 15 through 22, of the Gospel according to Saint Matthew, Jesus gave a provocative lesson about the moral duty to obey the government.

The Pharisees attempted to lay a trap for our Lord by sending Herodians to ask Jesus, "Is it lawful to give tribute unto Caesar, or not?" The question was a trap because if Jesus answered no—there is no obligation to give tribute to Caesar—the enemies of Christ would report Him to the Roman authorities who would charge Jesus with the capital crime of treason. If Jesus answered yes, then the Pharisees would discredit Him before the Jews. The tax was offensive to Jews because the coin for payment of the tribute, the denarius of Tiberius, represented the blasphemy of the Roman emperor as a deity.

Jesus avoided this trap with a surprising response that provides a fundamental tenet of Christianity:

> But Jesus perceived their wickedness, and said, Why tempt ye me, ye hypocrites? Shew me the tribute money. And they brought unto him a penny. And he saith unto them, Whose is this image and superscription? They say unto him, Caesar's. Then saith he unto them, Render therefore unto Caesar the things which are Caesar's; and unto God the things that are God's. When they had heard these words, they marveled, and left him, and went on their way.

Jesus avoided the trap of being accused of treason by admitting the lawfulness of paying tribute to Caesar, and He avoided blasphemy, in the eyes of the Jews, by recognizing the ultimate sovereignty of God.

Jesus did not say that giving the tax to Caesar was permissive; it was mandatory. As some versions of the New Testament state, Jesus spoke in terms of a duty to render to Caesar. "New Testament writers generally use the Greek verb translated 'to render' (apodidonai) to refer to the act of giving to someone that to which he is rightfully entitled."[1]

How could Jesus have taught that there was a duty to render tribute to Caesar when the Roman state was a pagan and occupation power? To put this question in a contemporary context, remember that Caesar would not have spent years debating Jewish authorities about the lawfulness of placing a monument of the Ten Commandments in a Roman building. Our federal and state governments are far superior to Caesar in providing justice and securing religious freedom. How could Jews have been expected by Jesus to render tribute to a tyrant like Caesar?

To gain a greater appreciation of Christ's teaching, we should turn to other passages in the New Testament. First consider chapter 13, verses 1 through 7, of the Epistle of the Apostle Paul to the Romans:

Let every soul be subject unto the higher powers. For there is no power but of God: the powers that be are ordained of God. Whosoever therefore resisteth the power, resisteth the ordinance of God: and they that resist shall receive to themselves damnation. For rulers are not a terror to good works, but to the evil. Wilt thou then not be afraid of the power? Do that which is good, and thou shalt have praise of the same: For he is the minister of God to thee for good. But if thou do that which is evil, be afraid; for he beareth not the sword in vain: for he is the minister of God, a revenger to execute wrath upon him that doeth evil. Wherefore ye must needs be subject, not only for wrath, but also for conscience sake. For this cause pay ye tribute also: for they are God's ministers, attending continually upon this very thing. Render therefore to all their dues: tribute to whom tribute is due; custom to whom custom; fear to whom fear; honour to whom honour.

Next consider the first Epistle of Peter, chapter 2, verses 13 through 17, which explains the same doctrine:

Submit yourselves to every ordinance of man for the Lord's sake: whether it be to the king, as supreme; Or unto governors, as unto them that are sent by him for the punishment of evildoers, and for the praise of them that do well. For so is the will of God, that with well doing ye may put to silence the ignorance of foolish men: As free, and not using your liberty for a cloak of maliciousness, but as the servants of God. Honour all men. Love the brotherhood. Fear God. Honour the king.

These epistles explain that because God is sovereign, our government exists by His will, and we have a moral obligation to obey the commands of our government. Our moral duty to obey the government, even when we believe its commands are unsound, is for our protection and common good. We live in a sinful world, as Heaven awaits, and the government exists to punish evil, although imperfectly. The government is God's institution for securing justice in our fallen world until we can enter Heaven through Christ's saving grace.

The Bible provides an important exception to this rule. In chapter 5 of the Acts of the Apostles, for example, Peter and John were imprisoned for preaching and healing the sick, and they returned to that preaching after being so instructed by an angel that freed them from prison. When they were arrested again and brought before the council, the high priest asked, "'Did not we straitly command you that ye should not teach in this name?' and, behold, ye have filled Jerusalem with your doctrine, and intend to bring this man's blood upon us. Then Peter and the other apostles answered and said, we ought to obey God rather than men."

If the government commands a citizen to violate a Christian duty or moral obligation, such as Peter's duty to preach, then the citizen, like Peter, is obliged to disobey the government. This obligation follows from the lesson of Jesus that we are to render unto God what belongs to God. We have no obligation to render unto the government an obligation that belongs to God.

I have long defended the constitutionality of depicting the Ten Commandments in a courthouse, and a depiction of the Ten Commandments hangs on the wall of my office, as it has for years. This month, I assisted the Governor in creating a display of several foundations of our law, including the Ten Commandments, in the old Supreme Court library of the State Capitol. I agree with the opinion written by Chief Justice Rehnquist two years ago that the Ten Commandments "have made a substantial contribution to our secular legal codes."[2] Because I consider the Ten Commandments to be the cornerstone of law for Western civilization, I do not consider their display in a courthouse, as they are displayed in the Supreme Court of the United States, to be an establishment of religion.

Nevertheless, in the recent controversy about the injunction of the federal court, I was obliged—morally and legally—to obey. Removing the monument of the Ten Commandments from the building of the government did not require me or another official to violate a Christian duty. Christ did not command us to maintain a monument of the Ten Commandments in the rotunda of the State Judicial Building. My Christian duty was not in conflict with my legal duty. The legality of a monument in the rotunda of Caesar's courthouse is a question for Caesar.

What about the second accusation? Did compliance with the injunction violate the civil rights of Christians? Were the protestors outside the State Judicial Building engaged in rightful civil disobedience? Was Chief Justice Moore the new Dr. King and I the modern day Bull Connor? The answer to all these questions is no.

The authoritative text on this issue, I submit, is the letter written by Dr. Martin Luther King Jr. from the Birmingham City Jail on Easter weekend 1963. The letter was addressed to liberal white clergy of Birmingham who opposed segregation but did not support King's nonviolent protests against racial discrimination. The white religious leaders argued that, as a Christian, King had a duty to obey the government.

King responded that he was not obliged to obey an immoral or unjust law. King argued, based on the writings of St. Augustine and St. Thomas Aquinas, that "[a]n unjust law is a human law that is not rooted in eternal law and natural law."[3] King contended that "segregation statutes are unjust because segregation distorts the soul and damages the personality."[4] He explained, "A law is unjust if it is inflicted on a minority that, as a result of being denied the right to vote, had no part in enacting or devising the law."[5] He concluded that a law is unjust when it is used "to deny citizens the First Amendment privilege of peaceful assembly and protest."[6] King's case was that segregation treated black persons as less than citizens and gave them no political recourse to remedy their injury.

Then King explained the difference between unjust defiance and just civil disobedience. He wrote,

> In no sense do I advocate evading or defying the law, as would the rabid segregationist. That would lead to anarchy. One who breaks an unjust law must do so openly, lovingly, and with a willingness to accept the penalty. I submit that an individual who breaks a law that conscience tells him is unjust, and who willingly accepts the penalty of imprisonment in order to arouse the conscience of the community over its injustice, is in reality expressing the highest respect for law.[7]

Dr. King's letter belies any comparison of the civil rights protests of 1963 in Birmingham and the protests of Chief Justice Moore's supporters in 2003 in Montgomery. The injunction to remove the monument did not distort the soul or personality of Christians, because our faith is not dependent upon the presence of a monument in a government building. The injunction did not represent a government denial of political recourse for Christians, because we still enjoy the constitutional rights to vote, hold office, speak, exercise our faith, and assemble. Indeed, the election of Chief Justice Moore and the peaceful protests for two weeks outside the State Judicial Building, complete with extensive freedom of the press, illustrate the vitality of the political rights of Christians.

The most fundamental distinction between Dr. King's example and the protests in Montgomery last month is the difference between defiance of the law and civil disobedience. Dr. King expected the law he called unjust to be enforced against him, but the protestors in Montgomery said that they expected our officials not to enforce the injunction. Dr. King was a private citizen who, in his words, "lovingly" accepted the punishment of an unjust law, but Chief Justice Moore is a public official who sought untimely stays of the order he refused to obey. Perhaps the greatest irony was the reaction of Moore's supporters following the removal of the monument from the rotunda. When we complied with the injunction, the supporters of Moore called on me to resign. As a public official, if I am ever unable to fulfill my oath and obey the command of a federal court directed against me, in my official capacity, then I should resign. This controversy, however, involved no balancing of my moral duty and my oath of office. My Christian duty required me to fulfill my oath.

The duty of a public official brings me to my response to Chief Justice Moore's final contention: that we were obliged to disobey the injunction as, he argued, we would disobey an order allowing slavery. After the associate justices unanimously ordered the building manager to comply with the injunction, Chief Justice Moore said, "If the rule of law means to do everything a judge tells you to do, we would still have slavery in this country." This assertion is contrary to the American history of the abolition of slavery, especially the example set by the Great Emancipator, Abraham Lincoln.

An infamous decision of the Supreme Court, of course, promoted slavery. In 1857, the Supreme Court ruled in *Dred Scott v.*

Sandford that the Missouri Compromise, which prohibited slavery in Western territories, was unconstitutional and that blacks were not citizens. Abraham Lincoln argued that Dred Scott was wrongly decided and must be opposed.

But Lincoln's perspective about the proper response to Dred Scott is instructive. In October 1858, Lincoln explained, in one of his famous debates with Stephen Douglas, as follows:

> We oppose the Dred Scott decision in a certain way. . . . [We] do not propose that when Dred Scott has been decided to be a slave by the court, we, as a mob, will decide him to be free. We do not propose that, when any other one, or one thousand, shall be decided by that court to be slaves, we will in any violent way disturb the rights of property thus settled; but we nevertheless do oppose that decision as a political rule which shall be binding on the voter to vote for nobody who thinks it wrong, which shall be binding on the members of Congress or the President to favor no measure that does not actually concur with the principles of that decision. . . . [We] propose so resisting it as to have it reversed if we can, and a new judicial rule established on this subject.[8]

Lincoln explained that there were two ways of opposing a decision of a court allowing slavery. One method of opposition was illegitimate and to be avoided. The other method of opposition was legitimate and necessary.

The illegitimate opposition was defiance of a final order of a court. Lincoln recognized that the Constitution, in article III, created a federal judiciary to resolve disputes, particularly involving the interpretation of the Constitution. Upon the resolution of their dispute, the parties to the lawsuit, in Lincoln's view, were obliged to follow the orders of the court, and nonparties were obliged to respect the resolution of that dispute between those parties. Public officials, sworn to uphold this constitutional framework for resolving disputes, were obliged to enforce the final orders of this process as between the parties, without regard to the public officials' opinion of the correctness of the ruling.

The legitimate method of opposition, according to Lincoln, was political. Voters should support candidates who would work to end slavery. Elected representatives should enact laws to end slavery. And, the judiciary should, in proper cases, reverse its erroneous decisions that promoted slavery.

Lincoln also supported another more provocative method of opposition. Lincoln refused to allow the Dred Scott decision to bind his administration. Lincoln required his administration, for example, to issue a passport to a black student and a patent to a black inventor. Lincoln supported policies of government that challenged the continued application of Dred Scott, because Lincoln considered those policies constitutional notwithstanding the erroneous precedent of Dred Scott. As Lincoln explained in his inaugural address, "the candid citizen must confess that if the policy of the Government upon vital questions affecting the whole people is to be irrevocably fixed by decisions of the Supreme Court, the instant they are made in ordinary litigation between parties in personal actions, the people will have ceased to be their own rulers, having to that extent practically resigned their Government into the hands of that eminent Tribunal."[9]

Slavery was eventually abolished, following a bloody civil war, with the adoption of the Thirteenth Amendment to the Constitution. Slavery did not end through the defiance of an injunction by a party to a lawsuit. Slavery ended and *Dred Scott* was discarded through armed conflict and political opposition that changed the law and set an example for posterity. The defiance and rebellion of the southern states is not the example to follow. When the judiciary interprets the Constitution erroneously, we still retain all the lawful tools of political opposition that President Lincoln employed. We can campaign for different policies. We can elect candidates who will enact our favored policies. Our elected officials can appoint judges faithful to the rule of law. We can bring new cases before the courts and urge the overruling of erroneous precedents. If necessary, we can even amend the Constitution.

I have said before, and I will say again, that my decision to comply with the injunction to remove the monument was not a tough call. My decision also was not a betrayal—far from it. I have taken the oath of office as attorney general three times, more often than any predecessor. When I first took the oath of office as the Attorney General of Alabama on January 2, 1997, I pledged, in a speech in our State Capitol, to "remain forever bound to the rule of law." I gave special tribute to the provision of the Constitution of Alabama that requires the separation of powers "'to the end that it may be a government of laws and not of men.'" I also expressed my hope, which I still maintain, that "[w]ith trust in God, and His Son, Jesus Christ, we will continue the American experiment of liberty in law." I have been and will strive to remain true to my oath of office, the rule of law, and my Christian duty. . . .

NOTES

1. Luis E. Lugo, "Caesar's Coin and the Politics of the Kingdom: A Pluralist Perspective," in *Caesar's Coin Revisited: Christians and the Limits of Government*, ed. Michael Cromartie (Grand Rapids, MI: Eerdmans, 1996), p. 8.

2. *City of Elkhart v. Books*, 532 US 1058, 1061 (2001) (C. J. Rehnquist, dissenting from denial of cert.); see also *Stone v. Graham*, 449 US 39, 45 (1980) (C. J. Rehnquist, dissenting): "It is equally undeniable . . . that the Ten Commandments have had a significant impact on the development of secular legal codes of the Western World."

3. Martin Luther King Jr., "Letter from Birmingham Jail" (April 16, 1963), p. 4. http://www.stanford.edu./group/King/popular_ requests/frequentdocs/birmingham.pdf.

4. Ibid.

5. Ibid., p. 5.

6. Ibid.

7. Ibid.

8. Abraham Lincoln, *The Collected Works of Abraham Lincoln*, ed. Roy P. Basler, (Rutgers University Press, 1953), p. 255. (Lincoln/Douglas Joint Debate at Quincy [October 13, 1858].)

9. "Abraham Lincoln's First Inaugural Address" (March 4, 1861), reprinted in Abraham Lincoln, *The Collected Works of Abraham Lincoln*, ed. Roy P. Basler, (Rutgers University Press, 1953), p. 258.

PART FOUR

CAPITAL PUNISHMENT
MORAL AND LEGAL ISSUES

SUPREME COURT OF THE UNITED STATES

LEONEL TORRES HERRERA

PETITIONER

V.

JAMES A. COLLINS

DIRECTOR, TEXAS DEPARTMENT OF CRIMINAL JUSTICE, INSTITUTIONAL DIVISION

REHNQUIST, C.J., delivered the opinion of the Court, in which O'CONNOR, SCALIA, KENNEDY, and THOMAS, JJ., joined. O'CONNOR filed a concurring opinion, in which KENNEDY, J., joined. SCALIA, J., filed a concurring opinion, in which THOMAS, J., joined. WHITE, J., filed an opinion concurring in the judgment joined. BLACKMUN, J., filed a dissenting opinion, in Parts I, II, III, and IV of which STEVENS and SOUTER, JJ., joined.

Chief Justice REHNQUIST delivered the opinion of the Court.

Petitioner Leonel Torres Herrera was convicted of capital murder and sentenced to death in January 1982. He unsuccessfully challenged the conviction on direct appeal and state collateral proceedings in the Texas state courts, and in a federal habeas petition. In February 1992—ten years after his conviction—he urged in a

506 US 390, no. 91-7328. Argued October 7, 1992. Decided January 25, 1993. Rehearing denied March 22, 1993.

second federal habeas petition that he was "actually innocent" of the murder for which he was sentenced to death, and that the Eighth Amendment's prohibition against cruel and unusual punishment and the Fourteenth Amendment's guarantee of due process of law therefore forbid his execution. He supported this claim with affidavits tending to show that his now-dead brother, rather than he, had been the perpetrator of the crime. Petitioner urges us to hold that this showing of innocence entitles him to relief in this federal habeas proceeding. We hold that it does not.

Shortly before 11 PM on an evening in late September 1981, the body of Texas Department of Public Safety Officer David Rucker was found by a passerby on a stretch of highway about six miles east of Los Fresnos, Texas, a few miles north of Brownsville in the Rio Grande Valley. Rucker's body was lying beside his patrol car. He had been shot in the head.

At about the same time, Los Fresnos Police Officer Enrique Carrisalez observed a speeding vehicle traveling west toward Los Fresnos, away from the place where Rucker's body had been found, along the same road. Carrisalez, who was accompanied in his patrol car by Enrique Hernandez, turned on his flashing red lights and pursued the speeding vehicle. After the car had stopped briefly at a red light, it signaled that it would pull over and did so. The patrol car pulled up behind it. Carrisalez took a flashlight and walked toward the car of the speeder. The driver opened his door and exchanged a few words with Carrisalez before firing at least one shot at Carrisalez's chest. The officer died nine days later.

Petitioner Herrera was arrested a few days after the shootings and charged with the capital murder of both Carrisalez and Rucker. He was tried and found guilty of the capital murder of Carrisalez in January 1982, and sentenced to death. In July 1982, petitioner pleaded guilty to the murder of Rucker.

At petitioner's trial for the murder of Carrisalez, Hernandez, who had witnessed Carrisalez's slaying from the officer's patrol car, identified petitioner as the person who had wielded the gun. A declaration by Officer Carrisalez to the same effect, made while he was in the hospital, was also admitted. Through a license plate check, it was shown that the speeding car involved in Carrisalez's murder was registered to petitioner's "live-in" girlfriend. Petitioner was known to drive this car, and he had a set of keys to the car in his pants pocket when he was arrested. Hernandez identified the car as the vehicle from which the murderer had emerged to fire the fatal shot. He also testified that there had been only one person in the car that night.

The evidence showed that Herrera's Social Security card had been found alongside Rucker's patrol car on the night he was killed. Splatters of blood on the car identified as the vehicle involved in the shootings, and on petitioner's blue jeans and wallet were identified as type A blood—the same type which Rucker had. (Herrera has type O blood.) Similar evidence with respect to strands of hair found in the car indicated that the hair was Rucker's and not Herrera's. A handwritten letter was also found on the person of petitioner when he was arrested, which strongly implied that he had killed Rucker.[1]

Petitioner appealed his conviction and sentence, arguing, among other things, that Hernandez's and Carrisalez's identifications were unreliable and improperly admitted.

[After an initial appeal and petition were denied,] Petitioner next returned to state court and filed a second habeas petition, raising, among other things, a claim of "actual innocence" based on newly discovered evidence. In support of this claim petitioner presented the affidavits of Hector Villarreal, an attorney who had represented petitioner's brother, Raul Herrera Sr., and of Juan Franco Palacious, one of Raul Senior's former cellmates. Both individuals claimed that Raul Senior, who died in 1984, had told them that he—and not petitioner—had killed Officers Rucker and Carrisalez. The State District Court denied this application, finding that "no evidence at trial remotely suggest[ed] that anyone other than [petitioner] committed the offense." The Texas Court of Criminal Appeals affirmed, and we denied certiorari.

In February 1992, petitioner lodged the instant habeas petition—his second—in federal court, alleging, among other things, that he is innocent of the murders of Rucker and Carrisalez, and that his execution would thus violate the Eighth and Fourteenth Amendments. In addition to proffering the above affidavits, petitioner presented the affidavits of Raul Herrera Jr., Raul Senior's son, and Jose Ybarra Jr., a schoolmate of the Herrera brothers. Raul

Junior averred that he had witnessed his father shoot Officers Rucker and Carrisalez and petitioner was not present. Raul Junior was nine years old at the time of the killings. Ybarra alleged that Raul Senior told him one summer night in 1983 that he had shot the two police officers. Petitioner alleged that law enforcement officials were aware of this evidence, and had withheld it in violation of *Brady v. Maryland* (1963) [requiring the prosecution to disclose exculpatory evidence].

The District Court dismissed most of petitioner's claims as an abuse of the writ. However, "in order to ensure that Petitioner can assert his constitutional claims and out of a sense of fairness and due process," the District Court granted petitioner's request for a stay of execution so that he could present his claim of actual innocence, along with the Raul Junior and Ybarra affidavits, in state court. Although it initially dismissed petitioner's *Brady* claim on the ground that petitioner had failed to present "any evidence of withholding exculpatory material by the prosecution," the District Court also granted an evidentiary hearing on this claim after reconsideration. The Court of Appeals vacated the stay of execution. It agreed with the District Court's initial conclusion that there was no evidentiary basis for petitioner's *Brady* claim, and found disingenuous petitioner's attempt to couch his claim of actual innocence in *Brady* terms. Absent an accompanying constitutional violation, the Court of Appeals held that petitioner's claim of actual innocence was not cognizable because, under *Townsend v. Sain*, "the existence merely of newly discovered evidence relevant to the guilt of a state prisoner is not a ground for relief on federal habeas corpus." We . . . now affirm.

Petitioner asserts that the Eighth and Fourteenth Amendments to the United States Constitution prohibit the execution of a person who is innocent of the crime for which he was convicted. This proposition has an elemental appeal, as would the similar proposition that the Constitution prohibits the imprisonment of one who is innocent of the crime for which he was convicted. After all, the central purpose of any system of criminal justice is to convict the guilty and free the innocent. But the evidence upon which petitioner's claim of innocence rests was not produced at his trial, but rather eight years later. In any system of criminal justice, "innocence" or "guilt" must be determined in some sort of a judicial proceeding. Petitioner's showing of innocence, and indeed his constitutional claim for relief based upon that showing, must be evaluated in the light of the previous proceedings in this case, which have stretched over a span of ten years.

A person when first charged with a crime is entitled to a presumption of innocence, and may insist that his guilt be established beyond a reasonable doubt. Other constitutional provisions also have the effect of ensuring against the risk of convicting an innocent person. In capital cases, we have required additional protections because of the nature of the penalty at stake. All of these constitutional safeguards, of course, make it more difficult for the State to rebut and finally overturn the presumption of innocence which attaches to every criminal defendant. But we have also observed that "[d]ue process does not require that every conceivable step be taken, at whatever cost, to eliminate the possibility of convicting an innocent person." *Patterson v. New York*. To conclude otherwise would all but paralyze our system for enforcement of the criminal law.

Once a defendant has been afforded a fair trial and convicted of the offense for which he was charged, the presumption of innocence disappears. Here, it is not disputed that the State met its burden of proving at trial that petitioner was guilty of the capital murder of Officer Carrisalez beyond a reasonable doubt. Thus, in the eyes of the law, petitioner does not come before the Court as one who is "innocent," but, on the contrary, as one who has been convicted by due process of law of two brutal murders.

Based on affidavits here filed, petitioner claims that evidence never presented to the trial court proves him innocent notwithstanding the verdict reached at his trial. Such a claim is not cognizable in the state courts of Texas. For to obtain a new trial based on newly discovered evidence, a defendant must file a motion within thirty days after imposition or suspension of sentence. . . .

Claims of actual innocence based on newly discovered evidence have never been held to state a ground for federal habeas relief absent an independent constitutional violation occurring in the underlying state criminal proceeding. Chief Justice Warren made this clear in *Townsend v. Sain* (emphasis added):

Where newly discovered evidence is alleged in a habeas application, evidence which could not reasonably have been presented
to the state trier of facts, the federal court must grant an evidentiary hearing. Of course, such evidence must bear upon the constitutionality of the applicant's detention; *the existence merely of
newly discovered evidence relevant to the guilt of a state prisoner is not
a ground for relief on federal habeas corpus.*

This rule is grounded in the principle that federal habeas courts
sit to ensure that individuals are not imprisoned in violation of the
Constitution—not to correct errors of fact. See, e.g., *Moore v. Dempsey*
(1923) (Holmes, J.) ("[W]hat we have to deal with [on habeas review]
is not the petitioners' innocence or guilt but solely the question
whether their constitutional rights have been preserved").

More recent authority construing federal habeas statutes
speaks in a similar vein. . . . The guilt or innocence determination
in state criminal trials is "a decisive and portentous event." *Wain-
wright v. Sykes.* "Society's resources have been concentrated at that
time and place in order to decide, within the limits of human fallibility, the question of guilt or innocence of one of its citizens." Ibid.
Few rulings would be more disruptive of our federal system than
to provide for federal habeas review of freestanding claims of
actual innocence.

Our decision in *Jackson v. Virginia* comes as close to authorizing
evidentiary review of a state-court conviction on federal habeas as
any of our cases. There, we held that a federal habeas court may
review a claim that the evidence adduced at a state trial was not
sufficient to convict a criminal defendant beyond a reasonable
doubt. But in so holding, we emphasized:

[T]his inquiry does not require a court to "ask itself whether *it*
believes that the evidence at the trial established guilt beyond a
reasonable doubt." Instead, the relevant question is whether, after
viewing the evidence in the light most favorable to the prosecution, *any* rational trier of fact could have found the essential elements of the crime beyond a reasonable doubt. This familiar standard gives full play to the responsibility of the trier of fact fairly
to resolve conflicts in the testimony, to weigh the evidence, and to
draw reasonable inferences from basic facts to ultimate facts.

We specifically noted that "the standard announced . . . does not permit a court to make its own subjective determination of guilt or innocence."

The type of federal habeas review sought by petitioner here is different in critical respects than that authorized by *Jackson*. First, the *Jackson* inquiry is aimed at determining whether there has been an independent constitutional violation—i.e., a conviction based on evidence that fails to meet the *Winship* standard. Thus, federal habeas courts act in their historic capacity—to assure that the habeas petitioner is not being held in violation of his or her federal constitutional rights. Second, the sufficiency of the evidence review authorized by *Jackson* is limited to "record evidence." *Jackson* does not extend to nonrecord evidence, including newly discovered evidence. Finally, the *Jackson* inquiry does not focus on whether the trier of fact made the *correct* guilt or innocence determination, but rather whether it made a *rational* decision to convict or acquit.

Petitioner is understandably imprecise in describing the sort of federal relief to which a suitable showing of actual innocence would entitle him. In his brief he states that the federal habeas court should have "an important initial opportunity to hear the evidence and resolve the merits of Petitioner's claim." Acceptance of this view would presumably require the habeas court to hear testimony from the witnesses who testified at trial as well as those who made the statements in the affidavits which petitioner has presented, and to determine anew whether or not petitioner is guilty of the murder of Officer Carrisalez. Indeed, the dissent's approach differs little from that hypothesized here.

The dissent would place the burden on petitioner to show that he is "probably" innocent. Although petitioner would not be entitled to discovery "as a matter of right," the District Court would retain its "discretion to order discovery . . . when it would help the court make a reliable determination with respect to the prisoner's claim." And although the District Court would not be required to hear testimony from the witnesses who testified at trial or the affiants upon whom petitioner relies, the dissent would allow the District Court to do so "if the petition warrants a hearing." At the end of the day, the dissent would have the District Court "make a case-by-case determination about the reliability of the newly discovered evidence under the circumstances," and then "weigh the evidence in favor of the prisoner against the evidence of his guilt."

The dissent fails to articulate the relief that would be available if petitioner were to meets its "probable innocence" standard. Would it be commutation of petitioner's death sentence, new trial, or unconditional release from imprisonment? The typical relief granted in federal habeas corpus is a conditional order of release unless the State elects to retry the successful habeas petitioner, or in a capital case a similar conditional order vacating the death sentence. Were petitioner to satisfy the dissent's "probable innocence" standard, therefore, the District Court would presumably be required to grant a conditional order of relief, which would in effect require the State to retry petitioner ten years after his first trial, not because of any constitutional violation which had occurred at the first trial, but simply because of a belief that in light of petitioner's newfound evidence a jury might find him not guilty at a second trial.

Yet there is no guarantee that the guilt or innocence determination would be any more exact. To the contrary, the passage of time only diminishes the reliability of criminal adjudications. . . . Under the dissent's approach, the District Court would be placed in the even more difficult position of having to weigh the probative value of "hot" and "cold" evidence on petitioner's guilt or innocence.

This is not to say that our habeas jurisprudence casts a blind eye toward innocence. In a series of cases culminating with *Sawyer v. Whitley*, decided last Term, we have held that a petitioner otherwise subject to defenses of abusive or successive use of the writ may have his federal constitutional claim considered on the merits if he makes a proper showing of actual innocence. This rule, or fundamental miscarriage of justice exception, is grounded in the "equitable discretion" of habeas courts to see that federal constitutional errors do not result in the incarceration of innocent persons. But this body of our habeas jurisprudence makes clear that a claim of "actual innocence" is not itself a constitutional claim, but instead a gateway through which a habeas petitioner must pass to have his otherwise barred constitutional claim considered on the merits.

Petitioner in this case is simply not entitled to habeas relief based on the reasoning of this line of cases. For he does not seek excusal of a procedural error so that he may bring an independent constitutional claim challenging his conviction or sentence, but rather argues that he is entitled to habeas relief because newly discovered evidence shows that his conviction is factually incorrect. The fundamental miscarriage of justice exception is available "only where the prisoner *supplements* his constitutional claim with a colorable showing of factual innocence." *Kuhlmann v. Wilson.* We have never held that it extends to freestanding claims of actual innocence. Therefore, the exception is inapplicable here.

Petitioner asserts that this case is different because he has been sentenced to death. But we have "refused to hold that the fact that a death sentence has been imposed requires a different standard of review on federal habeas corpus." *Murray v. Giarratano.* We have, of course, held that the Eighth Amendment requires increased reliability of the process by which capital punishment may be imposed. But petitioner's claim does not fit well into the doctrine of these cases, since, as we have pointed out, it is far from clear that a second trial ten years after the first trial would produce a more reliable result.

Perhaps mindful of this, petitioner urges not that he necessarily receive a new trial, but that his death sentence simply be vacated if a federal habeas court deems that a satisfactory showing of "actual innocence" has been made. But such a result is scarcely logical; petitioner's claim is not that some error was made in imposing a capital sentence upon him, but that a fundamental error was made in finding him guilty of the underlying murder in the first place. It would be a rather strange jurisprudence, in these circumstances, which held that under our Constitution he could not be executed, but that he could spend the rest of his life in prison. . . .

Alternatively, petitioner invokes the Fourteenth Amendment's guarantee of due process of law in support of his claim that his showing of actual innocence entitles him to a new trial, or at least to a vacation of his death sentence. "[B]ecause the States have considerable expertise in matters of criminal procedure and the criminal process is grounded in centuries of common-law tradition," we have "exercis[ed] substantial deference to legislative judgments in this area." *Medina v. California*. Thus, we have found criminal process lacking only where it "'offends some principle of justice so rooted in the traditions and conscience of our people as to be ranked as fundamental.'" Ibid (quoting *Patterson v. New York* [1977]).

The Constitution itself, of course, makes no mention of new trials. New trials in criminal cases were not granted in England until the end of the seventeenth century. . . .

In light of the historical availability of new trials, our own amendments to Rule 33 (imposing a two year time limit), and the contemporary practice in the States, we cannot say that Texas' refusal to entertain petitioner's newly discovered evidence eight years after his conviction transgresses a principle of fundamental fairness "rooted in the traditions and conscience of our people." *Patterson v. New York* (internal quotation marks and citations omitted). This is not to say, however, that petitioner is left without a forum to raise his actual innocence claim. For under Texas law, petitioner may file a request for executive clemency. Clemency is deeply rooted in our Anglo-American tradition of law, and is the historic remedy for preventing miscarriages of justice where judicial process has been exhausted. . . .

Our Constitution adopts the British model and gives to the President the "Power to grant Reprieves and Pardons for Offences against the United States." Art. II, § 2, cl. 1. In *United States v. Wilson* (1833), Chief Justice Marshall expounded on the President's pardon power:

> As this power had been exercised from time immemorial by the executive of that nation whose language is our language, and to whose judicial institutions ours bear a close resemblance; we adopt their principles respecting the operation and effect of a pardon, and look into their books for the rules prescribing the manner in which it is to be used by the person who would avail himself of it.
>
> A pardon is an act of grace, proceeding from the power entrusted with the execution of the laws, which exempts the individual, on whom it is bestowed, from the punishment the law inflicts for a crime he has committed. It is the private, though official act of the executive magistrate, delivered to the individual for whose benefit it is intended, and not communi-

cated officially to the court. It is a constituent part of the judicial system, that the judge sees only with judicial eyes, and knows nothing respecting any particular case, of which he is not informed judicially. A private deed, not communicated to him, whatever may be its character, whether a pardon or release, is totally unknown and cannot be acted on. The looseness which would be introduced into judicial proceedings, would prove fatal to the great principles of justice, if the judge might notice and act upon facts not brought regularly into the cause. Such a proceeding, in ordinary cases, would subvert the best established principles, and overturn those rules which have been settled by the wisdom of ages.

Of course, although the Constitution vests in the President a pardon power, it does not require the States to enact a clemency mechanism. Yet since the British Colonies were founded, clemency has been available in America. . . . Today, all thirty-six States that authorize capital punishment have constitutional or statutory provisions for clemency.

Executive clemency has provided the "fail safe" in our criminal justice system. . . . It is an unalterable fact that our judicial system, like the human beings who administer it, is fallible. But history is replete with examples of wrongfully convicted persons who have been pardoned in the wake of after-discovered evidence establishing their innocence. In his classic work, Professor Edwin Borchard compiled sixty-five cases in which it was later determined that individuals had been wrongfully convicted of crimes. Clemency provided the relief mechanism in forty-seven of these cases; the remaining cases ended in judgments of acquittals after new trials. E. Borchard, *Convicting the Innocent: Sixty-five Actual Errors of Criminal Justice* (Garden City, NY: Garden City Publishing, 1932). Recent authority confirms that over the past century clemency has been exercised frequently in capital cases in which demonstrations of "actual innocence" have been made. . . .

In Texas, the Governor has the power, upon the recommendation of a majority of the Board of Pardons and Paroles, to grant clemency. . . . The Texas clemency procedures contain specific guidelines for pardons on the ground of innocence. . . .

As the foregoing discussion illustrates, in state criminal proceedings the trial is the paramount event for determining the guilt or innocence of the defendant. Federal habeas review of state convictions has traditionally been limited to claims of constitutional violations occurring in the course of the underlying state criminal proceedings. Our federal habeas cases have treated claims of "actual innocence," not as an independent constitutional claim, but as a basis upon which a habeas petitioner may have an independent constitutional claim considered on the merits, even though his habeas petition would otherwise be regarded as successive or abusive. History shows that the traditional remedy for claims of innocence based on new evidence, discovered too late in the day to file a new trial motion, has been executive clemency.

We may assume, for the sake of argument in deciding this case, that in a capital case a truly persuasive demonstration of "actual innocence" made after trial would render the execution of a defendant unconstitutional, and warrant federal habeas relief if there were no state avenue open to process such a claim. But because of the very disruptive effect that entertaining claims of actual innocence would have on the need for finality in capital cases, and the enormous burden that having to retry cases based on often stale evidence would place on the States, the threshold showing for such an assumed right would necessarily be extraordinarily high. The showing made by petitioner in this case falls far short of any such threshold.

Petitioner's newly discovered evidence consists of affidavits. In the new trial context, motions based solely upon affidavits are disfavored because the affiants' statements are obtained without the benefit of cross-examination and an opportunity to make credibility determinations. Petitioner's affidavits are particularly suspect in this regard because, with the exception of Raul Herrera Jr.'s affidavit, they consist of hearsay. Likewise, in reviewing petitioner's new evidence, we are mindful that defendants often abuse new trial motions "as a method of delaying enforcement of just sentences." *United States v. Johnson.* Although we are not presented with a new trial motion per se, we believe the likelihood of abuse is as great—or greater—here.

The affidavits filed in this habeas proceeding were given over eight years after petitioner's trial. No satisfactory explanation has been given as to why the affiants waited until the 11th hour—and, indeed, until after the alleged perpetrator of the murders himself was dead—to make their statements. Equally troubling, no explanation has been offered as to why petitioner, by hypothesis an innocent man, pleaded guilty to the murder of Rucker.

Moreover, the affidavits themselves contain inconsistencies, and therefore fail to provide a convincing account of what took place on the night Officers Rucker and Carrisalez were killed. For instance, the affidavit of Raul Junior, who was nine years old at the time, indicates that there were three people in the speeding car from which the murderer emerged, whereas Hector Villarreal attested that Raul Senior told him that there were two people in the car that night. Of course, Hernandez testified at petitioner's trial that the murderer was the only occupant of the car. The affidavits also conflict as to the direction in which the vehicle was heading when the murders took place and petitioner's whereabouts on the night of the killings.

Finally, the affidavits must be considered in light of the proof of petitioner's guilt at trial-proof which included two eyewitness identifications, numerous pieces of circumstantial evidence, and a handwritten letter in which petitioner apologized for killing the officers and offered to turn himself in under certain conditions. That proof, even when considered alongside petitioner's belated affidavits, points strongly to petitioner's guilt.

This is not to say that petitioner's affidavits are without probative value. Had this sort of testimony been offered at trial, it could have been weighed by the jury, along with the evidence offered by the State and petitioner, in deliberating upon its verdict. Since the statements in the affidavits contradict the evidence received at trial, the jury would have had to decide important issues of credibility. But coming 10 years after petitioner's trial, this showing of innocence falls far short of that which would have to be made in order to trigger the sort of constitutional claim which we have assumed, *arguendo*, to exist.

The judgment of the Court of Appeals is
Affirmed.

Justice O'CONNOR, with whom Justice KENNEDY joins, concurring.

I cannot disagree with the fundamental legal principle that executing the innocent is inconsistent with the Constitution. Regardless of the verbal formula employed—"contrary to contemporary standards of decency," or offensive to a "'"'principle of justice so rooted in the traditions and conscience of our people as to be ranked as fundamental"'"' (opinion of the Court)—the execution of a legally and factually innocent person would be a constitutionally intolerable event. Dispositive to this case, however, is an equally fundamental fact: Petitioner is not innocent, in any sense of the word.

As the Court explains, petitioner is not innocent in the eyes of the law because, in our system of justice, "the trial is the paramount event for determining the guilt or innocence of the defendant," *ante*, p. 869. In petitioner's case, that paramount event occurred ten years ago. He was tried before a jury of his peers, with the full panoply of protections that our Constitution affords criminal defendants. At the conclusion of that trial, the jury found petitioner guilty beyond a reasonable doubt. Petitioner therefore does not appear before us as an innocent man on the verge of execution. He is instead a legally guilty one who, refusing to accept the jury's verdict, demands a hearing in which to have his culpability determined once again.

Consequently, the issue before us is not whether a State can execute the innocent. It is, as the Court notes, whether a fairly convicted and therefore legally guilty person is constitutionally entitled to yet another judicial proceeding in which to adjudicate his guilt anew, ten years after conviction, notwithstanding his failure to demonstrate that constitutional error infected his trial. In most circumstances, that question would answer itself in the negative. Our society has a high degree of confidence in its criminal trials, in no small part because the Constitution offers unparalleled protections against convicting the innocent. The question similarly would be answered in the negative today, except for the disturbing nature of the claim before us. Petitioner contends not only that the Constitution's protections "sometimes fail," but that their failure in his case will result in his execution—even though he is factually innocent and has evidence to prove it.

Exercising restraint, the Court and Justice WHITE assume for the sake of argument that, if a prisoner were to make an exceptionally strong showing of actual innocence, the execution could not go forward. Justice BLACKMUN, in contrast, would expressly so hold; he would also announce the precise burden of proof. . . . Resolving the issue is neither necessary nor advisable in this case. The question is a sensitive and, to say the least, troubling one. It implicates not just the life of a single individual, but also the State's powerful and legitimate interest in punishing the guilty, and the nature of state-federal relations. Indeed, as the Court persuasively demonstrates, throughout our history the federal courts have assumed that they should not and could not intervene to prevent an execution so long as the prisoner had been convicted after a constitutionally adequate trial. The prisoner's sole remedy was a pardon or clemency.

Nonetheless, the proper disposition of this case is neither difficult nor troubling. No matter what the Court might say about claims of actual innocence today, petitioner could not obtain relief. The record overwhelmingly demonstrates that petitioner deliberately shot and killed Officers Rucker and Carrisalez the night of September 29, 1981; petitioner's new evidence is bereft of credibility. Indeed, despite its stinging criticism of the Court's decision, not even the dissent expresses a belief that petitioner might possibly be actually innocent. Nor could it: The record makes it abundantly clear that petitioner is not somehow the future victim of "simple murder," but instead himself the established perpetrator of two brutal and tragic ones. . . .

*   *   *

Ultimately, two things about this case are clear. First is what the Court does *not* hold. Nowhere does the Court state that the Constitution permits the execution of an actually innocent person. Instead, the Court assumes for the sake of argument that a truly persuasive demonstration of actual innocence would render any such execution unconstitutional and that federal habeas relief would be warranted if no state avenue were open to process the claim. Second is what petitioner has not demonstrated. Petitioner has failed to make a persuasive showing of actual innocence. Not one judge—no state court judge, not the District Court Judge, none of the three judges of the Court of Appeals, and none of the Justices of this Court—has expressed doubt about petitioner's guilt. Accordingly, the Court has no reason to pass on, and appropriately reserves, the question whether federal courts may entertain convincing claims of actual innocence. That difficult question remains open. If the Constitution's guarantees of fair procedure and the safeguards of clemency and pardon fulfill their historical mission, it may never require resolution at all.

Justice SCALIA, with whom Justice THOMAS joins, concurring.

We granted certiorari on the question whether it violates due process or constitutes cruel and unusual punishment for a State to execute a person who, having been convicted of murder after a full and fair trial, later alleges that newly discovered evidence shows him to be "actually innocent." I would have preferred to decide that question, particularly since, as the Court's discussion shows, it is perfectly clear what the answer is: There is no basis in text, tradition, or even in contemporary practice (if that were enough) for finding in the Constitution a right to demand judicial consideration of newly discovered evidence of innocence brought forward after conviction. In saying that such a right exists, the dissenters apply nothing but their personal opinions to invalidate the rules of more than two-thirds of the States, and a Federal Rule of Criminal Procedure for which this Court itself is responsible. If the system that has been in place for two-hundred years (and remains widely approved) "shock[s]" the dissenters' consciences, perhaps they should doubt the calibration of their consciences, or, better still, the usefulness of "conscience shocking" as a legal test.

I nonetheless join the entirety of the Court's opinion, including the final portion, because there is no legal error in deciding a case by assuming, *arguendo*, that an asserted constitutional right exists, and because I can understand, or at least am accustomed to, the reluctance of the present Court to admit publicly that Our Perfect Constitution lets stand any injustice, much less the execution of an innocent man who has received, though to no avail, all the process that our society has traditionally deemed adequate.[2] With any luck, we shall avoid ever having to face this embarrassing question again, since it is improbable that evidence of innocence as convincing as today's opinion requires would fail to produce an executive pardon.

My concern is that in making life easier for ourselves we not appear to make it harder for the lower federal courts, imposing upon them the burden of regularly analyzing newly-discovered-evidence-of-innocence claims in capital cases (in which event such federal claims, it can confidently be predicted, will become routine and even repetitive). A number of Courts of Appeals have hitherto held, largely in reliance on our unelaborated statement in *Townsend v. Sain,* that newly discovered evidence relevant only to a state prisoner's guilt or innocence is not a basis for federal habeas corpus relief. I do not understand it to be the import of today's decision that those holdings are to be replaced with a strange regime that assumes permanently, though only *"arguendo,"* that a constitutional right exists, and expends substantial judicial resources on that assumption. The Court's extensive and scholarly discussion of the question presented in the present case does nothing but support our statement in *Townsend* and strengthen the validity of the holdings based upon it.

[Justice WHITE's concurring opinion is omitted.]

Justice BLACKMUN, with whom Justice STEVENS and Justice SOUTER join with respect to Parts I–IV, dissenting.

Nothing could be more contrary to contemporary standards of decency, or more shocking to the conscience, than to execute a person who is actually innocent.

I therefore must disagree with the long and general discussion that precedes the Court's disposition of this case. That discussion, of course, is dictum because the Court assumes, "for the sake of argument in deciding this case, that in a capital case a truly persuasive demonstration of 'actual innocence' made after trial would render the execution of a defendant unconstitutional." Without articulating the standard it is applying, however, the Court then decides that this petitioner has not made a sufficiently persuasive case. Because I believe that in the first instance the District Court should decide whether petitioner is entitled to a hearing and whether he is entitled to relief on the merits of his claim, I would reverse the order of the Court of Appeals and remand this case for further proceedings in the District Court.

I

The Court's enumeration of the constitutional rights of criminal defendants surely is entirely beside the point. These protections sometimes fail. We really are being asked to decide whether the Constitution forbids the execution of a person who has been validly convicted and sentenced but who, nonetheless, can prove his innocence with newly discovered evidence. Despite the State of Texas's astonishing protestation to the contrary, I do not see how the answer can be anything but "yes."

A

The Eighth Amendment prohibits "cruel and unusual punishments." This proscription is not static but rather reflects evolving standards of decency. I think it is crystal clear that the execution of an innocent person is "at odds with contemporary standards of fairness and decency." *Spaziano v. Florida*. Indeed, it is at odds with any standard of decency that I can imagine.

This Court has ruled that punishment is excessive and unconstitutional if it is "nothing more than the purposeless and needless imposition of pain and suffering," or if it is "grossly out of proportion to the severity of the crime." It has held that death is an excessive punishment for rape, and for mere participation in a robbery during which a killing takes place. If it is violative of the Eighth Amendment to execute someone who is guilty of those crimes, then it plainly is violative of the Eighth Amendment to execute a person who is actually innocent. Executing an innocent person epitomizes "the purposeless and needless imposition of pain and suffering."

The protection of the Eighth Amendment does not end once a defendant has been validly convicted and sentenced. . . .

The Court also suggests that allowing petitioner to raise his claim of innocence would not serve society's interest in the reliable imposition of the death penalty because it might require a new trial that would be less accurate than the first. *Ante*, p. 862. This suggestion misses the point entirely. The question is not whether a second trial would be more reliable than the first but whether, in light of new evidence, the result of the first trial is sufficiently reliable for the State to carry out a death sentence. Furthermore, it is far from clear that a State will seek to retry the rare prisoner who prevails on a claim of actual innocence. As explained in Part III, *infra*, I believe a prisoner must show not just that there was probably a reasonable doubt about his guilt but that he is probably actually innocent. I find it difficult to believe that any State would choose to retry a person who meets this standard.

I believe it contrary to any standard of decency to execute someone who is actually innocent. Because the Eighth Amendment applies to questions of guilt or innocence, and to persons upon whom a valid sentence of death has been imposed, I also believe that petitioner may raise an Eighth Amendment challenge to his punishment on the ground that he is actually innocent.

B

Execution of the innocent is equally offensive to the Due Process Clause of the Fourteenth Amendment. . . .

"The Due Process Clause of the Fifth Amendment provides that 'No person shall . . . be deprived of life, liberty, or property, without due process of law. . . .' [Editors' Note: The Fourteenth Amendment's Due Process Clause provides the same protection.] This Court has held that the Due Process Clause protects individuals against two types of government action. So-called 'substantive due process' prevents the government from engaging in conduct that 'shocks the conscience,' *Rochin v. California*, or interferes with rights 'implicit in the concept of ordered liberty.' *Palko v. Connecticut*. When government action depriving a person of life, liberty, or property survives substantive due process scrutiny, it must still be implemented in a fair manner. *Mathews v. Eldridge*. This requirement has traditionally been referred to as 'procedural' due process." *United States v. Salerno*. . . .

Just last Term, we had occasion to explain the role of substantive due process in our constitutional scheme. Quoting the second Justice Harlan, we said: "'[T]he full scope of the liberty guaranteed by the Due Process Clause cannot be found in or limited by the precise terms of the specific guarantees elsewhere provided in the Constitution. This "liberty" is not a series of isolated points. . . . It is a rational continuum which, broadly speaking, includes a freedom from all substantial arbitrary impositions and purposeless restraints. . . .'" *Planned Parenthood of Southeastern Pa. v. Casey* (1992).

Petitioner's claim falls within our due process precedents. In *Rochin*, deputy sheriffs investigating narcotics sales broke into Rochin's room and observed him put two capsules in his mouth. The deputies attempted to remove the capsules from his mouth and, having failed, took Rochin to a hospital and had his stomach pumped. The capsules were found to contain morphine. The Court held that the deputies' conduct "shock[ed] the conscience" and violated due process. "Illegally breaking into the privacy of the petitioner, the struggle to open his mouth and remove what was there, the forcible extraction of his stomach's contents—this course of proceeding by agents of government to obtain evidence is bound to offend even hardened sensibilities. They are methods too close to the rack and the screw to permit of constitutional differentiation." The lethal injection that petitioner faces as an allegedly innocent person is certainly closer to the rack and the screw than the stomach pump condemned in *Rochin*. Execution of an innocent person is the ultimate "'arbitrary impositio[n].'" It is an imposition from which one never recovers and for which one can never be compensated. Thus, I also believe that petitioner may raise a substantive due process challenge to his punishment on the ground that he is actually innocent.

C

Given my conclusion that it violates the Eighth and Fourteenth Amendments to execute a person who is actually innocent, I find no bar in *Townsend v. Sain*, to consideration of an actual-innocence claim. Newly discovered evidence of petitioner's innocence does bear on the constitutionality of his execution. Of course, it could be argued this is in some tension with *Townsend* 's statement that "the existence merely of newly discovered evidence relevant to the guilt of a state prisoner is not a ground for relief on federal habeas corpus." That statement, however, is no more than distant dictum here, for we never had been asked to consider whether the execution of an innocent person violates the Constitution.

II

The majority's discussion of petitioner's constitutional claims is even more perverse when viewed in the light of this Court's recent habeas jurisprudence. Beginning with a trio of decisions in 1986, this Court shifted the focus of federal habeas review of successive, abusive, or defaulted claims away from the preservation of constitutional rights to a fact-based inquiry into the habeas petitioner's guilt or innocence. The Court sought to strike a balance between the State's interest in the finality of its criminal judgments and the prisoner's interest in access to a forum to test the basic justice of his sentence. In striking this balance, the Court adopted the view of Judge Friendly that there should be an exception to the concept of finality when a prisoner can make a colorable claim of actual innocence. Friendly, "Is Innocence Irrelevant? Collateral Attack on Criminal Judgments," *University of Chicago Law Review* 38 (1970): 142, 160.

Justice Powell, writing for the plurality in *Wilson*, explained the reason for focusing on innocence:

> The prisoner may have a vital interest in having a second chance to test the fundamental justice of his incarceration. Even where, as here, the many judges who have reviewed the prisoner's claims in several proceedings provided by the State and on his first petition for federal habeas corpus have determined that his trial was free from constitutional error, a prisoner retains a powerful and legitimate interest in obtaining his release from custody if he is innocent of the charge for which he was incarcerated. That interest does not extend, however, to prisoners whose guilt is conceded or plain.

In other words, even a prisoner who appears to have had a *constitutionally perfect* trial "retains a powerful and legitimate interest in obtaining his release from custody if he is innocent of the charge for which he was incarcerated." It is obvious that this reasoning extends beyond the context of successive, abusive, or defaulted claims to substantive claims of actual innocence. Indeed, Judge Friendly recognized that substantive claims of actual innocence should be cognizable on federal habeas.

Having adopted an "actual-innocence" requirement for review of abusive, successive, or defaulted claims, however, the majority would now take the position that "a claim of 'actual innocence' is not itself a constitutional claim, but instead a gateway through which a habeas petitioner must pass to have his otherwise barred constitutional claim considered on the merits." In other words, having held that a prisoner who is incarcerated in violation of the Constitution must show he is actually innocent to obtain relief, the majority would now hold that a prisoner who is actually innocent must show a constitutional violation to obtain relief. The only principle that would appear to reconcile these two positions is the principle that habeas relief should be denied whenever possible.

III

The Eighth and Fourteenth Amendments, of course, are binding on the States, and one would normally expect the States to adopt procedures to consider claims of actual innocence based on newly discovered evidence. The majority's disposition of this case, however, leaves the States uncertain of their constitutional obligations.

A

Whatever procedures a State might adopt to hear actual-innocence claims, one thing is certain: The possibility of executive clemency is *not* sufficient to satisfy the requirements of the Eighth and Fourteenth Amendments. The majority correctly points out: "'A pardon is an act of grace.'" The vindication of rights guaranteed by the

Constitution has never been made to turn on the unreviewable discretion of an executive official or administrative tribunal. . . .

"The government of the United States has been emphatically termed a government of laws, and not of men. It will certainly cease to deserve this high appellation, if the laws furnish no remedy for the violation of a vested legal right." *Marbury v. Madison* (1803). If the exercise of a legal right turns on "an act of grace," then we no longer live under a government of laws. "The very purpose of a Bill of Rights was to withdraw certain subjects from the vicissitudes of political controversy, to place them beyond the reach of majorities and officials and to establish them as legal principles to be applied by the courts." *West Virginia Bd. of Ed. v. Barnette* (1943). It is understandable, therefore, that the majority does not say that the vindication of petitioner's constitutional rights may be left to executive clemency. . . .

C

The question that remains is what showing should be required to obtain relief on the merits of an Eighth or Fourteenth Amendment claim of actual innocence. I agree with the majority that "in state criminal proceedings the trial is the paramount event for determining the guilt or innocence of the defendant." I also think that "a truly persuasive demonstration of 'actual innocence' made after trial would render the execution of a defendant unconstitutional." The question is what "a truly persuasive demonstration" entails, a question the majority's disposition of this case leaves open.

In articulating the "actual-innocence" exception in our habeas jurisprudence, this Court has adopted a standard requiring the petitioner to show a "'fair probability that, in light of all the evidence . . . , the trier of the facts would have entertained a reasonable doubt of his guilt.'" In other words, the habeas petitioner must show that there probably would be a reasonable doubt.

I think the standard for relief on the merits of an actual-innocence claim must be higher than the threshold standard for merely reaching that claim or any other claim that has been procedurally defaulted or is successive or abusive. I would hold that, to obtain relief on a claim of actual innocence, the petitioner must show that he probably is innocent. . . .

IV

In this case, the District Court determined that petitioner's newly discovered evidence warranted further consideration. Because the District Court doubted its own authority to consider the new evidence, it thought that petitioner's claim of actual innocence should be brought in state court, but it clearly did not think that petitioner's evidence was so insubstantial that it could be dismissed without any hearing at all. I would reverse the order of the Court of Appeals and remand the case to the District Court to consider whether petitioner has shown, in light of all the evidence, that he is probably actually innocent.

I think it is unwise for this Court to step into the shoes of a district court and rule on this petition in the first instance. If this Court wishes to act as a district court, however, it must also be bound by the rules that govern consideration of habeas petitions in district court. A district court may summarily dismiss a habeas petition only if "it plainly appears from the face of the petition and any exhibits annexed to it that the petitioner is not entitled to relief." 28 U.S.C. § 2254 Rule 4. In one of the affidavits, Hector Villarreal, a licensed attorney and former state court judge, swears under penalty of perjury that his client Raul Herrera Sr. confessed that he, and not petitioner, committed the murders. No matter what the majority may think of the inconsistencies in the affidavits or the strength of the evidence presented at trial, this affidavit alone is sufficient to raise factual questions concerning petitioner's innocence that cannot be resolved simply by examining the affidavits and the petition.

I do not understand why the majority so severely faults petitioner for relying only on affidavits. It is common to rely on affidavits at the preliminary-consideration stage of a habeas proceeding. The opportunity for cross-examination and credibility determinations comes at the hearing, assuming that the petitioner is entitled to one. It makes no sense for this Court to impugn the reliability of petitioner's evidence on the ground that its credibility has not been tested when the reason its credibility has not been tested is that petitioner's habeas proceeding has been truncated by the Court of Appeals and now by this Court. In its haste to deny petitioner relief, the majority seems to confuse the question whether the petition may be dismissed summarily with the question whether petitioner is entitled to relief on the merits of his claim.

V

I have voiced disappointment over this Court's obvious eagerness to do away with any restriction on the States' power to execute whomever and however they please. I have also expressed doubts about whether, in the absence of such restrictions, capital punishment remains constitutional at all. Of one thing, however, I am certain. Just as an execution without adequate safeguards is unacceptable, so too is an execution when the condemned prisoner can prove that he is innocent. The execution of a person who can show that he is innocent comes perilously close to simple murder.

NOTES

1. The letter read: "To whom it may concern: I am terribly sorry for those I have brought grief to their lives. Who knows why? We cannot change the future's problems with problems from the past. What I did was for a cause and purpose. One law runs others, and in the world we live in, that's the way it is.

"I'm not a tormented person. . . . I believe in the law. What would it be without this [sic] men that risk their lives for others, and that's what they should be doing—protecting life, property, and the pursuit of happiness. Sometimes, the law gets too involved with other things that profit them. The most laws that they make for people to break them, in other words, to encourage crime.

"What happened to Rucker was for a certain reason. I knew him as Mike Tatum. He was in my business, and he violated some of its laws and suffered the penalty, like the one you have for me when the time comes.

"My personal life, which has been a conspiracy since my high school days, has nothing to do with what has happened. The other officer that became part of our lives, me and Rucker's (Tatum), that night had not to do in this [sic]. He was out to do what he had to do, protect, but that's life. There's a lot of us that wear different faces in lives every day, and that is what causes problems for all. [Unintelligible word].

"You have wrote all you want of my life, but think about yours, also. [Signed Leonel Herrera].

"I have tapes and pictures to prove what I have said. I will prove my side if you accept to listen. You [unintelligible word] freedom of speech, even a criminal has that right. I will present myself if this is read word for word over the media, I will turn myself in; if not, don't have millions of men out there working just on me while others—robbers, rapists, or burglars—are taking advantage of the law's time. Excuse my spelling and writing. It's hard at times like this." App. to Brief for United States as Amicus Curiae 3a–4a.

2. My reference is to an article by Professor Monaghan, which discusses the unhappy truth that not every problem was meant to be solved by the United States Constitution, nor can be. See Monaghan, "Our Perfect Constitution," *New York University Law Review* 56 (1981): 353.

SUPREME COURT OF THE UNITED STATES

KANSAS,

PETITIONER,

V.

MICHAEL LEE MARSH, II

T HOMAS, J., delivered the opinion of the Court, in which ROBERTS, C.J., and SCALIA, KENNEDY, and ALITO, JJ., joined. SCALIA, J., filed a concurring opinion. STEVENS, J., filed a dissenting opinion. SOUTER, J., filed a dissenting opinion, in which STEVENS, GINSBURG, and BREYER, JJ., joined.

Justice THOMAS delivered the opinion of the Court.

Kansas law provides that if a unanimous jury finds that aggravating circumstances are not outweighed by mitigating circumstances, the death penalty shall be imposed. We must decide whether this statute, which requires the imposition of the death penalty when the sentencing jury determines that aggravating evidence and mitigating evidence are in equipoise, violates the Constitution. We hold that it does not.

---

126 S. Ct. 2516, no. 04-1170. Argued April 25, 2006. Decided June 26, 2006.

I

Respondent Michael Lee Marsh II broke into the home of Marry Ane Pusch and lay in wait for her to return. When Marry Ane entered her home with her nineteen-month-old daughter, M. P., Marsh repeatedly shot Marry Ane, stabbed her, and slashed her throat. The home was set on fire with the toddler inside, and M. P. burned to death.

The jury convicted Marsh of the capital murder of M. P., the first-degree premeditated murder of Marry Ane, aggravated arson, and aggravated burglary. The jury found beyond a reasonable doubt the existence of three aggravating circumstances, and that those circumstances were not outweighed by any mitigating circumstances. On the basis of those findings, the jury sentenced Marsh to death for the capital murder of M. P. The jury also sentenced Marsh to life imprisonment without possibility of parole for forty years for the first-degree murder of Marry Ane, and consecutive sentences of fifty-one months' imprisonment for aggravated arson and thirty-four months' imprisonment for aggravated burglary.

On direct appeal, Marsh challenged § 21-4624(e), which reads:

> If, by unanimous vote, the jury finds beyond a reasonable doubt that one or more of the aggravating circumstances enumerated in [the statute] . . . exist and, further, that the existence of such aggravating circumstances is not outweighed by any mitigating circumstances which are found to exist, the defendant shall be sentenced to death; otherwise the defendant shall be sentenced as provided by law.

Focusing on the phrase "shall be sentenced to death," Marsh argued that § 21-4624(e) establishes an unconstitutional presumption in favor of death because it directs imposition of the death penalty when aggravating and mitigating circumstances are in equipoise.

The Kansas Supreme Court agreed, and held that the Kansas death penalty statute, § 21-4624(e), is facially unconstitutional. The court concluded that the statute's weighing equation violated the Eighth and Fourteenth Amendments of the United States Constitution because, "[i]n the event of equipoise, i.e., the jury's determination that the balance of any aggravating circumstances and any mitigating circumstances weighed equal, the death penalty would be required." ... We granted certiorari, and now reverse the Kansas Supreme Court's judgment that Kansas's capital sentencing statute is facially unconstitutional. ...

III

This case is controlled by *Walton v. Arizona* (1990). ... In that case, a jury had convicted Walton of a capital offense. At sentencing, the trial judge found the existence of two aggravating circumstances and that the mitigating circumstances did not call for leniency, and sentenced Walton to death. ...

Walton argued to this Court that the Arizona capital sentencing system created an unconstitutional presumption in favor of death because it "tells an Arizona sentencing judge who finds even a single aggravating factor, that death must be imposed, unless—as the Arizona Supreme Court put it in Petitioner's case—there are 'outweighing mitigating factors.'" Rejecting Walton's argument, this Court stated:

> So long as a State's method of allocating the burdens of proof does not lessen the State's burden to prove every element of the offense charged, or in this case to prove the existence of aggravating circumstances, a defendant's constitutional rights are not violated by placing on him the burden of proving mitigating circumstances sufficiently substantial to call for leniency.

This Court noted that, as a requirement of individualized sentencing, a jury must have the opportunity to consider all evidence relevant to mitigation, and that a state statute that permits a jury to consider any mitigating evidence comports with that requirement. The Court also pointedly observed that while the Constitution requires that a sentencing jury have discretion, it does not mandate that discretion be unfettered; the States are free to determine the manner in which a jury may consider mitigating evidence. So long as the sentencer is not precluded from considering relevant mitigating evidence, a capital sentencing statute cannot be said to impermissibly, much less automatically, impose death. Indeed, *Walton* suggested that the only capital sentencing systems that would be impermissibly mandatory were those that would "automatically impose death upon conviction for certain types of murder."

Contrary to Marsh's contentions and the Kansas Supreme Court's conclusions, the question presented in the instant case was squarely before this Court in *Walton*. Though, as Marsh notes, the *Walton* Court did not employ the term "equipoise," that issue undeniably gave rise to the question this Court sought to resolve, and it was necessarily included in Walton's argument that the Arizona system was unconstitutional because it required the death penalty unless the mitigating circumstances *outweighed* the aggravating circumstances. Moreover, the dissent in *Walton* reinforces what is evident from the opinion and the judgment of the Court— that the equipoise issue was before the Court, and that the Court resolved the issue in favor of the State. Indeed, the "equipoise" issue was, in large measure, the basis of the *Walton* dissent. See opinion of BLACKMUN ("If the mitigating and aggravating circumstances are in equipoise, the [Arizona] statute requires that the trial judge impose capital punishment. The assertion that a sentence of death may be imposed in such a case runs directly counter to the Eighth Amendment requirement that a capital sentence must rest upon a 'determination that death is the appropriate punishment in a specific case.'") Thus, although *Walton* did not discuss the equipoise issue explicitly, that issue was resolved by its holding. . . .

Accordingly, the reasoning of *Walton* requires approval of the Kansas death penalty statute. At bottom, in *Walton*, the Court held that a state death penalty statute may place the burden on the defendant to prove that mitigating circumstances outweigh aggravating circumstances. "A fortiori," Kansas's death penalty statute, consistent with the Constitution, may direct imposition of the death penalty when the State has proved beyond a reasonable doubt that mitigators do not outweigh aggravators, including where the aggravating circumstances and mitigating circumstances are in equipoise.

IV

A

Even if, as Marsh contends, *Walton* does not directly control, the general principles set forth in our death penalty jurisprudence would lead us to conclude that the Kansas capital sentencing system is constitutionally permissible. Together, our decisions in *Furman v. Georgia* (1972) (per curiam), and *Gregg v. Georgia* (joint opinion of Stewart, Powell, and STEVENS), establish that a state capital sentencing system must: (1) rationally narrow the class of death-eligible defendants; and (2) permit a jury to render a reasoned, individualized sentencing determination based on a death-eligible defendant's record, personal characteristics, and the circumstances of his crime. So long as a state system satisfies these requirements, our precedents establish that a State enjoys a range of discretion in imposing the death penalty, including the manner in which aggravating and mitigating circumstances are to be weighed.

The use of mitigation evidence is a product of the requirement of individualized sentencing. In *Lockett v. Ohio*, a plurality of this Court held that "the Eighth and Fourteenth Amendments require that the sentencer . . . not be precluded from considering, *as a mitigating factor*, any aspect of a defendant's character or record and any of the circumstances of the offense that the defendant proffers as a basis for a sentence less than death" (emphasis in original). . . .

In aggregate, our precedents confer upon defendants the right to present sentencers with information relevant to the sentencing decision and oblige sentencers to consider that information in determining the appropriate sentence. The thrust of our mitigation jurisprudence ends here. "[W]e have never held that a specific method for balancing mitigating and aggravating factors in a capital sentencing proceeding is constitutionally required." Rather, this Court has held that the States enjoy "'a constitutionally permissible range of discretion in imposing the death penalty.'"

B

The Kansas death penalty statute satisfies the constitutional mandates of *Furman* and its progeny because it rationally narrows the class of death-eligible defendants and permits a jury to consider any mitigating evidence relevant to its sentencing determination. It does not interfere, in a constitutionally significant way, with a jury's ability to give independent weight to evidence offered in mitigation.

Kansas's procedure narrows the universe of death-eligible defendants consistent with Eighth Amendment requirements. Under Kansas law, imposition of the death penalty is an *option* only after a defendant is convicted of capital murder, which requires that one or more specific elements beyond intentional premeditated murder be found. Once convicted of capital murder, a defendant becomes *eligible* for the death penalty only if the State seeks a separate sentencing hearing, and proves beyond a reasonable doubt the existence of one or more statutorily enumerated aggravating circumstances.

Consonant with the individualized sentencing requirement, a Kansas jury is permitted to consider *any* evidence relating to *any* mitigating circumstance in determining the appropriate sentence for a capital defendant, so long as that evidence is relevant. Specifically, jurors are instructed:

> A mitigating circumstance is that which in fairness or mercy may be considered as extenuating or reducing the degree of moral culpability or blame or which justify a sentence of less than death, although it does not justify or excuse the offense. The determination of what are mitigating circumstances is for you as jurors to resolve under the facts and circumstances of this case.
>
> The appropriateness of the exercise of mercy can itself be a mitigating factor you may consider in determining whether the State has proved beyond a reasonable doubt that the death penalty is warranted. § 21-4624 (c).

Jurors are then apprised of, but not limited to, the factors that the defendant contends are mitigating. They are then instructed that "[e]ach juror must consider every mitigating factor that he or she individually finds to exist."

Kansas's weighing equation merely channels a jury's discretion by providing it with criteria by which it may determine whether a sentence of life or death is appropriate. The system in Kansas provides the type of "'guided discretion,'" we have [previously] sanctioned. . . . Contrary to Marsh's argument, § 21-4624(e) does not create a general presumption in favor of the death penalty in the State of Kansas. Rather, the Kansas capital sentencing system is dominated by the presumption that life imprisonment is the appropriate sentence for a capital conviction. If the State fails to meet its burden to demonstrate the existence of an aggravating circumstance(s) beyond a reasonable doubt, a sentence of life imprisonment must be imposed. If the State overcomes this hurdle, then it bears the additional burden of proving beyond a reasonable doubt that aggravating circumstances are not outweighed by mitigating circumstances. Significantly, although the defendant appropriately bears the burden of proffering mitigating circumstances—a burden of production—he never bears the burden of demonstrating that mitigating circumstances outweigh aggravating circumstances. Instead, the State always has the burden of demonstrating that mitigating evidence does not outweigh aggravating evidence. Absent the State's ability to meet that burden, the default is life imprisonment. Moreover, if the jury is unable to reach a unanimous decision—in any respect—a sentence of life must be imposed. This system does not create a presumption that death is the appropriate sentence for capital murder.

Nor is there any force behind Marsh's contention that an equipoise determination reflects juror confusion or inability to decide between life and death, or that a jury may use equipoise as a loophole to shirk its constitutional duty to render a reasoned, moral decision, regarding whether death is an appropriate sentence for a particular defendant. Such an argument rests on an implausible characterization of the Kansas statute—that a jury's determination that aggravators and mitigators are in equipoise is not a *decision*, much less a decision *for death*—and thus misses the mark. Weighing is not an end; it is merely a means to reaching a decision. The decision the jury must reach is whether life or death is the appropriate punishment. The Kansas jury instructions clearly inform the jury that a determination that the evidence is in equipoise is a decision for—not a presumption in favor of—death. Kansas jurors, presumed to follow their instructions, are made aware that: a determination that mitigators outweigh aggravators is a decision that a life sentence is appropriate; a determination that aggravators outweigh mitigators *or* a determination that mitigators do not outweigh aggravators—including a finding that aggravators and mitigators are in balance—is a decision that death is the appropriate sentence; and an inability to reach a unanimous decision will result in a sentence of life imprisonment. So informed, far from the abdication of duty or the inability to select an appropriate sentence depicted by Marsh and Justice SOUTER, a jury's conclusion that aggravating evidence and mitigating evidence are in equipoise is a *decision for death* and is indicative of the type of measured, normative process in which a jury is constitutionally tasked to engage when deciding the appropriate sentence for a capital defendant.

V

Justice SOUTER argues (hereinafter the dissent) that the advent of DNA testing has resulted in the "exoneratio[n]" of "innocent" persons "in numbers never imagined before the development of DNA tests." Based upon this "new empirical demonstration of how 'death is different,'" the dissent concludes that Kansas's sentencing system permits the imposition of the death penalty in the absence of reasoned moral judgment.

But the availability of DNA testing, and the questions it might raise about the accuracy of guilt-phase determinations in capital cases, is simply irrelevant to the question before the Court today, namely, the constitutionality of Kansas's capital *sentencing* system. Accordingly, the accuracy of the dissent's factual claim that DNA testing has established the "innocence" of numerous convicted persons under death sentences—and the incendiary debate it invokes—is beyond the scope of this opinion.

The dissent's general criticisms against the death penalty are ultimately a call for resolving all legal disputes in capital cases by adopting the outcome that makes the death penalty more difficult to impose. While such a bright-line rule may be easily applied, it has no basis in law. Indeed, the logical consequence of the dissent's argument is that the death penalty can only be just in a system that does not permit error. Because the criminal justice system does not operate perfectly, abolition of the death penalty is the only answer to the moral dilemma the dissent poses. This Court, however, does not sit as a moral authority. Our precedents do not prohibit the States from authorizing the death penalty, even in our imperfect system. And those precedents do not empower this Court to chip away at the States' prerogatives to do so on the grounds the dissent invokes today.

*   *   *

We hold that the Kansas capital sentencing system, which directs imposition of the death penalty when a jury finds that aggravating and mitigating circumstances are in equipoise, is constitutional. Accordingly, we reverse the judgment of the Kansas Supreme Court, and remand the case for further proceedings not inconsistent with this opinion.

It is so ordered.

Justice SCALIA, concurring.

I join the opinion of the Court. I write separately to . . . respond at somewhat greater length first to . . . Justice SOUTER's claims about risks inherent in capital punishment.

*   *   *

III

. . . I must say a few words (indeed, more than a few) in response to Part III of Justice SOUTER's dissent. This contains the disclaimer that the dissenters are not (*yet*) ready to "generaliz[e] about the soundness of capital sentencing across the country," but that is in fact precisely what they do. The dissent essentially argues that capital punishment is such an undesirable institution—it results in the condemnation of such a large number of innocents—that any legal rule which eliminates its pronouncement, including the one favored by the dissenters in the present case, should be embraced.

As a general rule, I do not think it appropriate for judges to heap either praise or censure upon a legislative measure that comes before them, lest it be thought that their validation, invalidation, or interpretation of it is driven by their desire to expand or constrict what they personally approve or disapprove as a matter of policy. In the present case, for example, people might leap to the conclusion that the dissenters' views on whether Kansas's equipoise rule is constitutional are determined by their personal disapproval of an institution that has been democratically adopted by thirty-eight States and the United States. But of course that requires no leap; just a willingness to take the dissenters at their word. For as I have described, the dissenters' very argument is that imposition of the death penalty should be minimized by invalidation of the equipoise rule because it is a bad, "risk[y]," and "hazard[ous]" idea. A broader conclusion that people should derive, however (and I would not consider this much of a leap either), is that the dissenters' encumbering of the death penalty in *other* cases, with unwarranted restrictions neither contained in the text of the Constitution nor reflected in two centuries of practice under it, will be the product of their policy views—views not shared by the vast majority of the American people. The dissenters' proclamation of their policy agenda in the present case is especially striking because it is nailed to the door of the wrong church—that is, set forth in a case litigating a rule that has nothing to do with the evaluation of guilt or innocence. There are, of course, many cases in which the rule at issue *does* serve that function. But as the Court observes, see ibid., . . . guilt or innocence is logically disconnected to the challenge in *this* case to *sentencing* standards. The *only* time the equipoise provision is relevant is when the State has proved a defendant guilty of a capital crime.

There exists in some parts of the world sanctimonious criticism of America's death penalty, as somehow unworthy of a civilized society. (I say sanctimonious, because most of the countries to which these finger-waggers belong had the death penalty themselves until recently—and indeed, many of them would still have it if the democratic will prevailed.) It is a certainty that the opinion of a near-majority of the United States Supreme Court to the effect that our system condemns many innocent defendants to death will be trumpeted abroad as vindication of these criticisms. For that reason, I take the trouble to point out that the dissenting opinion has nothing substantial to support it.

It should be noted at the outset that the dissent does not discuss a single case—not one—in which it is clear that a person was executed for a crime he did not commit. If such an event had occurred in recent years, we would not have to hunt for it; the innocent's name would be shouted from the rooftops by the abolition lobby. The dissent makes much of the newfound capacity of DNA testing to establish innocence. But in every case of an executed defendant of which I am aware, that technology has *confirmed* guilt.

This happened, for instance, only a few months ago in the case of Roger Coleman. Coleman was convicted of the gruesome rape and murder of his sister-in-law, but he persuaded many that he was actually innocent and became the poster child for the abolitionist lobby. Around the time of his eventual execution, "his picture was on the cover of *Time* magazine ('This Man Might Be Innocent. This Man Is Due to Die'). He was interviewed from death row on *Larry King Live*, the *Today* show, *Primetime Live*, *Good Morning America* and *The Phil Donahue Show*." . . . Coleman ultimately failed a lie-detector test offered by the Governor of Virginia as a condition of a possible stay; he was executed on May 20, 1992.

In the years since then, Coleman's case became a rallying point for abolitionists, who hoped it would offer what they consider the "Holy Grail: proof from a test tube that an innocent person had been executed." But earlier this year, a DNA test ordered by a later Governor of Virginia proved that Coleman was guilty, even though his defense team had "proved" his innocence and had even identified "the real killer" (with whom they eventually settled a defamation suit). And Coleman's case is not unique. See Truth and Consequences: *The Penalty of Death, in Debating the Death*

Penalty: Should America Have Capital Punishment? The Experts on Both Sides Make Their Best Case, eds. H. Bedau and P. Cassell (New York: Oxford University Press, 2004), pp. 128–129 (discussing the cases of supposed innocents Rick McGinn and Derek Barnabei, whose guilt was also confirmed by DNA tests).

Instead of identifying and discussing any particular case or cases of mistaken execution, the dissent simply cites a handful of studies that bemoan the alleged prevalence of wrongful death sentences. One study (by Lanier and Acker) is quoted by the dissent as claiming that "'more than 110' death row prisoners have been released since 1973 upon findings that they were innocent of the crimes charged, and 'hundreds of additional wrongful convictions in potentially capital cases have been documented over the past century.'" For the first point, Lanier and Acker cite the work of the Death Penalty Information Center (more about that below) and an article in a law review jointly authored by Radelet, Lofquist, and Bedau (two professors of sociology and a professor of philosophy). For the second point, they cite only a 1987 article by Bedau and Radelet. See "Miscarriages of Justice in Potentially Capital Cases," *Stanford Law Review* 40: 21. In the very same paragraph which the dissent quotes, Lanier and Acker also refer to that 1987 article as "hav[ing] identified 23 individuals who, in their judgment, were convicted and executed in this country during the 20th century notwithstanding their innocence." Lanier and Acker, "Capital Punishment, the Moratorium Movement, and Empirical Questions," *Psychology, Public Policy & Law* 10 (2004): 593. This 1987 article has been highly influential in the abolitionist world. Hundreds of academic articles, including those relied on by today's dissent, have cited it. It also makes its appearance in judicial decisions—cited recently in a six-judge dissent in *House v. Bell* (C.A.6 2004) (en banc) (Merritt, J., dissenting), for the proposition that "the system is allowing some innocent defendants to be executed." The article therefore warrants some further observations.

The 1987 article's obsolescence began at the moment of publication. The most recent executions it considered were in 1984, 1964, and 1951; the rest predate the Allied victory in World War II. (Two of the supposed innocents are Sacco and Vanzetti.) (Bedau and Radelet, p. 73.) Even if the innocence claims made in this study were true, all except (perhaps) the 1984 example would cast no light upon the functioning of our current system of capital adjudication. The legal community's general attitude toward criminal defendants, the legal protections States afford, the constitutional guarantees this Court enforces, and the scope of federal habeas review, are all vastly different from what they were in 1961. So are the scientific means of establishing guilt, and hence innocence— which are now so striking in their operation and effect that they are the subject of more than one popular TV series. (One of these new means, of course, is DNA testing—which the dissent seems to think is primarily a way to identify defendants erroneously convicted, rather than a highly effective way to avoid conviction of the innocent.)

But their current relevance aside, this study's conclusions are unverified. And if the support for its most significant conclusion— the execution of 23 innocents in the twentieth century—is any indication of its accuracy, neither it, nor any study so careless as to rely upon it, is worthy of credence. The only execution of an innocent man it alleges to have occurred after the restoration of the death penalty in 1976—the Florida execution of James Adams in 1984— is the easiest case to verify. As evidence of Adams's innocence, it describes a hair that could not have been his as being "clutched in the victim's hand," (Bedau and Radelet, p. 91.) The hair was *not* in the victim's hand; "[i]t was a remnant of a sweeping of the ambulance and so could have come from another source." (Markman and Cassell, "Protecting the Innocent: A Response to the Bedau-Radelet Study," *Stanford Law Review* 41 [1988]: 131.) The study also claims that a witness who "heard a voice inside the victim's home at the time of the crime" testified that the "voice was a woman's" (Bedau and Radelet, p. 91). The witness's actual testimony was that the voice, which said """'In the name of God, don't do it'""" (and was hence unlikely to have been the voice of anyone but the male victim), "'sounded "kind of like a woman's voice, kind of like strangling or something . . .'" (Markman and Cassell, "Protecting the Innocent," p. 130). Bedau and Radelet failed to mention that upon arrest on the afternoon of the murder Adams was found with some $200 in his pocket—one bill of which "was stained with type O blood. When Adams was asked about the blood on the money, he said that it came from a cut on his finger. His blood was type AB, however, while the victim's was type O." (Ibid., p. 132.) Among the other unmentioned, incriminating details: that the victim's *eyeglasses* were found in Adams's car, along with jewelry belonging to the victim, and clothing of Adams's stained with type O blood. (Ibid.) This is just a sample of the evidence arrayed against this "innocent." (See ibid., pp. 128–133, 148–150.)

Critics have questioned the study's findings with regard to all its other cases of execution of alleged innocents for which "appellate opinions . . . set forth the facts proved at trial in detail sufficient to permit a neutral observer to assess the validity of the authors' conclusions." (Ibid., p. 134.) (For the rest, there was not "a reasonably complete account of the facts . . . readily available," ibid., p. 145.) As to those cases, the only readily verifiable ones, the authors of the 1987 study later acknowledged, "We agree with our critics that we have not 'proved' these executed defendants to be innocent; we never claimed that we had." (Bedau and Radelet, "The Myth of Infallibility: A Reply to Markman and Cassell," *Stanford Law Review* 41 [1988]: 164.) One would have hoped that this disclaimer of the study's most striking conclusion, if not the study's dubious methodology, would have prevented it from being cited as authority in the pages of the United States Reports. But alas, it is too late for that. Although today's dissent relies on the study only indirectly, the two dissenters who were on the Court in January 1993 have already embraced it. "One impressive study," they noted (referring to the 1987 study), "has concluded that 23 innocent people have been executed in the United States in this century, including one as recently as 1984." *Herrera v. Collins*, 506 US 390, 430, n. 1, 113 S.Ct. 853, 122 L.Ed.2d 203 (1993) (Blackmun, J., joined by Stevens and Souter, JJ., dissenting).

Remarkably avoiding any claim of erroneous executions, the dissent focuses on the large numbers of *non*-executed "exonerees" paraded by various professors. It speaks as though exoneration came about through the operation of some outside force to correct the mistakes of our legal system, rather than *as a consequence of the functioning of our legal system*. Reversal of an erroneous conviction on appeal or on habeas, or the pardoning of an innocent condemnee through executive clemency, demonstrates not the failure of the system but its success. Those devices are part and parcel of the multiple assurances that are applied before a death sentence is carried out.

Of course even in identifying exonerees, the dissent is willing to accept anybody's say-so. It engages in no critical review, but merely parrots articles or reports that support its attack on the American criminal justice system. The dissent places significant weight, for instance, on the Illinois Report (compiled by the appointees of an Illinois Governor who had declared a moratorium upon the death penalty and who eventually commuted all death sentences in the State [see Warden, "Illinois Death Penalty Reform: How It Happened, What It Promises," *Journal of Criminal Law & Criminology* 95 (2006): 406–407, 410]), which it claims shows that "false verdicts" are "remarkable in number." The dissent claims that this Report identifies 13 inmates released from death row after they were determined to be innocent. To take one of these cases, discussed by the dissent as an example of a judgment "as close to innocence as any judgments courts normally render": in *People v. Smith* (1999) the defendant was twice convicted of murder. After his first trial, the Supreme Court of Illinois "reversed [his] conviction based upon certain evidentiary errors" and remanded his case for a new trial. The second jury convicted Smith again. The Supreme Court of Illinois again reversed the conviction because it found that the evidence was insufficient to establish guilt beyond a reasonable doubt. The court explained: "While a not guilty finding is sometimes equated with a finding of innocence, that conclusion is erroneous. Courts do not find people guilty or innocent. . . . A not guilty verdict expresses no view as to a defendant's innocence. Rather, [a reversal of conviction] indicates simply that the prosecution has failed to meet its burden of proof."

This case alone suffices to refute the dissent's claim that the Illinois Report distinguishes between "exoneration of a convict because of actual innocence, and reversal of a judgment because of legal error affecting conviction or sentence but not inconsistent with guilt in fact." The broader point, however, is that it is utterly impossible to regard "exoneration"—however casually defined—as a failure of the capital justice system, rather than as a vindication of its effectiveness in releasing not only defendants who are innocent, but those whose guilt has not been established beyond a reasonable doubt.

Another of the dissent's leading authorities on exoneration of the innocent is Gross, Jacoby, Matheson, Montgomery, and Patil, "Exonerations in the United States 1989 through 2003," *Journal of Criminal Law & Criminology* 95 (2006): 523 (hereinafter Gross). The dissent quotes that study's self-congratulatory "criteria" of exoneration— seemingly so rigorous that no one could doubt the study's reliability. But in fact that article, like the others cited, is notable not for its rigorous investigation and analysis, but for the fervor of its belief that the American justice system is condemning the innocent "in numbers," as the dissent puts it, "never imagined before the development of DNA tests." Among the article's list of 74 "exonerees" (Gross, p. 529), is Jay Smith of Pennsylvania. Smith—a school principal— earned three death sentences for slaying one of his teachers and her two young children. His retrial for triple murder was barred on double jeopardy grounds because of prosecutorial misconduct during the first trial. But Smith could not leave well enough alone. He had the gall to sue . . . for false imprisonment. The Court of Appeals for the Third Circuit affirmed the jury verdict for the defendants, observing along the way that "our confidence in Smith's convictions is not diminished in the least. We remain firmly convinced of the integrity of those guilty verdicts." . . .

Of course, even with its distorted concept of what constitutes "exoneration," the claims of the Gross article are fairly modest: between 1989 and 2003, the authors identify 340 "exonerations" *nationwide*—not just for capital cases, mind you, nor even just for murder convictions, but for various felonies (Gross, p. 529). Joshua Marquis, a district attorney in Oregon, recently responded to this article as follows:

> [L]et's give the professor the benefit of the doubt: let's assume that he understated the number of innocents by roughly a factor of 10, that instead of 340 there were 4,000 people in prison who weren't involved in the crime in any way. During that same 15 years, there were more than 15 million felony convictions across the country. That would make the error rate .027 percent—or, to put it another way, a success rate of 99.973 percent. ("The Innocent and the Shammed," *New York Times* January 26, 2006, p. A23)

The dissent's suggestion that capital defendants are *especially* liable to suffer from the lack of 100 percent perfection in our criminal justice system is implausible. Capital cases are given especially close scrutiny at every level, which is why in most cases many years elapse before the sentence is executed. And of course capital cases receive special attention in the application of executive clemency. Indeed, one of the arguments made by abolitionists is that the process of finally completing all the appeals and reexaminations of capital sentences is so lengthy, and thus so expensive for the State, that the game is not worth the candle. The proof of the pudding, of course, is that as far as anyone can determine (and many are looking), *none* of [the] cases included in the .027 percent error rate for American verdicts involved a capital defendant erroneously executed.

Since 1976 there have been approximately a half million murders in the United States. In that time, 7,000 murderers have been sentenced to death; about 950 of them have been executed; and about 3,700 inmates are currently on death row. (See Marquis, "The Myth of Innocence," *Journal of Criminal Law & Criminology* 95 [2006]: 518.) As a consequence of the sensitivity of the criminal justice system to the due-process rights of defendants sentenced to death, almost two-thirds of all death sentences are overturned. "Virtually none" of these reversals, however, are attributable to a defendant's "'actual innocence.'" (Ibid.) Most are based on legal errors that have little or nothing to do with guilt. The studies cited by the dissent demonstrate nothing more.

Like other human institutions, courts and juries are not perfect. One cannot have a system of criminal punishment without accepting the possibility that someone will be punished mistakenly. That is a truism, not a revelation. But with regard to the punishment of death in the current American system, that possibility has been reduced to an insignificant minimum. This explains why those ideologically driven to ferret out and proclaim a mistaken modern execution have not a single verifiable case to point to, whereas it is easy as pie to identify plainly guilty murderers who have been set free. The American people have determined that the good to be derived from capital punishment—in deterrence, and perhaps most of all in the meting out of condign justice for horrible crimes—outweighs the risk of error. It is no proper part of the business of this Court, or of its Justices, to second-guess that judgment, much less to impugn it before the world, and less still to frustrate it by imposing judicially invented obstacles to its execution.

[The dissenting opinion of Justice STEVENS is omitted.]

Justice SOUTER, with whom Justice STEVENS, Justice GINS-BURG, and Justice BREYER join, dissenting.

I

Kansas's capital sentencing statute provides that a defendant "shall be sentenced to death" if, by unanimous vote, "the jury finds beyond a reasonable doubt that one or more aggravating circumstances . . . exist and . . . that the existence of such aggravating circumstances is not outweighed by any mitigating circumstances which are found to exist." (*Kan. Stat. Ann.* § 21-4624[e] [1995].) The Supreme Court of Kansas has read this provision to require imposition of the death penalty "[i]n the event of equipoise, [that is,] the jury's determination that the balance of any aggravating circumstances and any mitigating circumstances weighed equal." Given this construction, the state court held the law unconstitutional on the ground that the Eighth Amendment requires that a "'tie g[o] to the defendant' when life or death is at issue." (Ibid.) Because I agree with the Kansas judges that the Constitution forbids a mandatory death penalty in what they describe as "doubtful cases," when aggravating and mitigating factors are of equal weight, I respectfully dissent.[1]

II

More than thirty years ago, this Court explained that the Eighth Amendment's guarantee against cruel and unusual punishment barred imposition of the death penalty under statutory schemes so inarticulate that sentencing discretion produced wanton and freakish results. See *Furman v. Georgia* (1972) (per curiam) (Stewart, concurring) ("[T]he Eighth and Fourteenth Amendments cannot tolerate the infliction of a sentence of death under legal systems that permit this unique penalty to be . . . wantonly and . . . freakishly imposed" on a "capriciously selected random handful" of individuals). The Constitution was held to require, instead, a system structured to produce reliable, rational, and rationally reviewable determinations of sentence.

Decades of back-and-forth between legislative experiment and judicial review have made it plain that the constitutional demand for rationality goes beyond the minimal requirement to replace unbounded discretion with a sentencing structure; a State has much leeway in devising such a structure and in selecting the terms for measuring relative culpability, but a system must meet an ultimate test of constitutional reliability in producing "'a reasoned moral response to the defendant's background, character, and crime.'" *Penry v. Lynaugh.* The Eighth Amendment, that is, demands both form and substance, both a system for decision and one geared to produce morally justifiable results.

The State thinks its scheme is beyond questioning, whether as to form or substance, for it sees the tie-breaker law as equivalent to the provisions examined in [previous cases,] where we approved statutes that required a death sentence upon a jury finding that aggravating circumstances outweighed mitigating ones. But the crucial fact in those systems was the predominance of the aggravators, and our recognition of the moral rationality of a mandatory capital sentence based on that finding is no authority for giving States free rein to select a different conclusion that will dictate death.

Instead, the constitutional demand for a reasoned moral response requires the state statute to satisfy two criteria that speak to the issue before us now, one governing the character of sentencing evidence, and one going to the substantive justification needed for a death sentence. As to the first, there is an obligation in each case to inform the jury's choice of sentence with evidence about the crime as actually committed and about the specific individual who committed it. Since the sentencing choice is, by definition, the attribution of particular culpability to a criminal act and defendant, as distinct from the general culpability necessarily implicated by committing a given offense, the sentencing decision must turn on the uniqueness of the individual defendant and on the details of the crime, to which any resulting choice of death must be "directly" related.

Second, there is the point to which the particulars of crime and criminal are relevant: within the category of capital crimes, the death penalty must be reserved for "the worst of the worst." One object of the structured sentencing proceeding required in the aftermath of *Furman* is to eliminate the risk that a death sentence will be imposed in spite of facts calling for a lesser penalty, and the essence of the sentencing authority's responsibility is to determine whether the response to the crime and defendant "must be death." *Spaziano*. Of course, in the moral world of those who reject capital punishment in principle, a death sentence can never be a moral imperative. The point, however, is that within our legal and moral system, which allows a place for the death penalty, "must be death" does not mean "may be death."

Since a valid capital sentence thus requires a choice based upon unique particulars identifying the crime and its perpetrator as heinous to the point of demanding death even within the class of potentially capital offenses, the State's provision for a tie breaker in favor of death fails on both counts. The dispositive fact under the tie breaker is not the details of the crime or the unique identity of the individual defendant. The determining fact is not directly linked to a particular crime or particular criminal at all; the law operates merely on a jury's finding of equipoise in the State's own selected considerations for and against death. Nor does the tie breaker identify the worst of the worst, or even purport to reflect any evidentiary showing that death must be the reasoned moral response; it does the opposite. The statute produces a death sentence exactly when a sentencing impasse demonstrates as a matter of law that the jury does not see the evidence as showing the worst sort of crime committed by the worst sort of criminal, in a combination heinous enough to demand death. It operates, that is, when a jury has applied the State's chosen standards of culpability and mitigation and reached nothing more than what the Supreme Court of Kansas calls a "tie." It mandates death in what that court identifies as "doubtful cases." The statute thus addresses the risk of a morally unjustifiable death sentence, not by minimizing it as precedent unmistakably requires, but by guaranteeing that in equipoise cases the risk will be realized, by "placing a 'thumb [on] death's side of the scale' . . ."

In Kansas, when a jury applies the State's own standards of relative culpability and cannot decide that a defendant is among the most culpable, the state law says that equivocal evidence is good enough and the defendant must die. A law that requires execution when the case for aggravation has failed to convince the sentencing jury is morally absurd, and the Court's holding that the Constitution tolerates this moral irrationality defies decades of precedent aimed at eliminating freakish capital sentencing in the United States.

III

That precedent, demanding reasoned moral judgment, developed in response to facts that could not be ignored, the kaleidoscope of life and death verdicts that made no sense in fact or morality in the random sentencing before *Furman* was decided in 1972. Today, a new body of fact must be accounted for in deciding what, in practical terms, the Eighth Amendment guarantees should tolerate, for the period starting in 1989 has seen repeated exonerations of convicts under death sentences, in numbers never imagined before the development of DNA tests. We cannot face up to these facts and still hold that the guarantee of morally justifiable sentencing is hollow enough to allow maximizing death sentences, by requiring them when juries fail to find the worst degree of culpability: when, by a State's own standards and a State's own characterization, the case for death is "doubtful."

A few numbers from a growing literature will give a sense of the reality that must be addressed. When the Governor of Illinois imposed a moratorium on executions in 2000, 13 prisoners under death sentences had been released since 1977 after a number of them were shown to be innocent, as described in a report which used their examples to illustrate a theme common to all 13, of "relatively little solid evidence connecting the charged defendants to the crimes." State of Illinois, G. Ryan, Governor, Report of the Governor's Commission on Capital Punishment: Recommendations Only 7 (April 2002) (hereinafter Report). During the same period, 12 condemned convicts had been executed. Subsequently the Governor determined that 4 more death row inmates were innocent. See ibid., pp. 5–6; Warden, "Illinois Death Penalty Reform," *Journal of Criminal Law & Criminology* 95 (2005): 382, and n. 6.[2] Illinois had thus wrongly convicted and condemned even more capital defendants than it had executed, but it may well not have been otherwise unique; one recent study reports that between 1989 and 2003, 74 American prisoners condemned to death were exonerated. (Gross, Jacoby, Matheson, Montgomery, and Patil, "Exonerations in the United States 1989 through 2003," *Journal of Criminal Law & Criminology* 95 [2006]: 531 [hereinafter Gross]), many of them cleared by DNA evidence, ibid.[3] Another report states that "more than 110" death row prisoners have been released since 1973 upon findings that they were innocent of the crimes charged, and "[h]undreds of additional wrongful convictions in potentially capital cases have been documented over the past century." Lanier and Acker, "Capital Punishment, the Moratorium Movement, and Empirical Questions," *Psychology, Public Policy & Law* 10 (2004): 593. Most of these wrongful convictions and sentences resulted from eyewitness misidentification, false confession, and (most frequently) perjury, and the total shows that among all prosecutions homicide cases suffer an unusually high incidence of false conviction, probably owing to the combined difficulty of investigating without help from the victim, intense pressure to get convictions in homicide cases, and the corresponding incentive for the guilty to frame the innocent.

A number were subject to judgments as close to innocence as any judgments courts normally render. In the case of one of the released men, the Supreme Court of Illinois found the evidence insufficient to support his conviction. See *People v. Smith* (1999). Several others obtained acquittals, and still more simply had the charges against them dropped, after receiving orders for new trials.

At least 2 of the 13 were released at the initiative of the executive. We can reasonably assume that a State under no obligation to do so would not release into the public a person against whom it had a valid conviction and sentence unless it were certain beyond all doubt that the person in custody was not the perpetrator of the crime. The reason that the State would forgo even a judicial forum in which defendants would demonstrate grounds for vacating their convictions is a matter of common sense: evidence going to innocence was conclusive.

We are thus in a period of new empirical argument about how "death is different," *Gregg*: not only would these false verdicts defy correction after the fatal moment, the Illinois experience shows them to be remarkable in number, and they are probably disproportionately high in capital cases. While it is far too soon for any generalization about the soundness of capital sentencing across the country, the cautionary lesson of recent experience addresses the tie-breaking potential of the Kansas statute: the same risks of falsity that infect proof of guilt raise questions about sentences, when the circumstances of the crime are aggravating factors and bear on predictions of future dangerousness.

In the face of evidence of the hazards of capital prosecution, maintaining a sentencing system mandating death when the sentencer finds the evidence pro and con to be in equipoise is obtuse by any moral or social measure. And unless application of the Eighth Amendment no longer calls for reasoned moral judgment in substance as well as form, the Kansas law is unconstitutional.

NOTES

1. The majority views *Walton v. Arizona* (1990) as having decided this issue. But *Walton* is ambiguous on this point; while the Court there approved Arizona's practice of placing the burden on capital defendants to prove, "by a preponderance of the evidence, the existence of mitigating circumstances sufficiently substantial to call for leniency" (plurality opinion), it did not quantify the phrase "sufficiently substantial." . . .

2. The Illinois Report emphasizes the difference between exoneration of a convict because of actual innocence, and reversal of a judgment because of legal error affecting conviction or sentence but not inconsistent with guilt in fact. See Report 9 (noting that, apart from the 13 released men, a "broader review" discloses that more than half of the State's death penalty cases "were reversed at some point in the process"). More importantly, it takes only a cursory reading of the Report to recognize that it

describes men released who were demonstrably innocent or convicted on grossly unreliable evidence. Of one, the Report notes "two other persons were subsequently convicted in Wisconsin of" the murders. Ibid., p. 8. Of two others, the Report states that they were released after "DNA tests revealed that none of them were the source of the semen found in the victim. That same year, two other men confessed to the crime, pleaded guilty and were sentenced to life in prison, and a third was tried and convicted for the crime." Ibid. Of yet another, the Report says that "another man subsequently confessed to the crime for which [the released man] was convicted. He entered a plea of guilty and is currently serving a prison term for that crime." Ibid., p. 9.

3. The authors state the criteria for their study: "As we use the term, 'exoneration' is an official act declaring a defendant not guilty of a crime for which he or she had previously been convicted. The exonerations we have studied occurred in four ways: (1) In forty-two cases governors (or other appropriate executive officers) issued pardons based on evidence of the defendants' innocence. (2) In 263 cases criminal charges were dismissed by courts after new evidence of innocence emerged, such as DNA. (3) In thirty-one cases the defendants were acquitted at a retrial on the basis of evidence that they had no role in the crimes for which they were originally convicted. (4) In four cases, states posthumously acknowledged the innocence of defendants who had already died in prison. . . ." Gross, p. 524 (footnote omitted). The authors exclude from their list of exonerations "any case in which a dismissal or an acquittal appears to have been based on a decision that while the defendant was not guilty of the charges in the original conviction, he did play a role in the crime and may be guilty of some lesser crime that is based on the same conduct. For our purposes, a defendant who is acquitted of murder on retrial, but convicted of involuntary manslaughter, has not been exonerated. We have also excluded any case in which a dismissal was entered in the absence of strong evidence of factual innocence, or in which—despite such evidence—there was unexplained physical evidence of the defendant's guilt." Ibid., n. 4.

CHRIST, CHRISTIANS, AND CAPITAL PUNISHMENT

Mark Osler

INTRODUCTION

Rosmophin: "To what end is the Law ordained
if the true meaning thereof is not kept?"[1]

In part, we judge nations by whom their governments choose to kill. Primarily, there are two ways that governments choose to kill people intentionally: in war, and through the execution of criminals. Nations vary widely in how many people they choose to kill, how discriminate they are in choosing to kill, and whether or not they will intentionally kill people at all.

Whatever else may divide them, Presidents Bill Clinton and George W. Bush chose to kill abroad and at home, in that they supported both military actions abroad and the death penalty at home. They share another commonality as well, in that both are Christians and made their faith a part of their public and political personae.

Baylor Law Review 1 (Winter 2007).

This article explores an intriguing aspect of that common-ality—that Clinton and Bush have proclaimed a faith which has at its center a death penalty sentencing, and whose primary public symbol, the cross, is itself a representation of an instrument of execution. Even the press accounts of a condemned's last meal echo the Last Supper, which was the final meal of a man well aware he was to be executed. Oddly, lessons from the sentencing of Christ have not been a part of the American debate over the death penalty, even when the argument is between Christians. This article sets out to change that.

One reason we have much to learn from the criminal process afforded Christ is that it bears so many similarities to the criminal process employed in the United States today. Like many convicts sentenced to death in the here and now, Christ was given up to the authorities by a paid informant (Judas Iscariot), was arrested in a strategic manner by the authorities, given an arraignment and stood mute to the charges, was tried and convicted, sentenced to death, appealed to two separate sovereigns, and finally was refused a pardon.

While certainly I do not mean to compare the crime of which Christ was accused with the depraved acts of modern-day killers, I do think it is fair to compare the process leading to that execution and the process today, and note that less has changed than we might imagine. Though in so doing, I will be using Biblical texts in addressing a contemporary political question, it was not my choice to interject the Christian faith into national politics to level we see now. If candidates are to run for office while waving the flag of Christ, the reported encounters of Christ with the political actors of his day would seem to be an important part of the debate over the political issues those same flag-wavers address.

In reading the Gospel accounts of the trial of Christ as a death penalty process, certain aspects strike some Christians as unfair. I am one such Christian, and there are three primary aspects about the process undertaken (other than the innocence of Christ) which bother me: First, the process happened too quickly. Second, the role of the mob as a political force seems to determine a result out of momentary passion and independent of evidence or policy. Third, Jesus has no true advocate in the court.

Here, I will apply the same critique to modern capital sentencing, at two levels. First, the trial of Christ can be read as a moral basis for eliminating capital punishment altogether insofar as it involves the execution of an innocent, and raises one of the most compelling contemporary objections to capital punishment: that we may be executing those who are innocent among the larger mass of those who are guilty. Second, even if one remains an advocate of the death penalty, the trial of Jesus also offers a guide for specific elements of reform to address the unfairnesses Christians perceive about that trial (and described in the preceding paragraph). These reforms might include lengthening the trial process, reducing the role of political influences within at least some of the stages of the process, and providing better representation for those accused. Others, of course, have argued for similar reforms, but not as a Christian imperative derived from the singular life story of the Christian savior.

In section two of this article, I will set out the Gospel accounts of the trial of Christ, describing it as a process akin in many respects to what we employ today in capital cases, using Texas law as a reference. In section three, I will similarly examine the post-trial procedures allowed Christ, which included the rough equivalents of an appeal (to Pilate), a habeas petition to a separate jurisdiction's authority (Herod), and a final request for a pardon by the Governor (Pilate). Finally, in section four, I look for lessons from that trial in either barring or guiding capital sentencing today, and in section five conclude by briefly urging honest retrospection on this issue, particularly by people of faith.

CHRIST'S TRIAL AS DEATH PENALTY SENTENCING

The Trial of a Savior

Phytiphores: That righteousness which moveth sedition among the common people, is needless for the estate of the Country.[2]

The gospel accounts of the trial of Jesus vary in what they describe—that is, while they don't necessarily contradict one another, they do tell different parts of the same story. In analyzing those accounts, the reader will notice that I sometimes jump from one narrative to another, especially where a particular event is only reported in one of the gospels. For example, only the gospel of Luke includes the appearance of Christ before Herod, so I jump to that section to describe the encounter with Herod. In short, I have chosen to read the Gospel accounts in the manner of a guy who has bought several newspapers after some particularly interesting event, knowing that some will report facts ignored by others and allowing for a more complete picture of the event.

[Editors' Note: Sections on the investigation, arrest and arraignment have been eliminated in the interest of space.]

The Trial

Mesa: If he be just then let us join with him,
but if he be guilty let us root him out.[3]

. . . As in most modern criminal trials, the principal evidence against Jesus was the testimony of purported witnesses to the crimes. Also like many modern criminal cases, this testimony was not entirely consistent. In fact, according to the Gospel of Mark, though many gave testimony against him, "their testimony did not agree."[4] Specifically, the accusation was made that Jesus said "I will destroy this temple that is made with hands, and in three days I will build another, not built with hands,"[5] but the description of how or where this statement was made did not match.

Finally, having failed to establish their case through witnesses, the court tried to confront Jesus directly (at least according to the Gospel of Mark):

> Then the high priest stood up before them and asked Jesus, "Have you no answer? But why is it that they testify against you?" But he was silent and did not answer. Again the high priest asked him, "Are you the Messiah, the Son of the Blessed One?" Jesus said "I am"[6] . . .

In the Gospel of Luke, Jesus responds to the inquisitors in a more enigmatic way. When asked, "Are you, then, the Son of

God?"[7] he responds simply by saying, "You say that I am."[8] Once again, as at the arraignment, Jesus is seen to be leaving the authorities to their proofs, reminding us that while the Fifth Amendment granted us the right to remain silent, it did not create the ability to remain silent in the face of an accusation (provided we are willing to stand up to whatever coercion is employed).

What is significant is what Jesus does not have, in any of the Gospel accounts of the trial. He does not have counsel, or an advocate of any kind. He does not seem to have the ability to call witnesses, or have any role in the composition of the fact-finders. In short, it does not seem to be a very fair proceeding, or one intended to come to the truth rather than a conviction.

The Verdict

Caiaphas: All you know not what you say:
it is better that one man die than all the people perish.[9]

The Bible's account of the testimony against Christ is much more detailed than the description given of deliberation and verdict. . . . Mark and Matthew describe a single step in which Jesus is condemned to die, rather than a two-stage process in which a defendant is first found guilty and only then is sentencing considered. The two-step approach prevails now in the United States, but until very recently some states had mandatory sentencing statutes, which required execution once a defendant is convicted of a qualifying crime.

Caiaphas, now in the role of prosecutor, concludes the trial with a passion many modern prosecutors might admire:

> Then the high priest tore his clothes and said, "He has blasphemed! Why do we still need witnesses? You have heard his blasphemy. What is your verdict?" They answered, "He deserves death."[10]

The structure of this passage represents what an objective observer would immediately recognize as a closing argument. Further, as in a modern trial, Caiaphas is facing the panel serving as deciders of fact (the jury), and asks directly for their verdict. This replicates, in tone and substance (save for the tearing of clothes) what happens every day in American courtrooms.

Each aspect of Caiaphas' argument reflects a principle I included in my own closing arguments as a prosecutor (though I never did tear my clothes). For example "do we still need witnesses" has the same meaning as a boilerplate segment of every prosecutor's closing—that the evidence has been sufficient to meet the burden of proof. Similarly, "You have heard his blasphemy" is nothing more than the point any prosecutor would make—that a defendant who chose to represent himself simply proved the point of the prosecution through his statements.

The verdict is stunningly simple: "He deserves death." This, too, is like the sentence of an American jury, whose most profound decision is often reflected by simply checking a box in the verdict form, rather than in the lengthy opinions issued by judges, or the complex multi-part verdict forms completed by civil juries.

Certainly, this "trial" may have been nothing more than a brief hearing before religious officials in the courtyard of the home of the high priest. But let us have no delusions about the sometimes perfunctory proceedings in our own capital cases, which are often tried by inexperienced lawyers in the least populous and poorest parts of our country, in courtrooms smaller than that courtyard and before jurors less well educated than the Pharisees who were probably among the best educated of Jerusalem's citizens.

GOSPEL ACCOUNTS OF POST-TRIAL PROCEDURE

The Comparison to American Post-Trial Procedure

A defendant who is convicted of capital murder and sentenced to die in Texas has a well-defined series of procedural steps to follow prior to execution. First, he receives a mandatory appeal of right to the Court of Criminal Appeals, which is the Supreme Court in Texas for criminal matters, with no intermediate stop at the Court of Appeals. Were he (as usual) to lose his appeal in the Court of Criminal Appeals, he would next have the ability to petition the

Supreme Court of the United States to hear the case. After that, he could petition for habeas corpus in state court, which would immediately be decided by the Court of Criminal Appeals. Next, he could seek a writ of habeas corpus in federal court, and appeal the adverse decision there, possibly to the level of the United States Supreme Court. Finally, he can seek a pardon or commutation from the governor prior to the sentence.

Thus, in simpler terms, a defendant has the ability to appeal to both the state and federal authorities, and to seek a reprieve from the Governor before being put to death.

Jesus' post-sentence appeals were less lengthy and convoluted than those described above, and his first appeal and final request for commutation were from the equivalent of federal, not state authorities (reversing the order of appeals in American courts). Still, the fact remains that, like a Texas man sentenced to die, Jesus had appeals before representatives of two separate jurisdictions (Pilate as a representative of Rome, and Herod as ruler of Judea) and the opportunity for a final reprieve from the Governor before being put to death.

The Appeal to Pilate

Pilate: I, Pontius Pilate, Procounsel and Judge in Jerusalem, under the mightiest Emperor Tiberius . . . greeting. Sitting in judgment seat for the love of justice, by the Synagogue of the Jewish people, is presented before me Jesus of Nazareth, which with presumptuous words has named himself to be the Son of God, although he be born of a poor mother: He hath preached himself to be the King of the Jews, advancing to destroy Solomon's Temple, and to withdraw the people from the most approved Law of Moses. All this is considered and approved of, condemn him to the cross with the two murderers.[11]

Each of the gospel accounts describe Jesus being taken before Pilate, who was the Roman Procurator (or Governor) for the area at that time. . . .

It appears that Pilate has an immediate understanding of the issues at hand. Unlike a modern court of appeals, he hears evidence himself instead of relying on the report from the lower court. He immediately asks Jesus if he is the King of the Jews, and Jesus responds, "You say so."[12]

Pilate follows up by asking "Do you not hear how many accusations they make against you?"[13] Jesus makes no answer to this whatsoever, and Pilate is "amazed"[14] by the fortitude of the prisoner before him.

Here the Gospels diverge. Luke, alone, describes Pilate's reaction in greater detail, quoting Pilate as saying, "I find no basis for an accusation against this man."[15] Luke then describes Pilate's next move—sending Jesus to Herod for a further appeal, apparently based on his willingness to vacate the sentence of the Council below, and fear of the political consequences of doing so, given the passions of the chief priests.

[Editors' Note: A description of the appeal before Herod has been eliminated in the interest of space.]

The Denial of a Reprieve or Pardon

Ehiheris: Although he be just yet shall he die,
because the people are moved by his words.[16]

. . . Jesus has one last hope, the same last hope as many capital convicts today: That hope is that, somehow, the Governor will at the last minute pardon him or commute the sentence.

Thus, Jesus is sent back to Pilate,[17] who seems to want to give such a pardon or at least a different sentence, based on the lack of evidence:

> Pilate then called together the chief priests, the leaders, and the people, and said to them, "you brought me this man as one who was perverting the people; and here I have examined him in your presence and have not found this man guilty of any of your charges against him. Neither has Herod, and he sent him back to us. Indeed, he has done nothing to deserve death. I will therefore have him flogged and release him."[18]

Pilate is trying to mediate a fair outcome by suggesting a sentence less than death. It would appear that he does have the ability to grant such a commutation, given that the local authorities, on their own, do not have the ability to actually carry out an execution.

Further, Pilate had an additional option as well. At the Passover festival, it was a tradition that the Roman authorities would release a local prisoner. Pilate had two prisoners (at least) he could release under this tradition—Jesus and a murderer/ insurrectionist named Barabbas.

Thus, Pilate had at least two alternatives available: either stick with his initially declared commutation of the sentence (which would be within his inherent authority to deny the locals the courtesy of execution of a prisoner), or release Jesus as part of the festival tradition. However, Pilate lacks the will to stick with either solution in the face of grassroots political opposition and gives in to the desires of the mob despite his own conscience:

> Then they all shouted out together, "Away with this fellow! Release Barabbas for us!" (This was a man who had been put in prison for an insurrection that had taken place in the city, and for murder). Pilate, wanting to release Jesus, addressed them again; but they kept shouting "crucify him, crucify him!" A third time he said to them, "Why, what evil has he done?" . . . But they kept urgently demanding with loud shouts that he should be crucified, and their voices prevailed.[19]

Thus, his last appeals exhausted, Jesus was handed over for execution. The particulars of that execution have been well chronicled in both the popular and scholarly spheres.

LESSONS FROM THE TRIAL OF CHRIST

Saveas: A hypocrite is very dangerous in a commonwealth, therefore let him be rooted out from among the people.[20]

Lessons Regarding Moral Legitimacy of the Death Penalty

There are two types of lessons which can be drawn from a discussion of the trial of Christ as a death penalty process: first, lessons on the legitimacy or illegitimacy of the death penalty itself, and second, lessons on what procedures should be employed within a system which allows the death penalty. I will address each in turn.

The Trial of Christ in Support of the Death Penalty

Some, I would imagine, might turn the trial of Christ towards the goal of supporting capital punishment.

Of course, to many Christians, the full meaning of the faith was fulfilled only with the death of Christ and his resulting resurrection. Thus, capital punishment was not only a part of, but necessary to, the establishment of the Christian faith. While this argument certainly would apply to the killing of Jesus Christ, those who make it probably would not expand it to others subject to execution, because that would assume that they somehow also share that singular role of Christ—the ability to redeem the world through his death. The execution of others in the modern era seems to do nothing to propagate, promote or enhance any faith.

Apart from the "necessity" argument there was one incident in the Gospel accounts, after the trial and appeals and in the act of crucifixion itself, which could be taken as support for the general proposition of the death penalty. Crucifixion kills slowly, and it appears that Christ suffered for some time on the cross next to the two bandits who were crucified on either side of him. One of the bandits chides Jesus, saying, "Are you not the Messiah? Save yourself and us!"[21] The other bandit, however, rebukes him, saying, "[W]e indeed have been condemned justly, for we are getting what we deserve for our deeds, but this man has done nothing wrong,"[22] and asks Jesus to remember him "when you come into your kingdom."[23] Rather than condemn the punishment he is facing, Christ seems to honor the man's acceptance of his punishment, telling him "Truly I tell you, today you will be with me in Paradise."[24] Of course, it could also be that Jesus is honoring the man's recognition of him as the Son of God.

The Trial of Christ as a Basis for Opposition to the Death Penalty

Joram: Wherefore suffer we this innocent man to die, is it for his righteousness?[25]

Just as an argument for the death penalty drawn from the trial of Jesus Christ must imply lessons from that story, so must an argument against capital punishment—Christ did not take the opportunity to condemn the punishment in a general way at that time.

This is not to say, however, that Christ never directly addressed the question of capital punishment. The Gospel of John tells the remarkable story in which the scribes and Pharisees (no doubt in another attempt to trick Jesus into contravening the law) bring an adulteress before Jesus. They tell Jesus, correctly, that the Law of Moses requires that she be stoned to death, and ask what should be done. Famously, Christ answers "Let anyone among you who is without sin be the first to throw a stone at her."[26] One by one, they drift off, and in the end, the woman is left alone. It is hard to imagine a more direct condemnation of the death penalty than the Son of God coming across a lawful execution and stopping it by commanding that no man has the moral authority to carry it out.

The trial of Christ lacks a similar directness in condemning capital punishment and those who would authorize it. Jesus' trial does, however, lend support to a primary argument used by those who oppose the death penalty: that by its nature, the death penalty may lead to the execution of innocents, and this ultimate injustice is too high a cost to pay for the benefits which may come from the ability to kill the guilty.

The Bible itself takes pains to point out the innocence of Christ, an implicit criticism of this inherent risk of the death penalty. Specifically, two of the actors in the trial and execution seem stricken with guilt at their actions due to Christ's innocence—including not only one of the Roman centurians standing guard, but Pilate himself.

At the time of the execution, the Gospels describe the conversion of one of the executioners, a Roman centurian, who recognizes this crucial fact. After Jesus dies (which coincided with a darkness falling over the land), the centurian says "Certainly this man was innocent."[27] Pilate, in a more subtle way, also declares that Jesus may have been innocent. At the time of the crucifixion, a sign was placed over Jesus' cross saying "Jesus of Nazareth, the King of the Jews."[28] The chief priests urged Pilate to change the sign to read "This man said 'I am the King of the Jews,'"[29] but Pilate refused, saying "what I have written I have written."[30]

Within the modern debate over the death penalty, the issue of innocence is gaining increasing prominence as DNA evidence provides a means of calling capital convictions and even executions into question. For example Barry Scheck, Peter Neufeld, and Jim Dwyer's book *Actual Innocence* tells the stories of several people whose executions were overturned after DNA evidence established their innocence. More famously, the Republican Governor of Illinois, Jim Ryan, granted a blanket commutation to all death row prisoners in Illinois based on innocence questions.

Nor is the question of innocence necessarily limited to those who managed to avoid execution when the problem was identified. Recently, for example, prosecutors in St. Louis have reopened the trial of Larry Griffin, who was executed in Missouri in 1995. His conviction for murder rested on the testimony of a supposed eyewitness who was seeking to reduce his own charges, and contrary evidence has now come to light. This contrary evidence includes the fact that other eyewitnesses did not recall seeing a white man at the scene. That solitary eyewitness was white. Griffin may have been innocent.

Christian politicians, of course, may finesse this point by assuming that the criminal justice system is infallible and could not result in the execution of an innocent, an assumption that does not seem to be borne out by the facts. For example, Florida Governor Jeb Bush has justified his positions in opposition to abortion and in support of the death penalty through the familiar shibboleth that "[T]aking an innocent life is wrong."[31] I wonder if bulletproof evidence that innocents were being or had been executed would change the mind of such politicians, or if their consciences are hostage to the will of the population, as was Pilate's.

THE LESSONS OF CHRIST'S TRIAL FOR CAPITAL PROCEDURE

The Troubling Procedure Allowing For Execution

Even if the story of Christ's trial does not decide the issue of whether or not the death penalty is moral for any given individual, the similarities between the process leading to Christ's death and our modern procedures seem to suggest certain remedies short of abolition of the death penalty. By no means am I the first to suggest any of these reforms, but I am probably the first to urge them based on their similarities to the unfairnesses within the capital trial of Christ. I argue that we should not inflict on the "least of these"[32] the same procedural wrongs that were inflicted on Christ at his own trial.

Although I am sure there are others which could be identified, the procedural problems with the capital trial of Christ seem to include (1) a process which occurred too quickly, (2) a process in which the role of the public as a political force seems to determine a result independent of evidence or policy, and (3) a trial process in which he has no true advocate in the court to represent his interests.

A Rush to Judgment

It would appear that Jesus was tried and convicted within a single day's time. While some may find this shocking, defendants have been sentenced to die in the modern United States after a one-day trial, as well. But this was just one aspect of the deadly speed of the proceeding—also too quick, and probably more important, was the period from arrest to trial, from conviction to sentencing, and the course of appeals. I will address each or these in turn.

The Period from Arrest to Trial

Achias: The cause of the offender ought to be thoroughly examined Before sentence of death be given against him.[33]

It is easy to imagine the ways that Jesus was prejudiced by the fact he was swept up for arrest almost directly before his capital trial—he was unable to obtain assistance of counsel or friend, there was no chance to gather witnesses, and there was no time for passions to cool.

In the modern era, there is usually an adequate amount of time allowed for preparation of a capital case, though most jurisdictions do not provide a guaranteed time period. Rather, the opposite is true—speedy trial acts, including the federal act, go the other way—they mandate that the trial must be held within a certain number of days after arraignment. At the very least, judges should be liberal in granting continuances in capital cases if the defense requires them for preparation.

The Period from Trial to Sentencing

Jesus was sentenced immediately upon conviction—in fact, his conviction appears to include the sentence. While, at least since the overturning of mandatory death statutes, the conflation of adjudication and sentence does not exist in American law, there is often almost no gap between the two. For example, in Texas the sentencing phase of trial is required by statute to be held "as soon as practicable."[34] Clearly, this works to the prejudice of the defendant. Up to that point, defense counsel in a capital case have been working to disprove guilt. Suddenly, often within a day's time, they must shift gears abruptly and argue mitigation—that aspects of the defendant's life merit a sentence of life in prison rather than execution. Were even a week allowed between the two phases of trial, the defense could present a stronger case at sentencing.

This may, of course, work to inconvenience the jury, who would have to come back to the court having taken a week off. Given that the stakes at issue are the highest imaginable, this seems like a relatively reasonable cost.

The Period Allowed for Appeals

Within the past decade, all three branches of government seem nearly obsessed with reducing the time period allowed for capital appeals and habeas. Most strikingly, the [Antiterrorism and Effective Death Penalty Act] passed in 1996 by Congress and signed by Bill Clinton, has set strict and Byzantine restrictions on federal habeas petitions. It appears that Congress now appears eager to even more drastically restrict these time frames.

The same way the brevity of Jesus' appeals was wrong, to so restrict the appeals of the modern prisoner is wrong. To offer just one example, my colleague Bill Underwood handled the appeal and habeas petitions of a Texas prisoner for some 16 years. On its face, this may seem to be the kind of anecdote that those urging speedy death may rely on. However, the story takes a turn to the detriment of their argument. Bill's client was mentally retarded. On June 20, 2002, the Supreme Court reversed its own precedent and held that it was unconstitutional to execute the mentally retarded. As a result, Bill's client was resentenced to life—a life which would have long been over if the speedy appeals advocates had their way, and an execution which would have been unconstitutional under modern law. Delay may increase costs, but it also allows for justice to run its course.

The Role of the Mob

Ehiheris: Although he be just yet shall he die,
because the people are moved by his words.[35]

At each turn, powerful political actors urged those making the decision on Jesus' fate to have him killed. In the end, Pilate rejects commutation of the sentence in the face of the crowd's cries of "crucify him!"[36] The response of the judges to political pressure is clear. Are things so different today? One response to the story of Christ's trial is to provide more political insulation between those who make decisions on capital cases and the public who may be inclined to an emotional reaction to the crime rather than a balanced consideration of guilt and punishment.

Consider, for example, the case of Texas, where nearly all involved in a capital case are forced to be responsive to an electorate. The jurors must go back into the streets of the town where they live. The trial judge must stand for election, as do the judges of the Court of Appeals and the Court of Criminal Appeals (the Texas Supreme Court for criminal matters). When it is time for a stay of execution or commutation request, it goes to an elected governor. Were just one of these levels protected from the voices of retribution apart from careful reflection, perhaps just one egregious tragedy could be averted. . . .

The Need for Effective Representation

Joseph of Arimathea: What a shame is this, that in a whole city not one is to be found that will defend the innocent.[37]

Many have called for more effective representation at the trial level for capital defendants, and it may be that the level of representation for these defendants has improved. Nonetheless, the example of Christ demands increased scrutiny in this area.

One underlying problem related to representation is akin to the political pressures discussed in the preceding section. In Texas, defense attorneys in capital cases are most often selected by the judges who are to hear that capital case. While most judges will, of course, choose the most capable attorneys in their jurisdiction for this task, it remains true that the judge has complex interests.

For example, a judge naturally does not want to have decisions overturned on appeal. This goal is furthered if the defense attorney is competent, but not aggressive in making objections. These interests, of course, which favor an unaggressive defense, work to the detriment of the defendant, who benefits from a vigorous defense in two ways. First, it may result in more acquittals through the exclusion of evidence and passionate argument. Second, if the verdict is guilty, more issues will be preserved for appeal.

We can do better than judicial appointments of defense counsel. A system in which an independent body, such as a public defender's office, provides capital representation or chooses those who will avoids the problem of such conflicting interests.

CONCLUSION

Whether we like it or not, the bare fact is that religion, and specifically Christianity, is a political force in modern America, particularly in "religious values" areas such as the death penalty. The death of Christ portends nothing less—at the time of his death, the curtain in the temple, the curtain which separated the sacred from the profane, the secular from the religious, tore in two.

In holding the sacred story of Christ's trial up to the profane capital processes used in the United States in the place where that curtain has torn, one sees that present procedure, and perhaps the existence of the death penalty at all, do not match up with the lessons to be gleaned from the trial of Christ himself.

While each of us, in pride, are most likely to see ourselves as Christ in this drama, we are more likely akin to one of the others— Pilate, who subsumes his conscience to the political will; Peter, who pretends not to know or support the condemned when doing so would endanger his comfort; a part of the mob, crying out "crucify him!"; a member of the jury moved by Caiaphas' passionate closing argument; or perhaps one of those men a few days later walking on the dirt road to Emmaus, unaware that the stranger who had joined them was Jesus Christ himself.

NOTES

1. Gerardus Gossenius, *The Manner and Order of Proceeding Against Christ by the Judges* (English Broadside, 1586.) Original in the Society of Antiquaries.

2. Ibid.

3. Ibid.

4. Mark 14:56.

5. Mark 14:58, Matthew 26:61.

6. Mark 14:61.

7. Mark 14:70.

8. Ibid.

9. Gerardus Gossenius, *The Manner and Order of Proceeding Against Christ by the Judges.*

10. Matthew 26:65-66.

11. Gerardus Gossenius, *The Manner and Order of Proceeding Against Christ by the Judges.*

12. Matthew 27:11, Mark 15:2.

13. Matthew 27:13; Mark 15:4 is similar: "Have you no answer? See how many charges they bring against you."

14. Matthew 27:14, Mark 15:5.

15. Luke 23:4.

16. Gerardus Gossenius, *The Manner and Order of Proceeding Against Christ by the Judges*.

17. Luke 23:13, 16.

18. Luke 23:13–16.

19. Luke 23:18–25.

20. Gerardus Gossenius, *The Manner and Order of Proceeding Against Christ by the Judges*.

21. Luke 23:39.

22. Luke 23:41.

23. Luke 23:42.

24. Luke 23:43.

25. Gerardus Gossenius, *The Manner and Order of Proceeding Against Christ by the Judges*.

26. John 8:7.

27. Luke 23:47.

28. John 19:19.

29. John 19:21.

30. John 19:22.

31. Jeb Bush, Governor of Florida, interview by the Florida Baptist Witness, cited in Michael Rowan, "Minding Our Skepticism: A Conservative Approach to Capital Punishment," *Florida State University Law Review* 31 (2004): 377, 398, n. 139 (comment).

32. Matthew 25:45.

33. Gerardus Gossenius, *The Manner and Order of Proceeding Against Christ by the Judges*.

34. Texas Code of Criminal Procedure 37.071(2)(a)(1).

35. Gerardus Gossenius, *The Manner and Order of Proceeding Against Christ by the Judges*.

36. Luke 23:23.

37. Gerardus Gossenius, *The Manner and Order of Proceeding Against Christ by the Judges*.

PART FIVE

IMMIGRATION
MORAL AND LEGAL ISSUES

PRINCIPLED IMMIGRATION

Mary Ann Glendon

Not for the first time, the world finds itself in an age of great movements of peoples. And once again, the United States is confronted with the challenge of absorbing large numbers of newcomers. There are approximately 200 million migrants and refugees worldwide, triple the number estimated by the UN only seventeen years ago. In the United States alone, about a million new immigrants have entered every year since 1990, bringing the total immigrant population to more than 35 million, the largest number in the nation's history. Though Americans take justifiable pride in our history as a "nation of immigrants," the challenges are more complex than those the nation previously surmounted. For sending and receiving countries alike, this is a time of exceptional stress—and yet, a moment that offers opportunities as well.

All too often, these challenges and opportunities are discussed in narrowly economic terms, but an adequate understanding of

First Things 164 (June/July 2006): 23–26. Copyright © 2006.

today's migration patterns would also have to include their relation to the approaching "demographic winter" in the affluent societies of Europe and North America. Despite what population-con-
trol advocates had predicted in the 1960s and 1970s, the chief
demographic problem facing most countries today is not overpop-
ulation but its opposite. All over the world, even in developing
countries, populations are aging. In the wealthier nations, where
the process is most advanced, declining birth rates and increased
longevity mean that our populations now include a much smaller
proportion of children and a much larger proportion of disabled
and elderly persons than ever before.

The combination of low birth rates and greater longevity is
already bringing the health-care and social-security programs of
welfare states into crisis. Social-welfare systems were constructed
in the late nineteenth and early twentieth centuries on the basis of
a proportion of nine, or in some cases, seven active workers for
every pensioner. Now Europe is approaching three workers per
retiree, and those retirees are living much longer. (When those who
created the first social-security systems chose sixty-five as the age
of eligibility, they were counting on the fact that relatively few
people would live beyond that age to become burdens on the state.)
With increased longevity has also come increased need for medical
care, which has become vastly more expensive than anyone
dreamed when public health-care systems were first established.

Although Europe will experience the crunch first, the United
States will not be far behind. Our 78.2 million baby boomers are
fast approaching retirement age. Over the next twenty-five years,
the age structure of the whole country will come to resemble that
of "retirement states" like Florida, where a fifth of the population
is already over sixty-five. President Bush stressed the urgency of
the situation in his 2006 State of the Union Address, warning that
"the retirement of the baby-boom generation will put unprecedented strains on the federal government. By 2030, spending for
Social Security, Medicare, and Medicaid alone will be almost 60
percent of the entire federal budget. And that will present future
Congresses with impossible choices—staggering tax increases,
immense deficits, or deep cuts in every category of spending."

Although awareness of this impending demographic storm is

beginning to sink in, policymakers in Europe and the United States tend to frame it only as a "welfare crisis." The falling birth rates that are fueling the welfare crisis, however, are symptomatic of a deeper crisis in beliefs and attitudes—a crisis involving changes in the meanings and values that people attribute to aging and mortality, sex and procreation, marriage, gender, parenthood, relations among the generations, and life itself. That deeper crisis is part of the fallout from what Francis Fukuyama called "The Great Disruption," the revolution in behavior and ideas that came on us so suddenly in the late twentieth century that it was unforeseen by any demographer. Beginning in the mid-1960s, and over a mere twenty years, major demographic indicators in the United States and northern Europe rose or fell by a magnitude of 50 percent or more. Birth rates and marriage rates tumbled, while divorce rates, cohabitation rates, and births outside marriage climbed sharply.

Those same years, to be sure, saw impressive advances for many women and members of minority groups. But not all the innovations represented progress. Some tended to undermine the cultural foundations on which free, just, and egalitarian societies depend. For example, the notion gained wide acceptance that behavior in the highly personal areas of sex and marriage is of no concern to anyone other than the "consenting adults" involved. With the passage of time, however, it has become obvious that the actions of private individuals *in the aggregate* exert a profound influence on other individuals and on society as a whole. In fact, when enough individuals behave primarily with regard to their own self-fulfillment, the entire culture is transformed. Affluent Western nations have been engaged in a massive social experiment—an experiment that brought new opportunities and liberties to many adults but that has put mothers, children, and dependents generally at considerable risk.

The family breakdown has had ripple effects on all the social structures that traditionally depended on families for their support and that in turn served as resources for families in times of stress from schools, neighborhoods, and religious groups to local governments and workplace associations. The law has changed rapidly too, becoming less an element of stability and more of an arena for struggles among competing ideas about individual liberty, equality between men and women, human sexuality, marriage, and family life.

Now that the dependent population in affluent countries includes a much smaller proportion of children than ever before, increased pressure on social resources is already provoking generational conflict in the ambitious welfare states of northern Europe. If political deliberation about the impending welfare crisis remains within a framework based primarily on the idea of competition for scarce resources, the outlook for the most vulnerable members of society is grim—as witness the growing normalization of the extermination of persons who become inconvenient and burdensome to maintain at life's frail beginnings and endings.

Opinion leaders in the aging societies of Europe and the United States have generally avoided mentioning the relation between the birth dearth and the need for immigration. Consequently, there has been little discussion of what should be obvious: An affluent society that, for whatever reason, does not welcome babies is going to have to learn to welcome immigrants if it hopes to maintain its economic vigor and its commitments to the health and welfare of its population. The issue is not who will do jobs that Americans don't want. The issue is who will fill the ranks of a labor force that the retiring generation failed to replenish.

Meeting the challenge of the declining ratio between active workers and retirees will require many sorts of adaptations, but replacement migration will have to play a part in crafting effective responses. The good news is that America enjoys several advantages over Europe. To begin with, the United States has a fertility rate of 2.08 babies per woman, while in the European Union the estimated 2005 fertility rate was 1.47, well below the replacement figure of 2.1. More, the United States has a long history of successful experience in absorbing large numbers of new citizens from many parts of the world. (While the absolute number of new immigrants is currently the highest in United States history, it is proportionately less than in previous eras of large-scale immigration.)

A third advantage worth mentioning is that, while there is enormous diversity among the inhabitants of the American hemisphere, most migrants to the United States share certain important beliefs with most of the country's present inhabitants. Not least of these, in the case of Latin America, are religious in nature. According to a 2005 poll of the United States and nine of its closest allies where people were asked how important a role religion plays in their lives, Mexico and the United States came out on top, with 86 percent of Mexican and 84 percent of American respondents saying religion was important to them. European countries, by contrast, are understandably anxious about what will happen to the functioning of their democracies if sizeable groups of immigrants do not come to embrace the core concepts in which those regimes are grounded.

So why isn't the United States glad about Latin American immigration? Part of the answer is the economic cost of large-scale immigration. American wage earners often fear that migrants will drive down wages and take the jobs that remain. This fear is sometimes exaggerated, but it is not unfounded: The consensus among labor economists is that immigration has somewhat reduced the earnings of less-educated, low-wage workers. Many Americans are also concerned about the costs that illegal immigration imposes on taxpayers, with its strain on schools and social services, particularly in the border states. The desire to protect the national security of the United States, especially after the trauma of September 11, has played a role as well.

There are also some in the United States who want to close the door to newcomers simply because they are outsiders. Over the course of the twentieth century, that attitude seemed to be fading away, but in recent years sleeping nativist sentiments have been irresponsibly inflamed by anti-immigration groups. A few years ago, I wrote of the financial and ideological connections among extremist anti-immigration groups, radical environmentalists, and aggressive population controllers. What unites that loose coalition in what I called an "iron triangle of exclusion" is their common conviction that border controls and abortion are major defenses against an expanding, threatening, welfare-consuming, and nonwhite underclass. (I never suspected when I wrote those lines that they would cost me a half-year's salary. But on the basis of a promised grant from a foundation whose causes included environmental protection, I had taken an unpaid leave from Harvard. Shortly after my article was published, the foundation reneged on its promise. It turned out that their idea of protecting the environment included keeping out immigrants and keeping poor people from having children.)

Good-faith anxieties about large-scale immigration are sometimes expressed in terms of social costs, such as a feared deleterious effect on the nation's cultural cohesion or the stability of local communities. One would like to take comfort from the fact that similar concerns were expressed at the time of the great migrations of a century ago. Though marked by conflict and competition, the story of those earlier immigrants is, to a great extent, a story of successful integration.

But American culture in those days was characterized by a broader set of common understandings. The picture is more complicated today, with large-scale immigration taking place at a time when it is harder to specify, and therefore harder for a newcomer to discern, a widely shared view of what it means to be American.

To make matters worse, the community structures and religious groups that once played crucial roles in integrating immigrants have themselves been weakened. The old Democratic-party political machines that once brought new citizens into the political process at the local level have vanished. In their place, a new immigrant today encounters political institutions that were developed in response to the black civil-rights movement of the 1960s. The newcomer from Mexico, Brazil, or El Salvador becomes a generic "Latino" in preparation for initiation into the game of divisive racial minority politics.

Overshadowing all other concerns is alarm over the fact that there are 11 or 12 million immigrants in the United States who have entered or remained in the country illegally. To comprehend the depth of feeling attached to that issue, one has to keep in mind that there is no country on Earth where legal values play a more prominent role in the nation's conception of itself than the United States. That was one of the first things Tocqueville noticed in his travels here in the early 1830s, and, as the country has grown larger and more diverse, its reliance on legal values has become ever more salient. In the culture struggles of the late twentieth century, Americans had to rely more heavily than ever on the Declaration of Independence, the Constitution, and the rule of law to serve as unifying forces. Persons who come from societies bound together by shared history, stories, songs, and images can easily overlook or underrate the importance of this aspect of United States culture. Persons who come from societies where formal law is associated with colonialism may well find the United States' emphasis on legality rather strange. But no solution to the challenges of immigration is likely to succeed without taking it into account.

If the United States is to develop realistic, wise, and humane immigration policies, it will need a much fuller and better-informed public discussion. At present, the public debate is too often dominated by immigration alarmists who tend to ignore both our need for replacement migration and the human situations of the men and women who seek opportunities in the United States. Meanwhile, pro-immigration advocates show insufficient attentiveness to the legitimate concerns of citizens, while some others seem to want the economic benefits of migrant labor while turning a blind eye to the toll that the present situation takes on migrants and their families.

In the current atmosphere, it is extremely difficult to sort out the legitimate concerns from the sinister ones. There is thus an urgent need to increase public awareness both of the case for migration and of the likely social costs (both to migrants and the host country) when large-scale migration is not accompanied by well-thought-out strategies for integrating migrant families into the life of the communities where they settle.

To devise effective strategies, it will be necessary to forth-rightly confront the issue of legality. As political scientist Peter Skerry has pointed out, "The debate over immigration has been locked into a compelling but misleading framework that distinguishes sharply between legal and illegal immigration. It has been all but impossible to resist the prevailing paradigm which assigns all negative outcomes associated with immigration to illegal immigrants, and all benign or positive outcomes to legal immigrants. But the social-order effects of immigration do not easily fit into this neat legal-illegal paradigm."

Nevertheless, given the importance of the rule of law to most Americans, solutions will have to be found that avoid the appearance of rewarding law-breakers, yet shift the focus in individual cases to how the immigrants have comported themselves while in residence here. Proposals that draw on the time-honored concept of rehabilitation after paying one's debt to society seem to point toward a path between amnesty and punitiveness.

We will need to focus especially on the education of immigrant children, for schools are the first sustained point of contact with a new culture. Yet, that path is filled with pitfalls, for, as any parent can testify, integration into contemporary youth culture can pose problems of its own. If the United States is to rise to all these challenges, governments at all levels will have to rely heavily on local communities and organizations, including the faith-based organizations that have played such important roles in easing the transition of migrants in the past, even though these institutions are weaker today than they were in former times.

With migration inevitable, the only question worth asking seems to be: How can the process be influenced so as to maximize the potential advantages and minimize the disadvantages for all concerned? With so much at stake for the United States and Latin America, conditions ought to be favorable for intergovernmental negotiations of the sort begun by the Mexican and US governments in 2001. Those negotiations received a severe setback with the attacks of September 11, 2001. But the difficulties should not be permitted to obscure the many opportunities for cooperation based on the principle of shared responsibility for a shared problem. An honest and complete discussion of the legitimate concerns and objectives of the nations involved could highlight areas where our interests coincide, clarify areas of conflict, and lead to improved understanding of the options each country can reasonably be expected to consider.

The five principles set forth in the 2003 Joint Pastoral Letter issued by the Mexican and US bishops, *Strangers No Longer: Together on the Journey of Hope*, might be helpful in setting the stage for new approaches that could expand the pie for both sending and receiving countries. The letter asserts that (1) persons have the right to find opportunities in their homeland; (2) when opportunities are not available at home, persons have the right to migrate to find work to support themselves and their families; (3) sovereign nations have the right to control their boundaries, but economically stronger nations have a stronger obligation to accommodate migration flows; (4) refugees and asylum seekers fleeing wars and persecutions should be protected; and (5) the human dignity and rights of undocumented migrants should be respected.[1]

To those five principles, a sixth should be added: a principle recognizing the need for a highly diverse, rule-of-law society to be careful about the messages it sends to persons who wish to become part of that society. And the bishops might have done well to note, as Pope John Paul II did in *Solicitudo Rei Socialis*, that solidarity imposes duties on the disadvantaged as well as the advantaged: "Those who are more influential, because they have a greater share of goods and common services, should feel responsible for the weaker and be ready to share with them all they possess. Those who are weaker, for their part, in the same spirit of solidarity should not adopt a purely passive attitude, or one that is destructive of the social fabric, but, while claiming their legitimate rights, should do what they can for the good of all."[2]

Evidently, those general principles are in tension with each other in certain ways. To move from the level of principle to specific programs and policies will require enormous dedication, intelligence, creativity, and goodwill on the part of all concerned. It will require realistic discussion of the human and economic costs and benefits. But one thing seems certain: Given America's relative advantages in this age of great migrations, it would be a tragedy if the sending and receiving countries of our hemisphere did not join forces to explore how these advantages can be maximized in ways that are beneficial to all concerned. Whether we now live in countries of out-migration or in-migration, the choices we make now will determine what kind of societies we bring into being for those Americans, both of North and South, who come after us.

NOTES

1. Catholic Church, *Strangers No Longer: Together on the Journey of Hope: A Pastoral Letter Concerning Migration from the Catholic Bishops of Mexico and the United States* (United States Conference of Catholic Bishops, 2003).

2. Pope John Paul II, *Solicitudo Rei Socialis* (Pauline Books and Media, 1987), no. 41.

BORDERLANDS
AND IMMIGRANTS

George Friedman

The United States has returned to its recurring debate over
immigration. This edition of the debate, focused intensely on
the question of illegal immigration from Mexico, is phrased in a
very traditional way. One side argues that illegal migration from
Mexico threatens both American economic interests and security.
The other side argues that the United States historically has
thrived on immigration, and that this wave of migration is no different. As is frequently the case, the policy debate fails to take fundamental geopolitical realities into account.

To begin with, it is absolutely true that the United States has
always been an immigrant society. Even the first settlers in the
United States—the American Indian tribes—were migrants. Certainly, since the first settlements were established, successive
waves of immigration have both driven the American economy
and terrified those who were already living in the country. When

Stratfor (April 04, 2006).

the Scots-Irish began arriving in the late 1700s, the English settlers of all social classes thought that their arrival would place enormous pressure on existing economic processes, as well as bring crime and immorality to the United States.

The Scots-Irish were dramatically different culturally, and their arrival certainly generated stress. However, they proved crucial for populating the continent west of the Alleghenies. The Scots-Irish solved a demographic problem that was at the core of the United States: Given its population at that time, there simply were not enough Americans to expand settlements west of the mountains— and this posed a security threat. If the US population remained clustered in a long, thin line along the Atlantic seaboard, with poor lines of communication running north-south, the country would be vulnerable to European, and especially British, attack. The United States had to expand westward, and it lacked the population to do so. The Americans needed the Scots-Irish.

Successive waves of immigrants came to the United States over the next 200 years. In each case, they came looking for economic opportunity. In each case, there was massive anxiety that the arrival of these migrants would crowd the job market, driving down wages, and that the heterogeneous cultures would create massive social stress. The Irish immigration of the 1840s, the migrations from eastern and southern Europe in the 1880s—all triggered the same concerns. Nevertheless, without those waves of immigration, the United States would not have been able to populate the continent, to industrialize or to field the mass armies of the 20th century that established the nation as a global power.

POPULATION DENSITY AND ECONOMIC RETURNS

Logic would have it that immigration should undermine the economic well-being of those who already live in the United States. But this logic assumes that there is a zero-sum game. That may be true in Europe or Asia. It has not been true in the United States. The key is population density: The density of the United States, excluding Alaska, is 34 people per square kilometer. By comparison, the population density in the United Kingdom is 247 per square kilometer, 231 in Germany and 337 in Japan. The European Union, taken as a whole, has a population density of 115. If the United States were to equal the United Kingdom in terms of density, it would have a population of about 2 billion people.

Even accepting the premise that some parts of the United States are uninhabitable and that the United Kingdom is over-inhabited, the point is that the United States' population is still small relative to available land. That means that it has not come even close to diminishing economic returns. To the extent to which the population-to-land ratio determines productivity—and this, in our view, is the critical variable—the United States still can utilize population increases. At a time when population growth from native births is quite low, this means that the United States still can metabolize immigrants. It is, therefore, no accident that over the past 40 years, the United States has absorbed a massive influx of Asian immigrants who have been net producers over time. It's a big country, and much of it is barely inhabited.

On this level, the immigration issue poses no significant questions. It is a replay of a debate that has been ongoing since the founding of the country. Those who have predicted social and economic disaster as a result of immigration have been consistently wrong. Those who have predicted growing prosperity have been right. Those who have said that the national character of the United States would change dramatically have been somewhat right; core values have remained in place, but the Anglo-Protestant ethnicity represented at the founding has certainly been transformed. How one feels about this transformation depends on ideology and taste. But the simple fact is this: The United States not only would not have become a trans-continental power without immigration; it would not have industrialized. Masses of immigrants formed the armies of workers that drove industrialism and made the United States into a significant world power. No immigration, no United States.

GEOGRAPHY: THE DIFFERENCE WITH MEXICO

Now, it would seem at first glance that the current surge of Mexican migration should be understood in this context and, as such, simply welcomed. If immigration is good, then why wouldn't immigration from Mexico be good? Certainly, there is no cultural argument against it; if the United States could assimilate Ukrainian Jews, Sicilians, and Pakistanis, there is no self-evident reason why it could not absorb Mexicans. The argument against the Mexican migration would seem on its face to be simply a repeat of old, failed arguments against past migrations.

But Mexican migration should not be viewed in the same way as other migrations. When a Ukrainian Jew or a Sicilian or an Indian came to the United States, their arrival represented a sharp geographical event; whatever memories they might have of their birthplace, whatever cultural values they might bring with them, the geographical milieu was being abandoned. And with that, so were the geopolitical consequences of their migration. Sicilians might remember Sicily, they might harbor a cultural commitment to its values and they might even have a sense of residual loyalty to Sicily or to Italy—but Italy was thousands of miles away. The Italian government could neither control nor exploit the migrant's presence in the United States. Simply put, these immigrants did not represent a geopolitical threat; even if they did not assimilate to American culture—remaining huddled together in their "little Italys"—they did not threaten the United States in any way. Their strength was in the country they had left, and that country was far away. That is why, in the end, these immigrants assimilated, or their children did. Without assimilation, they were adrift.

The Mexican situation is different. When a Mexican comes to the United States, there is frequently no geographical split. There is geographical continuity. His roots are just across the land border. Therefore, the entire immigration dynamic shifts. An Italian, a Jew, an Indian can return to his home country, but only with great effort and disruption. A Mexican can and does return with considerable ease. He can, if he chooses, live his life in a perpetual ambiguity.

THE BORDERLAND BATTLEGROUND

This has nothing to do with Mexicans as a people, but rather with a geographical concept called "borderlands." Traveling through Europe, one will find many borderlands. Alsace-Lorraine is a borderland between Germany and France; the inhabitants are both French and German, and in some ways neither. It also is possible to find Hungarians—living Hungarian lives—deep inside Slovakia and Romania.

Borderlands can be found throughout the world. They are the places where the borders have shifted, leaving members of one nation stranded on the other side of the frontier. In many cases, these people now hold the citizenship of the countries in which they reside (according to recognized borders), but they think and speak in the language on the other side of the border. The border moved, but their homes didn't. There has been no decisive geographical event; they have not left their homeland. Only the legal abstraction of a border, and the non-abstract presence of a conquering army, has changed their reality.

Borderlands sometimes are political flashpoints, when the relative power of the two countries is shifting and one is reclaiming its old territory, as Germany did in 1940, or France in 1918. Sometimes the regions are quiet; the borders that have been imposed remain inviolable, due to the continued power of the conqueror. Sometimes, populations move back and forth in the borderland, as politics and economics shift. Borderlands are everywhere. They are the archaeological remains of history, except that these remains have a tendency to come back to life.

The US-Mexican frontier is a borderland. The United States, to all intents and purposes, conquered the region in the period between the Texan revolution (1835-36) and the Mexican-American war (1846-48). As a result of the war, the border moved and areas that had been Mexican territory became part of the United States. There was little ethnic cleansing. American citizens settled into the territory in increasing numbers over time, but the extant Mexican culture remained in place. The border was a political dividing line but was never a physical division; the area north of the border retained a certain Mexican presence, while the area south of the border became heavily influenced by American culture. The economic patterns that tied the area north of the Rio Grande to the area south of it did not disappear. At times they atrophied; at times they intensified; but the links were always there, and neither Washington nor Mexico City objected. It was the natural characteristic of the borderland.

It was not inevitable that the borderland would be held by the United States. Anyone looking at North America in 1800 might have bet that Mexico, not the United States, would be the dominant power of the continent. Why that didn't turn out to be the case is a long story, but by 1846, the Mexicans had lost direct control of the borderland. They have not regained it since. But that does not mean that the borderland is unambiguously American—and it does not mean that, over the next couple of hundred years, should Washington's power weaken and Mexico City's increase, the borders might not shift once again. How many times, after all, have the Franco-German borders shifted? For the moment, however, Washington is enormously more powerful than Mexico City, so the borders will stay where they are.

THE HEART OF THE MATTER

We are in a period, as happens with borderlands, when major population shifts are under way. This should not be understood as immigration. Or more precisely, these shifts should not be understood as immigration in the same sense that we talk about immigration from, say, Brazil, where the geographical relationship between migrant and home country is ruptured. The immigration from Mexico to the United States is a regional migration within a borderland between two powers—powers that have drawn a border based on military and political history, and in which two very different populations intermingle. Right now, the United States is economically dynamic relative to Mexico. Therefore, Mexicans tend to migrate northward, across the political border, within the geographical definition of the borderland. The map declares a border. Culture and history, however, take a different view.

The immigration debate in the US Congress, which conflates

Asian immigrations with Mexican immigrations, is mixing apples and oranges. Chinese immigration is part of the process of populating the United States—a process that has been occurring since the founding of the Republic. Mexican immigration is, to borrow a term from physics, the Brownian motion of the borderland. This process is nearly as old as the Republic, but there is a crucial difference: It is not about populating the continent nearly as much as it is about the dynamics of the borderland.

One way to lose control of a borderland is by losing control of its population. In general, most Mexicans cross the border for strictly economic reasons. Some wish to settle in the United States, some wish to assimilate. Others intend to be here temporarily. Some intend to cross the border for economic reasons—to work— and remain Mexicans in the full sense of the word. Now, so long as this migration remains economic and cultural, there is little concern for the United States. But when this last class of migrants crosses the border with political aspirations, such as the recovery of lost Mexican territories from the United States, that is the danger point.

Americans went to Texas in the 1820s. They entered the borderland. They then decided to make a political claim against Mexico, demanding a redefinition of the formal borders between Mexico and the United States. In other words, they came to make money and stayed to make a revolution. There is little evidence—flag-waving notwithstanding—that there is any practical move afoot now to reverse the American conquest of Mexican territories. Nevertheless, that is the danger with all borderlands: that those on the "wrong" side of the border will take action to move the border back.

For the United States, this makes the question of Mexican immigration within the borderland different from that of Mexican immigration to places well removed from it. In fact, it makes the issue of Mexican migration different from all other immigrations to the United States. The current congressional debate is about "immigration" as a whole, but that makes little sense. It needs to be about three different questions:

1. Immigration from other parts of the world to the United States

2. Immigration from Mexico to areas well removed from the southern border region

3. Immigration from Mexico to areas within the borderlands that were created by the US conquests

Treating these three issues as if they were the same thing confuses matters. The issue is not immigration in general, nor even Mexican immigration. It is about the borderland and its future. The question of legal and illegal immigration and various solutions to the problems must be addressed in this context.

IMMIGRATION QUOTAS VS. INDIVIDUAL RIGHTS

THE MORAL AND PRACTICAL CASE FOR OPEN IMMIGRATION

Harry Binswanger

This is a defense of phasing-in open immigration into the United States. Entry into the US should ultimately be free for any foreigner, with the exception of criminals, would-be terrorists, and those carrying infectious diseases. (And note: I am defending freedom of entry and residency, not the automatic granting of US citizenship).

An end to immigration quotas is demanded by the principle of individual rights. Every individual has rights as an individual, not as a member of this or that nation. One has rights not by virtue of being an American, but by virtue of being human.

One doesn't have to be a resident of any particular country to have a moral entitlement to be secure from governmental coercion against one's life, liberty, and property. In the words of the Declaration of Independence, government is instituted "to secure these rights"—to protect them against their violation by force or fraud.

Capitalism Magazine (April 2, 2006).

A foreigner has rights just as much as an American. To be a foreigner is not to be a criminal. Yet our government treats as criminals those foreigners not lucky enough to win the green-card lottery.

Seeking employment in this country is not a criminal act. It coerces no one and violates no one's rights (there is no "right" to be exempt from competition in the labor market, or in any other market).

It is not a criminal act to buy or rent a home here in which to reside. Paying for housing is not a coercive act—whether the buyer is an American or a foreigner. No one's rights are violated when a Mexican, or Canadian, or Senegalese rents an apartment from an American owner and moves into the housing he is paying for. And what about the rights of those American citizens who want to sell or rent their property to the highest bidders? Or the American businesses that want to hire the lowest cost workers? It is morally indefensible for our government to violate their right to do so, just because the person is a foreigner.

Immigration quotas forcibly exclude foreigners who want not to seize but to purchase housing here, who want not to rob Americans but to engage in productive work, raising our standard of living. To forcibly exclude those who seek peacefully to trade value for value with us is a violation of the rights of both parties to such a trade: the rights of the American seller or employer and the rights of the foreign buyer or employee.

Thus, immigration quotas treat both Americans and foreigners as if they were criminals, as if the peaceful exchange of values to mutual benefit were an act of destruction.

To take an actual example, if I want to invite my Norwegian friend Klaus to live in my home, either as a guest or as a paying tenant, what right does our government have to stop Klaus and me? To be a Norwegian is not to be a criminal. And if some American business wants to hire Klaus, what right does our government have to interfere?

The implicit premise of barring foreigners is: "This is our country, we let in who we want." But who is "we"? The government does not own the country. Jurisdiction is not ownership. Only the owner of land or any item of property can decide the terms of its use or sale. Nor does the majority own the country.

This is a country of private property, and housing is private property. So is a job.

American land is not the collective property of some entity called "the US government." Nor is there such thing as collective, social ownership of the land. The claim, "We have the right to decide who is allowed in" means some individuals—those with the most votes—claim the right to prevent other citizens from exercising their rights. But there can be no right to violate the rights of others.

Our constitutional republic respects minority rights. Sixty percent of the population cannot vote to enslave the other 40 percent. Nor can a majority dictate to the owners of private property. Nor can a majority dictate on whom private employers spend their money. Not morally, not in a free society. In a free society, the rights of the individual are held sacrosanct, above any claim of even an overwhelming majority.

The rights of one man end where the rights of his neighbor begin. Only within the limits of his rights is a man free to act on his own judgment. The criminal is the man who deliberately steps outside his rights-protected domain and invades the domain of another, depriving his victim of his exclusive control over his property, or liberty, or life. The criminal, by his own choice, has rejected rights in favor of brute violence. Thus, an immigration policy that excludes criminals is proper.

Likewise, a person with an infectious disease, such as smallpox, threatens with serious physical harm those with whom he comes into proximity. Unlike the criminal, he may not intend to do damage, but the threat of physical harm is clear, present, and objectively demonstrable. To protect the lives of Americans, he may be kept out or quarantined until he is no longer a threat.

But what about the millions of Mexicans, South Americans, Chinese, Canadians, etc. seeking entry who are not criminal and not bearing infectious diseases? By what moral principle can they be excluded? Not on the grounds of majority vote, not on the grounds of protecting any American's rights, not on the grounds of any legitimate authority of the state.

The Moral and the Practical: That's the moral case for phasing out limits on immigration. But some ask: "Is it practical? Wouldn't unlimited immigration—even if phased in over a decade—be disastrous to our economic well-being and create overcrowding? Are we being told to just grit our teeth and surrender our interests in the name of morality?"

This question is invalid on its face. It shows a failure to understand the nature of individual rights and of moral principles generally.

Individual rights are defined by determining what basic terms of social interaction are in the self-interest of all and require no one's sacrifice. The basic such condition is liberty. Rights prescribe freedom by proscribing coercion.

Rights reflect the fundamental alternative of voluntary consent or brute force. The reign of force is in no one's interest; the value of a system of voluntary consent is the precondition of everyone achieving their well-being.

To ignore the principle of rights means jettisoning the principled, "moral" resolution of conflicting desires, and substituting mere numbers (majority vote) for the rule of law. That is not to anyone's interest. Tyranny is not to anyone's self-interest.

Rights establish the necessary framework within which one defines his legitimate self-interest. One cannot hold that one's self-interest requires he be "free" to deprive others of their freedom, treating their interests as morally irrelevant. One cannot hold that recognizing the rights of others is moral but claim it is "not practical."

Rights are based on self-interest, on the requirements of man's life as a rational being. Rights define the conditions required by man's survival as man. There can be no conflict between the moral and the practical here: if respecting individual rights requires it, your interest requires it.

Freedom or force, reason or compulsion—that is the basic social alternative. Immigrants recognize the value of freedom—that's why they seek to come here.

The American Founders defined and implemented a system of rights because they recognized that man, as a rational being, must be free to act on his own judgment and to keep the products of his own effort. They did not intend to establish a system in which those who happen to be born here could use force to "protect" themselves from the competition of others.

ECONOMICS

One major fear of open immigration is economic: the fear of losing one's job to immigrants. It is asked: "Won't the immigrants take our jobs?" The answer is: "Yes, so we can go on to better, higher-paying jobs."

The fallacy in this protectionist objection lies in the idea that there is only a finite amount of work to be done. The unstated assumption is: "If Americans don't get to do that work, if foreigners do it instead, we Americans will have nothing to do."

But work is the creation of wealth. A job is a role in the production of goods and services—the production of food, of cars, computers, the providing of Internet content—all the items that go to make up our standard of living. A country cannot have too much wealth. The need for wealth is limitless, and the work that is to be done is limitless.

From a grand, historical perspective, we are only at the beginning of the wealth-creating age. The wealth Americans produce today is as nothing compared to what we'll have two hundred years from now—just as the standard of living 200 years in the past, in 1806, was as nothing to ours today.

Unemployment is not caused by an absence of avenues for the creation of wealth. Unemployment is caused by government interference in the labor market. Even with that interference, the number of jobs goes relentlessly upward, decade after decade. This bears witness to the fact that there's no end to the creation of wealth and thus no end to the useful employment of human intelligence and the physical effort directed by that intelligence. There is always more productive work to be done. If you can give your job to an immigrant, you can get a more valuable job.

What is the effect of a bigger labor pool on wage rates? If the money supply is constant, nominal wage rates fall. But real wage rates rise, because total output has gone up. Economists have demonstrated that real wages have to rise as long as the immigrants are self-supporting. If immigrants earn their keep, if they don't consume more than they produce, then they add to total output, which means that prices fall (if the money supply is constant).

And, in fact, rising real wages was the history of our country in the nineteenth century. Before the 1920s, there were no limits on immigration, yet our standard of living rocketed upward. Self-supporting immigrants were an economic benefit not an injury.

The protectionist objection that immigrants take away jobs and harm our standard of living is a solid economic fallacy.

WELFARE

A popular misconception is that immigrants come here to get welfare. To the extent that is true, immigrants do constitute a burden. But this issue is mooted by the passage, under the Clinton Administration of the Personal Responsibility and Work Opportunity and Reconciliation Act (PRWORA), which makes legal permanent residents ineligible for most forms of welfare for 5 years. I support this kind of legislation.

Further, if the fear is of non-working immigrants, why is the pending legislation aimed at "employers" of immigrants?

OVERCROWDING

America is a vastly underpopulated country. Our population density is less than one-third of France's.

Take an extreme example. Suppose a tidal wave of immigrants came here. Suppose that half of the people on the planet moved here. That would mean an unthinkable eleven-fold increase in our population—from 300 million to 3.3 billion people. That would make America almost as "densely" populated as today's England (360 people/sq. km. vs. 384 people/sq. km.). In fact, it would make us less densely populated than the state of New Jersey (453 per sq. km.). And these calculations exclude Alaska, Hawaii, and counts only land area.

And contrary to widespread beliefs, high population density is a value not a disvalue. High population density intensifies the division of labor, which makes possible a wider variety of jobs and specialized consumer products. For instance, in Manhattan, there is a "doll hospital"—a store specializing in the repair of children's dolls. Such a store and the many specialized, niche businesses require a high population density to have a market. Try finding a doll hospital in Poughkeepsie. In Manhattan, one can find a job as a Pilates Method teacher or as a "Secret Shopper" (2 jobs actually listed on Craig's List). Not in Paducah.

People want to live near other people, in cities. One-seventh of England's population lives in London. If population density is a bad thing, why are Manhattan real-estate prices so high?

THE VALUE OF IMMIGRANTS

Immigrants are the kind of people who refresh the American spirit. They are ambitious, courageous, and value freedom. They come here, often with no money and not even speaking the language, to seek a better life for themselves and their children.

The vision of American freedom with its opportunity to prosper by hard work serves as a magnet drawing the best of the world's people. Immigrants are self-selected for their virtues: their ambitiousness, daring, independence, and pride. They are willing to cast aside the tradition-bound roles assigned to them in their native lands and to re-define themselves as Americans. These are the people America needs in order to keep alive the individualist, hard-working attitude that made America.

Here is a short list of some great immigrants: Alexander Hamilton, Alexander Graham Bell, Andrew Carnegie, most of the top scientists of the Manhattan Project, Igor Sikorsky (the inventor of the helicopter), Ayn Rand.

Open immigration: the benefits are great. The right is unquestionable. So let them come.

ILLEGAL IMMIGRATION IS A MORAL ISSUE

Victor Davis Hanson

As President Bush's guest worker proposals slog through Congress, new reports suggest that there may be not 8 million, but almost 20 million illegal aliens in the United States, a population larger than most entire states. Four hundred billion dollars in taxes—almost the current annual budget deficit —are not collected due to a growing underground cash economy.

Mexico brazenly issued a survival guide for its intrepid citizens on how to cross illegally into the United States. A 2,000-mile border is porous at a time when stealthy terrorists count on such laxity to enter the United States.

The hallowed assimilationist formula has too few overt defenders these days—even though measured, legal immigration, English emersion, multiracialism instead of multiculturalism, and integration have ensured that past legal immigrants from Mexico are among America's finest citizens.

Tribune News Services, January 24, 2005. Copyright © 2005 Victor Davis Hanson.

The laissez-faire right still lectures on open borders as if it were a matter of robust lawful immigration—emphasizing global competitiveness that accrues from cheap labor. The minimum wage, not illegality, supposedly is its only problem: if only the self-correcting market could be set free to adjudicate wages, $2 an hour might not tempt any more from rural Mexico.

The therapeutic left will not even talk of "illegal immigration"—taboo nomenclature that supposedly denotes racism. "Undocumented workers" is the politically correct terminology, even though not all aliens are working or simply misplaced their certification.

If employers count on inexpensive industrious laborers in the shadows, chauvinists envision a revolving, but still permanent unassimilated constituency to enhance their own agendas. In response to the tired rhetoric, perhaps it is better to envision illegal immigration from Mexico not as a question of divisive politics, but of collective morality. Is it ethical for the Mexican government to export annually 1 million to 2 million of its unwanted citizens to avoid long-overdue reform—hoping to free itself of dissidents and earn $12 billion in subsidies from its poorest abroad? No wonder Mexico talks of the problem in terms of US imperialism in lieu of its own cynicism.

Is it moral for employers to count on illegal industrious workers, usually without English or education, to undercut the wages of American citizens—as if a laborer remains youthful and hale in perpetuity with no need of social entitlements when disabled or impoverished years later? No wonder employers claim that they are only providing a service to Mexico's poor.

Is it so liberal that governments must pay for those who ignore the law while citizens go without? In California, the money to incarcerate more than 14,000 felonious illegal aliens from Mexico—well over $400 million—would fund the start-up costs of 20 university campuses like the new University of California at Merced, at a time when Americans (including many first-generation Mexican-American citizens) who are eligible for higher education cannot find access or financial support.

Is it so fair to assume that the unemployed in our midst—over 10 percent of the work force in many counties of the American

Southwest that are most affected by illegal immigration—cannot find entry-level work? No wonder we insist that no one can discover a citizen to mow the lawn or cook his food—as if 30 years ago our yards were weedy and we did not eat out, as if states without illegal aliens have poor landscaping and empty restaurants. Picking an illegal worker up at the local lumber yard, paying him in cash for a day of digging, and then dumping him on the curb at twilight—"out of sight, out of mind"—is neither liberal nor humane even if done in Santa Cruz or Carmel.

And is it equitable that laws must be sacred for most, but not for some? Do we really want a bureaucratic system near collapse from fraudulent Social Security numbers, off-the-books wages, false names, cars without registration and insurance, even as millions abroad queue up to enter our shores lawfully? Are we to tell waiting Punjabis or Filipinos to certify their education, skills and method of support—even as we ask far less of those who break the law to cross the border from Mexico?

Who, then, is the real moralist? Is it the police officer who stops an illegal alien but cannot call immigration authorities? The contractor who knowingly accepts falsified identification and pays untaxed cash wages? The La Raza ("The Race") activist who promotes ethnic chauvinism for those to whom it will prove most deleterious? Perhaps the grandstanding Mexican consul who faults the United States for his own country's callousness? Or is it the rest of us, who in fear of being slurred as "racists" or "nativists" often keep silent—just when candor and honesty on all sides are needed now if we are to avoid becoming an amoral apartheid society with a permanent underclass in the shadows?

COMPREHENSIVE IMMIGRATION REFORM

Cardinal Theodore E. McCarrick

T he US Senate is poised to consider legislation which could change how our country responds to the newcomer, to the downtrodden, and to the oppressed who come to our shores seeking a better life. It is an important time, and it is vital that all American citizens, most particularly members of faith communities, understand the present moment in which we live and act to ensure that our nation does not forsake her immigrant history.

As we all know, immigration is not a simple issue, but one that evokes strong passions and economic, legal, social, and national security debates. We are here today, representing our individual faith communities, because we believe that immigration is not just a theoretical policy issue, but ultimately a humanitarian issue that impacts the basic dignity and life of the person, created in the image and likeness of God. It is because of its impact on basic human dignity and human life that we believe immigration is, first and foremost, a moral issue.

Interfaith Press Event (March 1, 2006).

All sides in the debate agree on one thing: our nation's immigration policy is flawed and needs to be repaired. It is a matter of human justice. Every day, we in the Catholic Church see the human consequences of this flawed system. Our parishes, agencies, hospitals, and pastoral ministries are called upon daily to respond to the many needs of new immigrants, hard-working people who have fled their homeland in despair and fear. They ask us for a loving heart, a helping hand, for medical care, legal assistance, and counseling. We see families separated, workers exploited, and migrants abused by smugglers and who sometimes even die in the desert.

Changing the status quo is an issue of moral gravity. Our nation must create an immigration response that is humane, while also serving our nation's economic and national security needs. Any legislation must include:

- policy directions which address the root causes of migration, such as economic development, so that migrants can remain in their home countries to support themselves and their families;

- reform of our legal immigration system, including the adoption of an earned legalization program for undocumented workers and their families; a temporary worker program with appropriate protections for both US and foreign workers; and reform of the family preference system, so families can be reunited in a timely fashion;

- restoration of due process protections for immigrants to allow them to have "their day in court," consistent with American values.

These elements are best embodied in S. 1033/H.R. 2330, the Secure America and Orderly Immigration Act of 2005. As the Senate Judiciary Committee and the full US Senate begin consideration of a Senate bill, we ask that principles embodied in the Secure America and Orderly Immigration Act receive strong consideration and support. We also ask that the Agricultural Jobs, Opportunity, Benefits, and Security Act (AgJOBS) legislation, which helps our nation's farm workers, and the DREAM Act, which assists undocumented students who came to our nation through no fault of their own, and the Unaccompanied Alien Child Protection Act are included in any final legislative package.

In our view, only a comprehensive approach to immigration reform will effectively address our nation's immigration crisis. This is why the US Conference of Catholic Bishops (USCCB) strongly opposes H.R. 4437, the Border Protection, Anti-Terrorism, and Illegal Immigration Act of 2005, an enforcement-only bill which was passed by the House of Representatives in December.

Let me be clear. The Catholic Church acknowledges and supports the right of a sovereign nation to secure its borders, most particularly at a time in which national security is in question. However, we believe H.R. 4437 goes well beyond the issue of national security, is overly broad and punitive, and would bring undue harm to immigrants, asylum-seekers, and refugees.

If enacted, H.R. 4437 would alter basic American values of fairness and due process and severely weaken our asylum and refugee protection system. Its scope and reach would extend to US citizens as well, including those, such as our own parishioners, who offer, in an act of mercy, basic sustenance to an undocumented migrant. In short, H.R. 4437 would fundamentally change the heritage of our nation as a welcoming, compassionate, and open society, a heritage which has made us the strong nation we are today. We urge its defeat.

Today is Ash Wednesday, when Christians around the world observe the beginning of Lent. During this period Catholics pray, fast, and prepare for the coming of Easter and the Resurrection of New Life. These 40 days of Lent recall the time Jesus spent in the desert fasting and praying.

Today, many of our brothers and sisters find themselves in their own desert—sometimes literally. They risk their lives to support their families, and they bring to our nation a strong work ethic, family values, and a deep spirituality. It is my prayer that we do not abandon them, that we embrace their many gifts, and that, in the very near future, their suffering will end.

In closing, then, I urge Congress and President Bush to work together in the days ahead to create a new immigration system which protects our national security, respects our common humanity, and reflects the values—fairness, compassion, and opportunity—and the people, including the immigrants, upon which our nation was built. Thank you.

WHEN ILLEGAL IS RIGHT, WHAT IS WRONG?

Kathleen Parker

There's nothing like the sight of 500,000 protesters on US turf, demanding rights in Spanish while waving Mexican flags, to stir Americans from their siestas. In Los Angeles, the iconic phrase may be "Si se puede," but in Muncie, it's "What the . . . ?"

Suddenly, in the flash of a newscast, polite political debate about guest-worker programs visually morphed into what seemed like a full-blown invasion.

Demonstrations have the desired effect of focusing attention on an idea—and television cameras can tighten that focus so that a slow drip looks like a tsunami. But the same imagery can backfire. I suspect that the sight of so many people demanding rights to which they have no legal claim will not help the cause of illegals in this country, even if it motivates politicians to act, well, politically.

Let's just say that convincing others of one's desire to become an American citizen would be more effective if one were to do so

Waco Tribune Herald (April 4, 2006).

in English—while waving an American flag. Just imagine how welcome 500,000 Bubbas waving American flags and chanting, "Hell no, we won't go," would be in Mexico City.

Now before I'm accused of being biased against Latinos, let me be clear. *Yo quiero a los latinos.* I could go on in Espanol, but when in America, I always say, do as the Americans do. Speak English. Otherwise, I'm over-the-top pro-Latino and pro-immigrant.

I grew up in Florida with Cubans as my closest friends, and my stepfather is Mexican—a legal immigrant who came to this country at age 16 to attend medical school.

I am, in other words, an unapologetic Hispanophile.

But, like a majority of Americans who think Congress should secure our borders, I'm a fan of laws and of those who respect them—even though I occasionally turn right on red when the sign says not to.

The question of what to do with some 11 million to 20 million illegal immigrants already living and working in this country may be too problematic for mere politicians. The issue is exacerbated by our refusal to speak plain, non-PC English about what's what. Illegal immigrants are not "undocumented workers." They're illegal. And, if we're to use the legal language accurately, they're "aliens."

Then again, when we talk about illegal aliens, it is useful to remind ourselves that we're also talking about human beings. To see television images of shadows crossing the desert into the US is to see criminals intent on misdeeds rather than poor people, hundreds of whom die each year in the process, trying to find jobs and plenty to eat.

As we've been told hundreds of times, these people do the work Americans won't do, which is both true and not true. It is true that Americans don't want to work for the low wages that illegal workers gratefully earn, but not necessarily true that no American would do those jobs under any circumstances.

Steven Camarota, research director for the Center for Immigration Studies (cis.org), says that unemployment figures tell the truer story of how native workers are being crowded out of the market by cheap labor: 11 percent of American construction workers are unemployed, as are 9 percent of workers in food processing and 11 percent in cleaning and maintenance.

"The least educated Americans are getting hurt," he says.

Standing around a Washington, DC, Metro station the other day, I watched a Latino sweeping the tiled floor. He was one of those people you barely notice—an invisible soul, dignified, unobtrusive—but plainly attentive to his job. I don't know if he's here legally, but I do know the floor was spotless. I tried to imagine any other American doing the same job. A college student? Another minority? Is there really an involuntarily unemployed American citizen keeping warm on a street grate because this small brown man is sweeping the floor of an underground tunnel?

Before I bleed to death or start writing poetry, let me balance this romantic view of the illegal immigrant with another nugget: About 27 percent of all inmates in the federal prison system are criminal aliens, according to government figures. Then again, millions of illegals who are otherwise law-abiding people have lived here for 10 to 20 years, buying houses, attending parent-teacher meetings and giving birth to native-born Americans.

Although there seems no simple solution to such a complex issue, two nagging thoughts persist: 1) The right to protest was a gift from America's Founding Fathers to the nation's citizens, ergo, non-citizens should protest in their own countries; and 2) the purpose of the legislative branch of government is to pass laws that serve the best interests of the nation's citizens.

Which may mean, *No se puede.*

CONTRIBUTORS

HARRY BINSWANGER, Professor of Philosophy at the Objectivist Academic Center, Ayn Rand Institute.

RONALD DWORKIN, Frank Henry Sommer Professor of Law and Professor of Philosophy, New York University; Bentham Professor of Jurisprudence, University College London.

GEORGE FRIEDMAN, Founder, Chairman, and Chief Intelligence Officer, STRATFOR, Strategic Forecasting Inc.

ROBERT P. GEORGE, McCormick Professor of Jurisprudence and Director of the James Madison Program in American Ideals and Institutions, Princeton University.

MARY ANN GLENDON, Learned Hand Professor of Law, Harvard University.

VICTOR DAVIS HANSON, Classicist; Military Historian; Senior Fellow at the Hoover Institution, Stanford University; and Professor Emeritus, California State University, Fresno.

OLIVER WENDELL HOLMES JR. (1841–1935), American jurist, appointed to the United States Supreme Court in 1902.

SAMUEL J. LEVINE, Professor of Law, Pepperdine University School of Law.

CARDINAL THEODORE E. MCCARRICK, Archbishop of Washington, DC.

LINDA MEYER, Professor of Law, Quinnipac School of Law.

MARTHA MINOW, Professor of Law, Harvard University.

CHARLES OGLETREE, Jesse Climenko Professor of Law, Harvard University; Founder and Executive Director, Charles Hamilton Houston Institute for Race and Justice.

MARK OSLER, Professor of Law, Baylor University.

KATHLEEN PARKER, syndicated columnist and Director of the School of Written Expression, Buckley School of Public Speaking and Persuasion.

IRA H. PEAK JR., Senior Minister, First Christian Church of Beech Grove, Indiana; Adjunct Professor, Department of Philosophy, University of Indianapolis.

RUSSELL G. PEARCE, Professor of Law, Fordham University School of Law; Codirector, Louis Stein Center for Law and Ethics.

WILLIAM H. PRYOR JR., Judge, United States Court of Appeals, Eleventh Circuit.

CASS R. SUNSTEIN, Karl N. Llewellyn Distinguished Service Professor of Jurisprudence, University of Chicago School of Law; Contributing Editor, *The New Republic*.

AMELIA J. UELMEN, Director of the Institute on Religion, Law & Lawyer's Work, Fordham University School of Law.

JOHN J. WORLEY, Professor of Law, South Texas College of Law.